History on the Margins

History *on the* Margins

*People and Places
in the Emergence
of Modern France*

JOHN MERRIMAN

University of Nebraska Press

LINCOLN & LONDON

Acknowledgments for the use of copyrighted material appear on pages 147–48, which constitute an extension of the copyright page.

Library of Congress Cataloging-in-Publication Data
Names: Merriman, John M., author.
Title: History on the margins: people and places in the emergence of modern France / John Merriman.
Description: Lincoln: University of Nebraska Press, [2018] | Includes bibliographical references.
Identifiers: LCCN 2018027402
ISBN 9780803295896 (pbk.: alk. paper)
ISBN 9781496213082 (epub)
ISBN 9781496213099 (mobi)
ISBN 9781496213105 (pdf)
Subjects: LCSH: France—History—19th century. | France—Historiography.
Classification: LCC DC251 .M472 2018 | DDC 944.06—dc23 LC record available at https://lccn.loc.gov/2018027402

Set in Minion Pro by Mikala R. Kolander.

In memory of Carol Merriman (1950–2016).
And, again, for Laura Merriman and Chris Merriman.

CONTENTS

ACKNOWLEDGMENTS

I would like to thank Alisa Plant, editor-in-chief at the University of Nebraska Press, for her encouragement and wonderful editing. Thanks to Ann Baker and Hannah Gokie at the Press. Chris Merriman provided excellent suggestions for the essay "History on the Margins."

Thanks also to Peter McPhee, Michelle Perrot, Dominique Kalifa, Chris Johnson, Charles Keith, Mark Lawrence, Dave Bushnell, Don Lamm, Ken Loiselle, Jim Collins, David Bell, Steve Pincus, Sue Stokes, Paul Hanson, Rachel Chrastil, Darrin McMahon, Phil Kalberer, Andrzej Kaminski, Hervé, Françoise, and Élodie Parain, Victoria Johnson, Eric Fruleux, Mathieu Fruleux, Lucien and Catherine Mollier, Jeanne Innes, Jean-Claude Petilon, Sven Wanegffelen, and Bruno Cabanes for inspiration and friendship. And of course, Laura Merriman and Chris Merriman.

I owe so much to three people who sadly are no longer with us: Chuck Tilly, Peter Gay, and, above all, Carol Merriman.

An indulgent university and teaching in France have made it possible for me to have spent the equivalent of decades in the country I so much love. So many wonderful cities, towns, and villages, hotels, restaurants, cafés, and archives. And more important, so many friends in Balazuc, Paris, Lyon, *et un peu partout*. I have been very fortunate indeed.

Balazuc
May 11, 2018

When I was about eleven or twelve, I decided to write a history of the world. I used encyclopedias and random books, beginning with the letter "A" (Albania, Armenia, etc.) and hoping to march all the way through the alphabet. I actually got to the letter "E," and thus not to "F," as in France. Friends of my mother gave me as birthday presents books by groundbreaking historians Henri Pirenne and Henry Steele Commager. I never did get too far into reading them at that age. I was far more interested in *Sports Illustrated.*

At Jesuit High School in Portland, Oregon, I was interested in (and played) sports, but also history and some English literature. My freshman year I wrote assignments in history that went well beyond fifty pages, even nearing a hundred, although they were not very original and I doubt that they were very good. I did okay in those subjects but not in much else. The Jesuits did not know what to do with me. I seemed to work only in subjects that interested me. A couple of them were excellent teachers with whom I am still in touch. I had a good many A's and B's, but also six C's and five D's. I defensively add that this was before grade inflation. I graduated 39th in a class of 125 boys. I probably have never taught a student at Yale with such a mediocre high school record. On my transcript school authorities dissed me by giving me a "Satisfactory" and not "Excellent" in "character and citizenship." Many years later my Yale-educated offspring, Laura and Chris, found much that was amusing in my high school transcript.

When it came to applying for college, I applied to only one place—the University of Michigan—and was admitted, probably because my grandfather, mother, father (whom I never knew), great-uncle, and aunt had gone there. After four years in a repressed Catholic high school, my first semester at Michigan was a catastrophe. I returned to Portland for Christmas break (my first airplane trip, which seems strange to me now after decades of constant air travel and well more than three hundred times across the Atlantic), carrying with me an "F"—in French! When I showed up for the midterm in that course, the teacher did not know who I was because I had been there to be tortured at eight in the morning on only a few occasions. At the end of the semester I received the "F," two "C's," and a "B"—in history. My grade point average was 1.93. My mother, who had been an excellent student at Michigan, saw my grades and said she had not realized that Michigan had gone to a two-point system! Sadly, it had not.

My schoolwork went better after that. I think Asian Studies 102 during my second semester saved me. Chairman Mao was very much in the news and I wanted to know more. I did well enough in the following semesters and was fortunate to have counted the historian of China Albert Feuerwerker and the historian of Germany Gerhard Weinberg among my professors, despite partying and spending at least three hours playing basketball in the gym every day. My junior year I was honored to win the award for "Best All-Around Athlete in Intramural Competition," which included varsity athletes. The life of the mind still took second place for me.

I went to Europe for the first time as a Eurail-carrying young tourist, arriving in Paris on my twenty-first birthday. Early in my wanderings I met a sculptress on a bus to Dachau, near Munich. She arranged for me to have dinner in Paris with Paloma Picasso. I never met the great man himself. If I had it would have been terrific if he had scrawled a drawing on a napkin or something. Upon my return to Portland, my mother—a professional portrait and landscape painter—could hardly believe it when I told her about meeting Picasso's daughter.

Back in Ann Arbor, I took a course in French history one summer term. It was taught by Guillaume de Bertier de Sauvigny, historian of Restoration France and genial priest (he was also a direct descendent of one of the founders of the Chevaliers de la Foi, which had helped prepare the way for the return of the monarchy. Going to France twice as a tourist gave me something of an appreciation for the country's regional differences, including, of course, its food and wine (seems to be a theme here). But I can't say that the spark of wanting to study France had been lit.

I started graduate school in 1968 because I wanted to stay in Ann Arbor to play baseball in a summer league. I had applied on a whim and without much of an idea of graduate studies. Admitted, but without any funding at all, I mulled over the idea of going into Chinese history, but this was before U.S. scholars—or pretty much anyone—could go to China for research or anything else. I knew only that I was interested in social and political change but I did not know where this would lead me. I was sort of a marginal character among some very determined (and reasonably well-funded) graduate students.

No young graduate student in history could have been more fortunate than me as a second year. During my first year I had developed vague aspirations of working in French history, particularly the nineteenth century. Michigan's history department included a very kind historian of modern France, but he did not research or write and could not speak French. One Saturday morning, while recovering from a Friday night in Ann Arbor, I read Charles Tilly's *The Vendée*, the path-breaking study of counter-revolution in France. Suddenly change could be explained. Tilly had just arrived from the University of Toronto to the University of Michigan. He was stationed in the Department of Sociology, with a joint appointment in history. My second semester of this second year I nervously began Tilly's seminar.

Tilly taught us to keep our eyes on the big picture: the economic, social, political, and indeed cultural dynamics over the *longue durée*. *The Vendée*, originally published in English in 1964, had an enormous influence on social history (and, for that matter, on political science). Social history already rocked and at that time ruled. Tilly and the rest of us mere mortals believed that history had causes and that those causes could be determined. Nor was history limited to elites. The histories of ordinary people could be analyzed, described, and evoked. Chuck—as I and everyone came to know him—once said, "It is bitter hard to write the history of remainders" and being able to bring to life people who over the centuries rioted to protest the high price of grain in most every European country or the Captain Swing rebels in southern England in 1829–30 who are so spectacularly analyzed and described by Eric Hobsbawm and George Rudé. This idea I have never forgotten. Tilly once described himself as inhabiting that no-man's land between history and sociology. He virtually created the field of historical sociology. He often presented sweeping *problématiques,* so it is entirely fitting that one of the fifty-one books he authored or edited carries the title *Big Structures, Large Processes, Huge Comparisons.*

When I first met Chuck I was stunned—as were all his students—by his brilliance. He was a jovial genius, that's for sure. I knew next to nothing about sociology and had to scramble to get what was then an honorable "C" in an introductory course at the University of Michigan in my disastrous first undergraduate semester.

I was fortunate enough to have been part of the emergence of the field of French social history. However, when I started out there were topics that young folks like me did not work on. A big one was the middle-classes, the bourgeoisie—we did not think that we liked *them.* At the time not many aspiring academics studied imperialism in a historical sense, although many of us were resisting our own country's engagement in precisely that in Southeast Asia. And not many historians of France, at least in the United States, worked on religion, although happily there were some exceptions. Other than the French Revolution and the Napoleonic era, there was not much work being done on war and society. Many historians of my generation also dissed military history, in part because much of it seemed confined to the "who stood where" variety. Since 2000 or so, especially in the case of the French Revolution, studies of war and society have thrived.

The complexities of national, ethnic, and cultural identities have also emerged as important fields of research. What we used to call "diplomatic history" has now become international or relational history, inevitably merging with the deepening influence of globalization. Fascinating work on and within these themes suggests that Tilly—and others who insisted on keeping our eyes on the big dynamics of change, including state-making, large-scale industrialization, the dynamics of religion, and the complexities of cultural identity—got it right.

My grad school gang tended to study workers, particularly "the crowds" within movements of social and political protest, following the lead of the late George Rudé, whose *The Crowd in the French Revolution* (1959) had paved the way. My first conference presentation (at the American Historical Association's meeting in New Orleans in December 1972) and subsequent article carried the title, almost inevitably, of "The Crowd in the *Affaire de Limoges* (April 27, 1848)." I was very proud that Rudé came to the session and later more proud to call him a friend. I still read Berthold Brecht's magnificent poem "A Worker Reads History" at the end of the first lecture in every course at Yale. It celebrates the place of ordinary people in history, while textbooks tend to pay homage to "the names of kings."

Chuck Tilly was a "quantifier," which I am not, but he also had a strong sense of the importance of what French geographers in the early twentieth century called "humanistic geography"—basically the influence of space, the physical landscape, on politics. I moved more in that direction. Tilly had received a substantial grant from the U.S. Science Foundation to study French collective violence over the *longue durée,* and he had amassed an imposing number of reels of microfilmed archival documents on the subject. Because of this collection I was able to research and write a seminar paper on the events in Limoges following the February Revolution in Paris in 1848, and in doing so I found my dissertation topic: "Radicalization and Repression: The Experience of the Limousin, 1848–51"—a very 1970s title. I went off to France to do my research, beginning in Paris.

During most of my first year in Paris I lived in a room in the Hôtel Stella, 41 rue Monsieur-le-Prince, two blocks from Odéon and with the Jardin du Luxembourg close by. From the hotel I could walk to the Archives Nationales in the Marais, a wonderful trek that took me past Notre Dame, the Hôtel-de-ville and the Bazar de l'Hôtel-de-ville department store, and then up the rue des Archives. My room went for 11 francs a night, then about $2.25. Beneath the hotel there was and still is the restaurant Polidor. Legend says the great socialist prime minister Jean Jaurès dined from time to time in this classic eating establishment. Now, alas, it is far from what it once was. Back then one could have a terrific meal for 14 francs. Extremely ordinary but drinkable wine went for 2.50 francs a bottle. Sunday nights at Polidor were always chaotic, with rugby teams partying loudly in the back room.

The first day that I went to the Archives Nationales I was quite nervous. Graduate students and historians from the United States working in France were then quite rare. I managed to figure out how to order cartons without annoying the then-generally grim, blue-smocked personnel. When Jules Michelet worked in "the catacombs of manuscripts" in the Archives Nationales he wanted to bring the long-deceased back to life again. And, "as I breathed their dust," he wrote, "I saw them rise up."[1]

I asked for BB30 361 in the rich series of the Ministry of Justice. It contains precious documentation on events in Limoges in the spring of 1848, when porcelain workers rose up and briefly held power in the porcelain city following the first elections of the Second French Republic. After a lengthy wait the carton arrived at my share of one of the tables at which researchers worked. I stared at the very old carton and with great excitement opened it up. Michelet had been right: clouds of dust almost exploded from it—the carton evidently had not been opened in quite a long time. But, there before me, were two huge dossiers concerning Limoges in 1848. I distinctly remember thinking, "I will indeed have a dissertation." I held in my hands real reports tendered by the prefect of Haute-Vienne, by the *procureur général* of Limoges, and by local gendarmes. (Now that more and more of French archives have been microfilmed and are only available in that form, part of the thrill of research arguably is gone.) As I read the reports the past came to life. I loved it and I began taking copious notes on *fiches Bristol*.

Directly across from the main entrance to the Archives Nationales on the corner of rue Francs-Bourgeois and the rue des Archives stood a small café. Monsieur and Madame Charles Bonis, who ran Le Petit Berri, were not from the region of Berri at all, but rather from Auvergne. Charles Bonis was from Cantal and was very proud of being a Cantalien or Cantalou. Madame Charles was from Aveyron, further south in Auvergne. Both had grown up in extremely modest villages. Each had more than ten brothers and sisters, some of whom had not survived infancy or childhood. They had met in Paris at an Auvergnat dance on rue de Lappe, a street on which many people from the region then lived. In the twentieth century, particularly after World War II, many Auvergnats became *cafetiers* in Paris. News of available cafés passed by word of mouth or were listed in Auvergnat publications in the capital. Thanks to a timely loan from a neighbor back in Cantal who had no children, the Bonis couple managed to take over Le Petit Berri in 1964 and kept the name.

Many clients of Le Petit Berri were researchers, some of whom, like me, had their first espresso there before the enormous doors of the archives swung opened at 9:00 a.m. and a second one later in the morning. Some returned for lunch, which back then was never more than a sandwich for me. Depending who was researching in Paris on a given year or over breaks in the academic calendar, within a few years a group of historians would gather for a drink or two after work. Monsieur and Madame Charley had no idea and could not have cared less about who was working on what or who had recently published a book. Happily the place was not like that at all—no academic snobs to be seen. My late friend Richard Cobb, the amazing historian, liked to go there for a drink or two. Thanks to Monsieur Charley and his spouse I learned about a region that I had at that point never seen, but where I have been many times since. Several employees of the *caisse municipale* were there virtually every night for a drink. Everyone got along very well. It was nice hanging out with historians, of course, but I enjoyed the company of people whose lives and interests were far from the cartons BB30 and F7 across the street.

Monsieur and Madame Charley were wonderfully nice to me and patient with my then-halting French. I knew virtually no one in Paris when I started working on my dissertation and they made me feel welcome after I had completed the picturesque walk from rue Monsieur-le-Prince to the rue Francs-bourgeois. We gradually became friends. Monsieur and Madame Charley hosted a small gathering at the café for my wife Carol and me shortly after our marriage in New Haven in May 1980. Six years later, Carol would often meet me at the café with baby Laura at the end of my archival day. After they retired in the late 1990s we met up in the same café— which had taken on a different name and had become part of the late-night scene in the Marais. Long after that meeting, I went there one final time and have never been back since. It was very different than before and, in any case, the Archives Nationales for the post-1789 period have moved out to a distant suburb. Charley passed away from a terrible illness in June 2008. I went to Paris for the funeral as did the historian Michael Broers, a good friend of the couple who came from Oxford. It is impossible not to be nostalgic about those days when the archives were full of researchers and *Le Petit Berri* was there for everyone.

Let me reiterate that when I went first to France in September 1970, I knew no one there and was quite shy. Chuck Tilly told me to look up the renowned historian Emmanuel LeRoy Ladurie. I could not imagine doing that. What would I ask the famous historian of Ancien Régime France? I had nothing to say and I doubted that he would have the slightest interest in an American graduate student working on his dissertation on the experience of the Limousin between 1848 and 1851.

One day early in my stay, I saw that great man in the magnificent reading room of the Bibliothèque Nationale, which was still an overwhelming presence on rue Richelieu. Vacillating between fear and panic, I did what my mentor had instructed me to do. I went up to Monsieur le professeur LeRoy Ladurie and clumsily introduced myself as a doctoral student of Charles Tilly. I can't remember exactly the expression on his face—probably because I was staring at my own shoes. He said rather indifferently, "*Très bien . . .* Meet me here in the foyer at *quatorze heures*," and he turned and left. The next day brought me intense uncertainty and nervousness. I went out to the foyer at 1:45 to be sure not to miss him. The clock marched slowly on. 14:00 came and went. So did 14:15. And so did 14:30. And 15:00, in turn. Maybe I had misunderstood *quatorze heures* for *quatre heures*? So I waited some more. 16:00 ticked by. Then 16:30. I realized that Professor Ladurie was not going to show up. Something more interesting had come along—almost anything, I guess, from his point of view. I was vaguely disappointed but also a little angry, even bitter. I vowed that I would never promise something and not follow through particularly when it came to a student, whether one of mine or anyone else's. I had learned something valuable. About a year later, back in Ann Arbor, I ran into a fellow graduate student of Chuck's in the lobby of a movie theater showing Clint Eastwood's film *Dirty Harry.* The student was with LeRoy Ladurie and introduced me to him. It seemed absolutely pointless to mention to the great man that we had met quite briefly once before in Paris, although not really.

While carrying out research in the Limousin, I sometimes returned to Paris for the weekends. I have friends in Le Perreux-sur-Marne in the eastern suburbs of the capital and made a habit of staying there. Late one evening I was with friends at *Le Petit Pont*, an old haunt across the Seine from Notre-Dame. *Le Petit Pont* had already been transformed from a modest establishment of character into a place catering to tourists with money to burn. I happily stayed late to drink another glass of wine or two but the trade-off was that I missed the last possible *métro* to Nation, then the last RER to Nogent-sur-Marne, and finally the last bus to Le Perreux. So I found myself at 1:30 in the morning without a way back to Le Perreux. I walked and ran to Nation, a quite manageable trek, but then was faced with getting to Vincennes and then to Nogent-sur-Marne and finally Le Perreux. At that point I was not really sure how to find Le Perreux. I hitchhiked a ride a little past Vincennes. My hitchhiking benefactors did not know of Le Perreux, and they deposited me where we thought it might be on a road with houses on both sides. It seemed like the middle of nowhere. In vain I looked for a reassuring sign.

After a while I came upon a green and white Paris bus parked along a wide street. In those days no buses ran at night, at least in the suburbs. The bus was obviously out of service. But inside the bus was a bus driver, complete with uniform and cap. He was reading. I never learned why he was there— perhaps it was a *problème de couple*, a family argument. In any case, he seemed quite content reading his book. I walked up to the bus window and, hoping against hope, asked if the bus was still in service. He replied logically and with a bit of scorn, "Of course not!" I asked him how I could find Le Perreux. "*C'est par là!*" he replied, pointing me in the right direction. It was a good distance away. I thanked him and began to run down the road. A few minutes later, I heard a "beep, beep" behind me. I looked back up and there was the same bus. "*Montez, Chef,*" said the driver. He then asked me where I was going in Le Perreux. "Boulevard d'Alsace-Lorraine," I replied in amazement. We reached the boulevard and he had to make a difficult turn to back up toward number 97 where my friends live. He took me right up to the door. I didn't know how to thank him and, perhaps still a bit deadened by wine, I reached for a bus ticket as if to put it in the machine to cancel it. The driver laughed. A ticket wasn't necessary. I thanked him. He drove off in his bus, probably to continue reading somewhere else. The Parisian suburbs had proved very welcoming indeed.

When working in Tulle in the Archives Départementales de la Corrèze (where there were not more than two or three weeks of documents for me), I gradually learned what had happened there during the World War II German occupation of Vichy France in 1944. German SS troops abruptly left one day in early June. There had been many *maquis* in the region, among them André Malraux. As soon as the Germans had gone townspeople poured into the streets of the long, narrow town along the river. But then the unmistakable sound of motorized vehicles was heard. The SS was back. The Germans hung men and even boys—ninety-nine of them—from the lampposts of Tulle. (Those same s s troops soon after headed north, where some of them massacred hundreds of men, women, and children in Oradour-sur-Glane on June 10. That large village became the *site de mémoire* for Nazi atrocities in France.)

In Tulle, as elsewhere, the archives closed for lunch for two full hours. I had nothing to do and virtually zero money to spend on lunch. From time to time, I would have an ice cream cone sold by a vendor who had a small wagon parked along the river. My improving French was good enough for some conversation with the nice ice cream man. One day I brought up the dreadful day of the hangings. I asked if he had been there. Yes, he had, he was fourteen or so then. What had he done when the German troops suddenly reappeared? He had run and hidden under the porch of a house above the river. He had been very lucky. While he was relating this to me, a woman came up and ordered some sort of berry ice-cream cone. The ice-cream man said, "Oh, you remember that awful day, don't you, Madame?" She replied, "I sure do. They hung my husband from that pole right there." The pole stood next to the vendor's wagon. I almost lost my ice-cream. I never will forget it.

During that year my French improved considerably. I played basketball for a team that thankfully no longer exists. I do not even remember what league we played in—we were not paid but had our meals picked up now and then and that was about it. We practiced and played home games at the very large Stade Coubertin in Porte Saint-Cloud. Thousands of people did not come to watch us play. Each team could have only two foreigners. Ours were a giant Serb who was a *pivot,* or center, and me. The Serb and I would meet up for coffee before home games and complain about our French teammates. I don't have many good memories of the whole experience. For one thing, the president of the club intervened constantly in the coaching. Our coach had played on the French national team but this was all way before basketball took off in France. Only later did the Tony Parkers and Nicholas Batums head to the U.S. to play. The coach knew what he was doing but the president, however amiable, did not. We played in cold places most everywhere—I remember thinking we were literally going to freeze before the game started one evening in Beauvais. My role on the team was to shoot and score. I won our first game with a last-second shot, but things never subsequently worked out as I hoped, although I had some good games. One evening we lost and I had shot something like five of sixteen from the field. On the way back to the dressing room, I muttered, "*J'étais terrible.*" "*Non,*" one of my teammates replied, "*Tu étais horrible.*" *On apprend comme ça.*

I returned to Ann Arbor after nine months of fun research and three months of traveling in Europe and sleeping on Mediterranean beaches from Greece to Portugal with a couple of friends. Back in Michigan between trips to the gym I organized my notes and slowly wrote some pages. Struggling with a chapter on urban-rural networks of revolutionary mobilization during the eventful French Second Republic, I went to see Chuck. "Let's go for a walk," he said. I poured out my dilemmas. Tilly stopped walking and said, "Look, in this analysis, you have three fragmentary linkages." I had absolutely no idea what he talking about. I just stood there staring at him. Perplexed by my stunned silence, he said, somewhat patiently, dealing with a mere mortal, "Look, John, you have three fragmentary linkages." Again silence. Now Chuck expressed a little irritation. "You have *three fragmentary* linkages!" To which I could only reply, "Cool." End of conversation. But I titled my chapter "Three Fragmentary Linkages" . . .

I was so proud.

One night in March, after I had been back from France a little more than six months and had written only eighty mediocre pages, I woke up in the middle of the night in terror and began writing. I worked virtually around the clock for twelve days and finished my dissertation. Most of it was a first draft, and anyone who looks at it will easily discover that this is so. I was so tired at the end that I misspelled grateful as "greatful" in the acknowledgements and the thesis has no page 51, as a note inserted in the text by The University Microfilms staff documents.

I hesitantly applied for teaching positions that year but no jobs came my way. I didn't even get a single interview. The following academic year, thanks to Tilly, the University of Michigan pieced together a part-time teaching appointment for me in the departments of history and sociology. That December, I attended the American Historical Association's annual conference in New Orleans (where a man with a rifle, not a historian, got on a roof the last day of the meeting and shot dead a couple of people, including historians). I had several over-the-table interviews and two real ones, including one with R. R. Palmer from Yale. An on-campus interview at Yale followed, as well as a second interview at another liberal arts college in Massachusetts. I was fortunate enough to be hired at Yale, receiving a letter notifying me in early February.

It was intimidating coming to Yale. The University of Michigan was a wonderful, magical place but it wasn't the Ivy League. I could not imagine what Yale would be like. I contemplated this while driving out to New Haven in my recently purchased small car with everything I owned packed into it. (When the department's administrative assistant asked me to provide my moving expenses, the total bill was 13 dollars for gas. She looked at me as if I were from another planet—which I guess I was, yet again sort of a marginal presence—but I later received a check for $13.00.) Would people in the History Department of an Ivy League school accept someone with a doctorate not granted by Yale, Harvard, or Princeton? Would the students be snobs all trained at Andover, Exeter, Deerfield, or some such elite place? Certainly there were cultural differences. In Payne Whitney Gymnasium I came upon a sign on the inside of an exit door: "Do not open for ingress." Most other gyms would have a sign that read, "Don't let no one in this door!" The sign is still there in Payne Whitney, albeit a bit battered by time.

The history department of Yale was in those days the greatest anywhere, boasting C. Vann Woodward, Edmund Morgan, David Brion Davis, John Morton Blum, Peter Gay, Robert Lopez, Jonathan Spence, R.R. Palmer, Robin Winks, John Hall, and Jack Hexter, among others, all as tenured professors of the department. Alas, there was only one tenured female professor, Emilia Viotti da Costa, a historian of Brazil, who began in 1973, the same year as I did. The extremely distinguished historian of China, Mary Wright, who had passed away several years before my arrival in New Haven, only carried the title of lecturer in the History Department, whereas her husband, Arthur Wright, had been named a full professor. Happily, Nancy Cott joined the department in 1975 and things gradually began to change for the better.

The transition to gender balance at Yale was in some ways seamless and in other ways not. When I arrived at the university about 35 percent of the students were female, women having only been first admitted to Yale College in 1969. I heard stories about well-meaning senior male instructors in seminar settings struggling with the change, asking a female student, "Could you please give us a gal's perspective on Chaucer?" or some such question. The percentage of female faculty members was embarrassingly low. Old Yale in many ways lived on, despite the intention of many well-intentioned colleagues. The year before I came to Yale, a young female assistant professor in the Department of History in her first year was invited to dinner at the house of a senior colleague. She was single and all the other women there were spouses of professors in the department. For virtually the entire painful evening no one said a word to her. Finally, as dessert was being consumed, an eminent scholar sitting across the table from her asked, "To whom do you belong?"

During my own first year at Yale, I met a graduate student who was in the job market. I heard he had an on-campus interview, so I asked him how it had gone. "Well enough," came the answer. "Where was the interview?" I asked. He couldn't quite remember! "It was in one of those states that begins with an "I," he replied. Coming from one of those states that begins with an "O," I felt a little aggrieved. But I understood, I guess. None of those states are near I-95.

Yet things went along smoothly enough for me. The great historians were invariably nice and welcoming, even to someone just starting out at age twenty-six. (One had to be more careful of those my late colleague and good friend Robin Winks called the "second-raters"—which is still the case.) But, to repeat, having so many distinguished colleagues was at first intimidating. Ed Morgan offered me advice: "Got a minute? Write a line." It was a bit scary. Not long afterwards Peter Gay told me the first thing he thought about when he woke up in the morning was what he was going to write that day. Even more scary. Back then, the first thing I contemplated was when I could head to the gym to play basketball. A bit later, it was what I would eat that day. And before too long, it was what wine I would drink later that day. Yet soon, although I am no Edmund Morgan or Peter Gay, my first thoughts indeed began to be about what I would write that day.

I held a position at an extremely prestigious place, but I did not have much money. My starting salary was $10,000, out of which I paid $150 a month to live in a virtually unheated beach cottage in Branford, Connecticut. For the following five years, not including a year in France, as well as a few vacations, I lived in Yale's Calhoun College—now happily renamed Hopper College—as a resident fellow (and had a great time there). When in 1979 I was fortunate enough to land a Guggenheim Fellowship, I must have been one of the few recipients whose salary was barely above the amount of the fellowship (the difference was only $500). An accountant friend of mine in Paris did my taxes in exchange for a modest dinner at the restaurant Trumilou on the quai de l'Hôtel de ville because he said he did not have any other client who made so little money. He convinced me to start deducting my expenses for attending academic conferences. Until then, I had only deducted expenses if I had not had a good time at the conference.

In 1980 Carol and I were married and I was fortunate enough to receive tenure. I met Carol in late 1976 on the occasion of the Harvard-Yale football game in Cambridge. I don't pay attention to that game, however fabled, and Carol never liked football— perhaps because she had grown up in Lincoln, Nebraska, where it is omnipresent. A mutual friend introduced us there, nonetheless. A year after we married, it seemed to Carol that it was time for us to move out of Calhoun College and buy a home. We found a nice, small, mid-nineteenth-century house in rural Northford, half an hour from Yale. The next step was to get a mortgage. Since I had tenure, I was, in principle, entitled to one quarter of a percentage point off a mortgage. So we went to a bank, but disappointing news came back: no mortgage. Why? We did not have enough money and tenure did not replace available funds, of which we had about zero.

Old Yale did not seem to have many professors of modest means. Stories swirled about "dollar-a-year men," colleagues for whom any sort of salary was an afterthought. George Pierson, historian of Yale and long-time chair of the history department who had retired the year before my arrival in New Haven, had been rumored to be such a person. On one occasion years earlier, a young assistant professor made an appointment to see him to ask for a small raise. His wife was soon to give birth to a second or third child and money was tight. Pierson did not understand the nature of his junior colleague's visit. After several halting sentences from his extremely nervous visitor, Pierson finally understood. It was about money! "Well," said the chair, "there comes a time in a young man's life when he has to take that certain decision! He has to dip into capital!"

Carol and I had no capital in which to dip. Therefore, no mortgage. The next Tuesday my friend David Large and I were eating lunch in the Fellows Lounge with other members of the history department after another perfectly dreadful Tuesday "sherry hour" in the College Common Room. Pierson was sitting two places away, and no one was sitting with him or between us. David asked what had happened about our mortgage. I relayed the outcome. We needed another five or six thousand dollars. Could we pull that off? David asked. I expressed no optimism on that score. Pierson looked over with a look of contempt and condescension. He said to me, "I couldn't help overhearing your conversation. I have a friend out in Hamden who owns quite a lot of property. I suppose if I call him, he might let you and your wife live in a trailer on his back forty." In Old Yale there were still people around to let you know your place. Some of us younger faculty occasionally noted that Yale rhymes nicely with Jail. (Eventually Carol and I managed to put together some money and ended up with the house.)

In the meantime I continued to spend all vacations and leaves carrying out research in France. When I had worked in Limoges, Guéret, and Tulle for my dissertation research, I fell in love with departmental archives in part because working in them gave me the opportunity to explore different French cities. One of the joys of doing research and living in France was to arrive by train or car and check out possible hotels, restaurants, cafés, and, of course, the location of the archives. Then I would walk and walk, sometimes a green *Guide Michelin* in hand. When I arrived by car, I could explore the regions of each *chef-lieu*. I could never imagine writing about a place or even a street that I had not myself experienced in some way. Nor could I imagine teaching about France if I had not been virtually everywhere in the hexagon.

Subsequent research projects took me to a host of other

departmental archives, and therefore cities. I hope Carol forgave me for going to work in the Archives du Département de la Meurthe-et-Moselle in Nancy while we were on our honeymoon. Being somewhat *maniaque*, I decided that I would work in every departmental archive in France. To be sure, the departmental archives of the Manche, the Aisne, the Loiret, the Pas-de-Calais, and the Ardennes were all severely damaged or largely destroyed by the world wars (the Charleville-Mezières got it in both wars). Fires destroyed valuable archives in Pau and Mende. In La Rochelle—one of my favorite cities anywhere and thus a place where I wanted to work for an extended time—I was told that termites or some other little creatures had devoured much of the "M" series, which was essential for studying the nineteenth century. Nonetheless I went to all of these places to be sure that there was nothing or not much left of interest to me. Eventually I had worked in every departmental archive in the country (excluding several *départements* that were not created in the Paris region until 1968, when the Seine-et-Oise was broken up into several *départements*).

After completing my dissertation I became interested in the series of devastating arson fires that swept through Normandy and parts of northern France in 1829 and 1830, primarily in the context of the mobilization of liberals against the Restoration monarchy of Charles X. I researched these fires in Vincennes and wrote an article about them which I submitted to *French Historical Studies*. A reader for the journal responded condescendingly that I should decide if I wanted to write "real" French history or "rural sociology." (David Pinkney, the editor of *French Historical Studies* and subsequently my good friend, ignored the review and published the article, which is included in this volume.)

Working in the military archives in the Château de Vincennes had its challenges. The reading room was very small. (It also was the first French archive in my experience to require readers to place their personal items in a locker outside the reading room because of a thriving industry of cutting out Napoleon's signature from documents or simply stealing entire reports.) But once you got used to the place, you could do very well there. Many readers were ordinary French men and women searching for their ancestors who had fought in French armies. I loved reading the reports submitted by junior officers who were responsible for mapping and planning imaginary defenses of towns in France or North Africa. They counted up the number of artisans useful for the defense of besieged places such as saddlemakers, metal-workers, and so on. They surveyed entrances to these towns, describing humble auberges. They tried to assess what percentage of the population spoke French well or somewhat well. These are fascinating reports (series MR)—although they often offered a somewhat condescending, relatively elite, and northern view of more southern places. Eugen Weber used these documents in his brilliant but misleading classic *Peasants into Frenchmen*, which argues that "peasants" could not really be "Frenchmen" until three agencies of modernization—railroads, military conscription, and schooling in French—had intervened in their lives. By this view, Gascons, Bretons, Auvergnats, Catalans, Limousins, and others could go off to die as Frenchmen in the Great War only after singing the "Marseillaise" in acceptable French. Of course the reality in much of France was considerably different. Bilingualism survived and indeed thrived in many places. As Jean-François Chanet has shown convincingly, many schoolteachers reported to their superiors that they taught in French, while in fact they continued to use local languages, dialects, and patois to communicate with their pupils.

Certainly one of the reasons I loved reading the *reconnaissances militaires* written by junior officers awaiting promotion was that I liked to do exactly what the officers did as they came up with imaginary defenses of the cities to which they had been assigned. They walked most everywhere, reading the stones of cities and towns and the lay of the land.

When studying the political repression that followed the Revolution of 1848, thus during the Second French Republic (1848–1851), I wanted to consult the series on "military justice" (often a contradiction in terms, *quand même*). I could not find in the bound inventories exactly what I needed, but I knew the documents were stored somewhere among the thousands of hefty boxes in the Vincennes archives. *Madame la présidente de la salle*, apparently the wife or widow of a military officer, was of no help at all; she seemed to have little idea about the archives over which she presided. She simply sat there, seemingly oblivious to readers, resources, everything. I knew these cartons existed, but I could not simply stroll into the vast storage area looking for them.

Another frequent visitor to Vincennes told me that the *gardien*, a genial young soldier who brought cartons that had been ordered to the readers, collected stamps. Naturally I received letters from the United States, as well as from friends in the Peace Corps in various distant places. Some of these missives sported exotic stamps. So I casually left the letters and envelopes out on my work table. One day the *gardien* stopped and said, "My, what beautiful stamps you have there!" "Oh," I replied, "would you like to have them?" A couple of days later, I asked him about the Military Justice series. He told me to wait until *Madame la Présidente* went out at noon—rumor had it she had a daily tryst, at least during the workweek. Then he escorted me back into the storage area. I found the cartons (and also, chained in an enclosed cage, the sensitive documents concerning the French army mutinies in 1917, the consultation of which was then viewed as dangerous for French national pride, although they were subsequently released to scholars). It all worked out, but in the world of French archives, getting the materials you need can take time.

One day I opened a carton in the F1 series (the Second Republic, 1848–51). When I was researching my dissertation, I had gone through the reports carefully, but now I wanted to double check something. The first thing I came upon was not a report from the gendarmerie about events during the heady months of the spring of 1848, but rather a case for reading glasses. "Some poor soul left his or her glasses case in the carton," I sneered to myself. Then my eyes fell on the source of the empty case: "Kennedy and Perkins, New Haven Connecticut." I had been that poor soul. On another occasion I found a magnifying glass in a carton. Briefly tempted to take it with me, I left it with the *président de la salle*. One often leaves something in a place to which one wants to return, and in this case, the archives was that place.

Geographic marginalization—the relegation to the periphery of unwanted activities and people—has been an important theme in my work, so I find it sad that during the years I have been working in *archives départementales*, they, too, have been relegated to the margins of French cities and towns. Arguably one of the reasons for the abandonment of quaint old archive buildings in the center of town has been to provide more storage space for ever-expanding documental holdings, more tables and chairs for *chercheurs,* and more parking spaces to accommodate an expanding clientele, particularly local people and visitors from other regions researching genealogies. Unfortunately many of the more recently constructed departmental buildings are structures of questionable taste, completely *privé d'âme*—with neither soul nor character. At a time when some scholars embracing the popularity of techniques borrowed from literary criticism seek to marginalize—or at least relegate to the bin of the old-fashioned—research into the lives of real people in space and time, physical access to French archives has, in some places, become increasingly difficult.

In 2013 the Archives Nationales moved—at least for *histoire contemporaine*—from the Hôtel Soubise out to Pierrefitte, beyond Saint-Denis, which is a long trek from central Paris. Around the same time, the Archives de la Préfecture de Police left the friendly (although not exactly *rigolo*) confines of the police *commissariat* near place Maubert out to a location several blocks from *métro* Hoche, a good forty-five minute ride from "downtown" Paris.

In the mid-1980s, the Archives Départementales de la Haute-Vienne moved a good distance out of Limoges to a site near the university (another example, in the years since 1968, of the relegation of people—students—unwanted in the center to the periphery of urban life). The archives in Perpignan had already moved outside the city, near the apartment complex of Moulin-à-Vent. At noon, *chercheurs* without a car had to take the bus into town to find something to eat. The grand champion of inconvenience may be the departmental archives of Haute-Marne. When I worked there the archives were found in the *commune* of Choigne—beyond Chaumont, beyond a garbage dump, and not even near a bus stop. Genealogists usually have cars, yet many historians and graduate students do not. When I worked briefly in the Archives Départementales du Doubs, I had to enter the archives through a parking lot at the Mammouth *hypermarché*.

To be sure, charming and centrally located departmental (and municipal) archives remain, such as those in Nîmes, Poitiers, Rodez, Dijon (where Mozart once gave a concert in the elegant room that served as the *salle de lecture* when I was there), the Vaucluse in Avignon (virtually in the Palais des Papes, although surrounded by the increasingly greedy commercialization of mass tourism), Eure-et-Loire (in the shadow of the magnificent cathedral of Chartres), and Indre-et-Loire (in a *quartier* in Tours described by Balzac). Greater convenience for some users does not make up for the charm and intimacy of the old buildings of character. Yet at least in departmental archives, whether relegated to the periphery or not, the documents themselves are still to be found.

In addition to Chuck Tilly, the historians of France who are in my private pantheon and who shaped the social and political histories of modern France include my friends Michelle Perrot (whose work on women and the world of work, and much else, remains fundamental), Alain Corbin, the most imaginative of all French historians, the late Maurice Agulhon, Yves Lequin, and Robert Darnton.

Richard Cobb has also been an inspiration to me, although perhaps in other ways. Following his brilliant study of *Les Armées révolutionnaires* and his persuasive *The Police and the People*, Richard largely turned to writing essays based on his decades of experiences in France, going back to the 1930s. Richard's writing is wonderfully evocative; he bounces back and forth in his texts between English and French, even refusing to translate French quotations. His essays on "Paris Xe"—no one then wrote about the tenth arrondissement, where Richard for a time lived—and "DAN 34-25"—his phone number when he lived on rue Tournon just below the Luxembourg Gardens—are among my favorites. Above all Richard had a supreme sense of place (*People and Places* is the title of one of his books). He dismissed the work of Albert Soboul and George Rudé, once his friends, both of whom I knew and liked very much. They wrote about social movements, and, above all, about quantification in history. Richard had contempt for the whole idea of "*les sans-culottes.*" He cherished the individual in history—their daily routines, personal itineraries, and trajectories. Despite Tilly's work in quantitative history, Cobb had much more than a grudging respect for him because Chuck insisted on the significance of the lay of the land in his work. (Cobb even wrote a review of *The Vendée* in which he described Tilly roaming through Anjou and the Vendée in Bermuda shorts).

I got to know Richard, who was both an amazing historian and quite a character. Stories of Cobb's drinking episodes, one of which occurred at Yale, are legend. His former doctoral students emerged as the most eminent and—like Richard himself—most readable historians of the French Revolution (along with Timothy Tackett in the United States and Peter McPhee in Australia): Alan Forrest, Colin Jones, Peter Jones, and Michael Broers. Richard knew France and spoke superb French, and he insisted that his students do so as well. One of my favorite of his many books is *A Second Identity*, in which he grapples with living in two very different worlds, as I suppose I do as well.

After completing my dissertation, I paused to organize an edited book, *1830 in France,* which included "The *Demoiselles* of the Ariège, 1829-31" (reprinted in this book). When that was finished, I was eager to research and write an account of "radicalization and repression" in France as a whole, organizing the study both thematically and with chapters on other regions to which I could compare what had occurred in Limousin. There was nothing unusual in deciding on such a subject for a book-length study, particularly as I had already fallen in love with departmental archives, as well as with the Archives Nationales in Paris and the Military Archives in Vincennes. That research and curiosity led to *The Agony of the Republic: The Repression of the Left in Revolutionary France, 1848–1851*.

Once that book was completed, after considerable research, it was time to think about my next project. Cities, towns, and *bourgs* (small market towns) had led the social, political, and cultural transition of modern France. I wanted to write the history of a single city—Limoges—over the course of the nineteenth century, combining colorful narrative—what used to be called "thick description"—and analysis. The experiences of ordinary people in space and time provide a valid means of understanding sweeping change. I argued that Limoges, not Paris, was the real "*ville rouge*" during this period (and Narbonne as well). In every revolution, Limoges was the forefront. It was the scene of dramatic strikes in 1905, during which French soldiers shot and killed a porcelain worker. While researching my thesis, I had become aware of the historical role of the butchers of Limoges, who were members of five families that had controlled the trade for centuries. They resided—appropriately enough—on the rue de la Boucherie and adjoining streets. Whereas Limoges, and indeed virtually the entire Limousin, had become increasingly dechristianized, the butchers remained relentlessly faithful to the Catholic Church, an identity symbolized by the statue of the Virgin Mary that stands outside the butchers' chapel in old Limoges.

I subsequently learned that at one point during the massive 1905 strikes in Limoges, porcelain workers had left their barricades in the working-class faubourgs that lay beyond the place Denis Dussoubs and had marched to the butchers' quartier. Their goal was to smash the butchers' statue of the Virgin Mary—the last such statue standing in a public place in the city. The butchers were armed and ready. The statue is still there.

This "Incident at the Statue of the Virgin Mary" (reprinted in this volume) provided me with an entry into researching and writing *The Red City: Limoges and the French Nineteenth Century*. In my narrative and analysis, I focused on these two communities: the butchers in their tiny quartier, and the porcelain workers, the majority of whom lived in the working-class faubourgs and had roots in the rural world of the southern Haute-Vienne, speaking patois—not French—in daily life. This strategy allowed me to avoid the diffuse nature of a French *thèse*, which would be congenial neither for publishers nor readers. I sought to bring these communities and neighborhoods to life.

I decided to spend considerably more time in Limoges to complete this research. The porcelain city has always had something of a poor reputation in France. The verb *"limoger"* means to fire, dismiss, or cashier. If a general was sent to Limoges it was considered a disgrace. When I first went to Limoges I spent some Sunday nights sleeping in the Gare des Bénédictins, arriving from Paris at about 3:30 a.m. The goal was to save the 11 francs I would otherwise be paying for a room at the very modest Hôtel d'Isly, which no longer exists. At 8:30 I would drop my little bag at the hotel and head up the hill to the archives. I knew virtually no one in Limoges, which was as cold as the people there with whom I came into contact. The city had done virtually nothing to maintain the rue de la Boucherie and other potential tourist sites. British tourists heading to Dordogne further south rarely stopped to see anything as they passed through the city.

I had nothing to occupy my free time in Limoges except watch miserable films in a theater near the archives. I am not a film person, but I had to have something to do. Once, on my third visit to the theater in a week, the woman at the *caisse* looked at me and exclaimed, *"C'est toujours vous, mon pauvre monsieur!"* Since my time, Limoges has embraced its interesting past, and the place Denis Dussoubs (named after a Montagnard representative from Haute-Vienne shot dead on a barricade defending the Second Republic against the coup d'état of Louis Napoleon

Bonaparte in December 1851) is full of interesting cafés. This was not the case when I first stayed and worked there.

Upon returning for more research in the Archives Départementales de la Haute Vienne over the next couple of years, I began to like Limoges more and more because I knew the place very well and had walked—as always—almost every street thinking about the past. A sense of familiarity with the place had developed. I later took my kids there when they were quite young and showed them the statue of the Virgin Mary and the butchers' chapel, but they were not terribly interested, although later that changed. When I was invited back to Limoges in 2002 to receive an honorary doctorate, I went alone.

Three years later it was an enormous pleasure to be asked back again to give a lecture on the centenary of the Limoges strikes of 1905. The influence of the left was such that the event was held in the elegant hall where the Conseil Régional meets. I anticipated thirty or forty people in attendance. To my surprise, there were hundreds there, not because of me, but because of the importance of the porcelain industry and the extent to which the strikes still loom large in the collective memory of the city. The Haviland Company, once the largest producer of Limoges porcelain, had recently thrown in the towel. (Several years earlier I had participated in a documentary for FR3 television, filmed on an impossibly hot day—unusual for Limousin—in which I stood among broken plates and dead pigeons in what was left of one of the two Haviland factories undergoing demolition.) Only Bernardaud remained of the major producers of porcelain, and rumors had it that the company was moving its operations to Poland. A women's choral group wearing red scarves was there, singing revolutionary songs from the turn of the twentieth century. One of them, tears streaming down her cheeks, read a letter from her grandmother to her mother, describing the death of the porcelain worker Camille Vardelle. For me, it was unforgettable. The day, which began with drinks about half past ten in the morning at the Maison du peuple, ended in the early morning hours in a restaurant that had stayed open late for us. Limoges rocked.

I was fortunate in that the Archives départementales in Limoges are extraordinarily rich. Unclassified censuses and other documents in the attic of the *hôtel-de-ville* also proved useful. Jean-Claude Peyronnet, historian at the Université-de-Limoges, longtime president of the Conseil Général de la Haute-Vienne, subsequently also president of the Conseil Régional, and later senator representing the Haute-Vienne, helped me carry the heavy 1905 census to a taxi and then out to the university so I could make photocopies of the entire set. When we were done, I of course returned them to the attic of the town hall.

I remain attached to the imposing challenges and terrific pleasures of archival research. Thus I fully agree with Arlette Farge, a distinguished historian of Ancien Régime France: "The archival document is a tear in the fabric of time, an unplanned glimpse offered into an unexpected event. In it, everything is focused on a few instants in the lives of ordinary people who were rarely visited by history, unless they happened to form a mob and make what would later be called history." She asks,

> How can we rescue from oblivion these lives that were never made note of even when they were alive (or if they were recognized it was only in order to punish them)? . . . The taste for the archive is rooted in these encounters with the silhouettes of the past, be they faltering or sublime. There is an obscure beauty in so many existences barely illuminated by words, in confrontation with each other . . . [which] can at least evoke alternate outcomes, margins of freedom for possible futures, if only by conveying a sense of human dignity and working to measure the depth of sorrow and pain.[2]

Approaches to the study of French and other histories rise and fall like great powers and empires (and history departments). In 1974 I attended my first meeting of the Society of French Historical Studies, held at Johns Hopkins University in Baltimore. I encouraged Peter Gay to attend a session—they were all plenary back then—on themes in recent social history, at the time so much in vogue. Christopher Johnson spoke about his project on the prodigious industrialization and de-industrialization of the Lower Languedoc. Peter seemed increasingly bored, even antsy. After about fifteen minutes, he had written nothing on his large yellow legal pad. Finally, in exasperation, he wrote on it in large letters and passed it to me: "Hell with this stuff! I want to hear about Flaubert!" But Peter soon was reading lots of social history, preparing his monumental multi-volume history of "the bourgeois experience," Victorian and otherwise. And he loved to read Chris Johnson's work. Parenthetically, it was Peter who, despairing of what he called the *via regia* of intellectual history— the study of how one idea met up with another off in space somewhere and begat another idea—had only a few years earlier called for a "social history of ideas." This is what Robert Darnton did so brilliantly, as did Johnson in his wonderful study of the ideological constituency of Étienne Cabet, the Icarian utopian socialist.[3]

Our craft went through a phase of heavy-duty "new" cultural history, closely tied to the famous "linguistic turn." I must admit that during the heyday of this kind of approach, I found myself thinking sympathetically about Peter Gay's reaction to my friend's talk at the gathering of the Society for French Historical Studies. At our conferences I sometimes wanted to cry out, "To hell with this stuff—I want to hear about the Lot-et-Garonne, I want to hear about Alsace! I want to hear about seasonal migration!"

At the very end of the 1990s, I had to prepare a job talk for a position at a renowned university in the eastern United States. Looking at the roster of colleagues there, it occurred to me that I had better have something to say about language, and had better sharpen up my knowledge of the "new" cultural history. I put together a paper about language—"*Les mots de la ville*" (reprinted in this volume), building on *Aux marges de la ville: faubourgs et banlieues en France, 1815–1871*. Just before I hopped on the train, I realized that I also needed to be ready to answer questions that would surely be posed by a leading cultural historian of modern Europe. I said to myself, "You *cannot possibly* go down to The Seminar if you are not ready to answer a question about 'visual signifiers.'" Sure enough, I was asked what my descriptions and analyses had to say about visual signifiers. The answer was obvious: the *octrois* of French cities—until World War II, the point of entry where one paid taxes on goods brought into town, thus financing most of the municipal budget. I had been very fortunate to have guessed correctly, and I appeared to be more in the flow of what was considered cool than I actually was. At the end of my presentation (and the article that ensued), I made what I still consider an important point: language can itself be a dynamic of change, but it is absolutely essential to remember that real economic, social, political, and cultural change alter the meaning of words and terms, and not the other way around. For all the benefits of new cultural history, the claims of history—of the real experiences of people in space and time—were, I think, sometimes lost.

Some of the "new" cultural history did indeed give me the impression that reading between the lines in selected texts risked losing knowledge about the historical experience of France and the French people in the process. Indeed, I once heard an excellent practitioner of the approach express great pride in knowing next to nothing about France or contemporary French culture. Long ago David Pinkney, one of the founding fathers of the Society for French Historical Studies, argued provocatively that it was difficult for Americans to do serious work in France because France is relatively far from the United States. I never took his contention seriously. Yet because *problématiques* have changed, today there are far fewer American historians of France than twenty or thirty years ago working in the Archives Nationales or in departmental archives, even those that were once frequented in fairly impressive numbers, including the Rhône, the Loire, the Hérault, the Haute-Garonne, and the Gironde. (Moreover, the cost of research in France is even greater than in the past.) It is worth noting that because of continued interest in the complexities of cultural identities, the Bas-Rhin (Strasbourg) still attracts attention. There are also many fewer *chercheurs français*. It seems to me that all too often, American graduate students and professors fly to France, go to an archive or library, take numerous photos of documents, get back on another plane, and return to North America. What is missing from their research is France.

To my mind, the real triumphs of cultural history include the work of Peter, Roger Chartier, and Daniel Roche, among others. Robert Herbert's brilliant *Impressionism: Art, Leisure, and Parisian Society* reflects the influence of the history of art, which has sometimes been dominated by connaisseur-ship and questions such as where Cézanne got his red ochre. Herbert largely created the social history of French painting. Debra Silverman's fantastic study of art nouveau also combines the best of interdisciplinary approaches.[4]

In thinking about French history from 1815 to the present, one thing now seems perfectly clear to me. As time moves relentlessly along, the century between 1815 and World War I is in some ways far less visible than it was when I became a historian. One day a couple of years ago I was down at the giant FNAC bookstore, in the monstrously failed Forum des Halles, looking for a book on the Paris Commune. For years the shelves had been organized chronologically: the French Revolution and Napoleon, then the nineteenth century, subdivided, and then the Great War. But the sections now jumped from Napoleon to the Great War! What had happened to the long nineteenth century? (What happened to my books?) A helpful clerk led me to a shelf beneath one of the tables. I had to get down on my knees to search for the period from 1815 to 1914. To be sure, this was just one bookstore, but the new arrangement was revealing. It was a rather sad moment for me. The revolutions of 1830 and 1848, which had so engaged folks like me for quite some time, seemed to have had their day.

Since the early 1970s, historians have undertaken an incredible amount of excellent research and have crafted superb studies of the two world wars, the dismantling of European empires in the twentieth century, and other important topics. In France, the fifty-year prohibition for accessing archival documents limited what sources historians could read. Robert Paxton's path-breaking *Vichy France*, first published in 1972 in English and French, was largely based on captured German documents, newspapers, and memoir literature because the French archival holdings were blocked. On one occasion, an archivist informed Paxton in a departmental archive that he was a "troublemaker" for seeking documents related to right-wing agricultural movements in the 1930s. Some of those powerful families were still very much alive in the region. As such documents became available—what Tilly once referred to rather provocatively as "Clio's striptease," the gradual revealing of the past—Henry Rousso published his influential *Vichy Syndrome*. Vichy France became a major focus for many terrific historians in France, Great Britain, and the United States. More recently, the Great War also became a crucial topic, even more so with the centenary of World War I.

After publishing *The Red City: Limoges and the French Nineteenth Century* (*Limoges, la ville rouge*), I started a project on the so-called "dangerous and laboring classes" in French cities during the first half of the nineteenth century. My goal was to demonstrate that the great historian of Paris, Louis Chevalier, had got it right about the image the upper classes had of ordinary, working Parisians, but quite wrong in arguing that the "dangerous classes" and "laboring classes" were the same—in other words, that revolution was basically an extension of purse-snatching.[5]

I began working on the project in the Archives Nationales and various *archives départementales*. But I was struggling. The work was not coalescing. Much of what I was seeing in judicial, police, and other reports seemed perfectly obvious. The "dangerous classes" were largely in the imagination of the French elite. One morning I was sitting in the Archives Départementales de la Meuse in Bar-le-Duc, a town most well-known as the origin of the *voie sacrée* that carried supplies to French forces fighting northeast of nearby Verdun in 1916. (I must say that my *voie sacrée* that day was the one that would get me out of there as quickly as possible.) It was pouring rain outside, and I glumly contemplated what to do for lunch when the archives closed at noon for two hours. Then I came across a police report that dramatically changed the *problématique* of my study.

The report described the ill-fated procession of several prostitutes, indeed the most miserable of the poorest prostitutes in Verdun, on June 23, 1825. They passed through the gates of the fortified town and marched, "somewhat drunk," along the rue des Ramparts de la Porte Saint-Victor, between the lower and upper sections of the strategically important town that the great military engineer Vauban had fortified in the seventeenth century. The walls all too arbitrarily marked the end of the countryside's modest vineyards. It was generally beyond the walls that the prostitutes plied their trade. The procession mocked the coronation of Charles X, which had been held the previous May 29 in Reims. The prostitutes wore their best clothes, basically rags, replacing candles with parts of broken broomsticks. One of them led the way, using an ordinary stick for a bishop's staff, while another followed, lifting the back of her friend's long dress above the dust of the town's poor periphery as if it were a robe of silk. The prostitutes sang "unintelligibly" to the tune of a church hymn or canticle. Their first "station" was not of the cross but a cabaret on rue Saint-Victor, from which they were quickly expelled. They tried to get others "from the same class" to follow them, but their little procession attracted only a small following of six children. The police arrested the prostitutes, who each received six months in prison and a fine of 300 francs (which obviously they could never pay), a stiff sentence but one in tune with the times in Restoration France.[6]

This action took place on the margins of urban life, similar to other episodes about which I had written in nineteenth-century Limoges. The prostitutes were perched on the periphery, unwanted by the center. We never hear their side of the story. Outraged indignation seeps through the document which was highly biased against the poor women; they were accused of sacrilegious behavior. I realized that the police account was typical of reports that reflected official and elite fears of the "disorder" associated with people who were considered "marginal," both socially and spatially. "Marginal" thus assumed a social and geographical sense: on or beyond the fringe of bourgeois society, or at or beyond the frontiers of its urban world. The prostitutes mocked the king of France and, in doing so, mocked the denizens of the *beaux quartiers* of Verdun as well. We can take this case as an incidence of solidarity and deliberate resistance articulated by the supposedly inarticulate poor, a mockery of social hierarchy and authority at a time when the Restoration monarchy was challenged not only by liberal opposition but also by ordinary people. The prostitutes had their own solidarity which was shaped by the experience of being outsiders. They were *faubouriennes* in a town without faubourgs (since Verdun was a *ville forte*, one could not build beyond its ramparts). Most probably they lived well beyond its walls. Their joyful, though ill-fated, procession in Verdun was something of a symbolic, *carnivalesque* conquest of the fortified town launched from the outside, the ambiguous land standing between city and country. The prostitutes were identified with the growing faubourgs and *banlieues* of France's cities and towns.

My old *problématique* disappeared. I ate my pizza with gusto and with a new topic, but one still focused on the lives of ordinary people. I had had the good fortune of coming upon a remarkable document leading me to a very different book than the one with which I had started the day. The richness of French archives had again been proven. I set out to explore *The Margins of City Life* during the first half of the nineteenth century.

The study of *faubourgs* and *banlieues* led me to study the relationship between city and country, the place of the edge of cities in political and social contention, changing attitudes toward the margins of city life and the concomitant stigmatization of the urban periphery, and much more. My immediate question was: which cities and towns should I select as examples that would evoke the complexity of the margins of city life? Obviously Paris and its burgeoning suburbs would comprise one focus. Saint-Étienne, a *ville-faubourg* because of its dramatic growth during the early nineteenth century, was an equally obvious choice. I had to put aside the temptation to pick my favorite cities, such as La Rochelle, whose seventeenth-century glory was long gone, as was much of Series M. I selected Reims—most known for its cathedral where French kings, including Charles X, had been crowned—not only because of its champagne but because of its growing industrial suburbs which accompanied the displacement of textile production to the edge of the city. I selected Châtellerault in the *département* of Vienne because of its similarly expanding industrial faubourg (dedicated to arms manufacture) and because nearby Poitiers, which remained an ecclesiastical center as well as *chef lieu,* offered an interesting comparison. Perpignan offered another fascinating contrast. As it was an *agro-ville,* the capital of French Catalonia did not have faubourgs stretching beyond the massive ramparts of the *ville-forte.* However, poor people who in other towns would be living in faubourgs here lived within the walls of the fortified town, because military authorities would not permit houses just beyond Perpignan's ramparts for fear that they could be used advantageously by an invading army. I began to study the gardeners living in quartier Saint-Jacques and the agricultural laborers living in quartier Saint-Mathieu—perpetual enemies, *quartier blanc, quartier rouge.* Both spoke Catalan and were thus culturally marginalized, out of tune with the French-speaking administration as well as the elite of the city.

I then selected La Roche-sur-Yon, a town built on the ruins of a small bourg destroyed during the Counter-Revolution. Napoleon had wanted it to serve as the *chef lieu* of the Vendée in order to bring "civilization"—at least as the emperor defined it—to the previously insurrectionary royalists. La Roche-sur-Yon was constructed with building materials not conducive to the climate and hurriedly put together in a grid pattern with only straight lines permitted. I found it strange to be staying there while working in the *archives départementales,* as it was a town without much of a past, boasting not much more than a national stud farm and a factory producing refrigerators. The Yon River, which provided the town's name, could be hopped in one easy jump. Nîmes appeared as an attractive site for study because in a town so-often bitterly divided between Protestants and Catholics, poor Catholic workers clustered in the faubourg of the Enclos Rey beyond the boulevard that encircled the old town.

When I first went to France I was ashamed to be a citizen of the United States. The Vietnam War was raging, and protests rocked European cities just as they did in New York, Washington, Berkeley, Ann Arbor, and Madison, among many other places. There were ample reasons to protest the policies being carried out by the United States government. Back in those days, Americans in Europe could be pretty easily identified by their jeans and, for some, their tennis shoes. But I went out of my way not to carry the *International Herald Tribune* (which I read for the baseball line scores) in public. Obviously there was nothing I could do about my accent when I spoke French.

Over the years, and then decades, however, I began to feel far more at home in France than in the United States. I now know France far better than I know the United States, although I have also had the chance to travel widely in the country of my birth. I still have something of an American accent—less and less after several glasses of wine—and I can fake an Ardéchois accent. The first time or two that I was on "Les lundis de l'histoire," thanks to Michelle Perrot, the producers sent me a recording of the program, and when I listened my accent seemed to jump out at me.

Our daughter, Laura, first went to France when she was three months old and has spent half of her life there. Our son, Chris, arrived in Lyon and then Balazuc at the age of ten days. Chris, like Laura, was in school so often in France that they avoided having any sort of accent. When Laura was interviewed by *France Culture* in New York during "Occupy Wall Street," in which she participated, she had no accent. A French journalist wrote a piece on Chris a few years back and asked him if he felt more French or American. "*Français, mais pas par nationalité*," he replied, reasonably enough. As he and Laura were both born in Connecticut, neither has French citizenship. Carol and I filled out the forms to become French, and then she worried about taxes (although we pay them in both countries), so we foolishly did not begin the process. But I still feel more French than American, despite my passion for Michigan football and having taught at Yale (but also in France) for many years. I have been very fortunate, thanks to an indulgent university and teaching from time to time in France, to have spent at least half my adult life in the country I love. (Poland, where I have spent about a month every year for the past decade because of a series of very mobile conferences considering manuscripts on that country's history, and some of its neighbors, has now moved up to second place).

We purchased a house in Balazuc in 1987. I had been in Ardèche on several occasions because we had friends with residences in the old Protestant town of Les Vans, on the edge of the Cévennes. Tired of going up and down the stairs with a baby carriage, kitty litter, and assorted provisions to our apartment right off rue du Temple in Paris, we rented one of their houses for a month. Michelin in hand, we went over to visit Balazuc *"un des plus beaux villages en France."* Walking down the narrow *ruelle*, carrying baby Laura, to the twelfth-century Romanesque Church and the small, rocky square that stands before it, we were amazed by the incredible beauty of the village and its surroundings. Just above the stairs leading down to the church we came upon a handwritten sign below the terrace of a house indicating that it was for sale directly through the owner. Carol wanted to take a look so the next day we did, and the following day we came back a second time and several days later we signed a contract to purchase the house in Balazuc, one of the best moves we ever made. Since then, we have been fortunate to have spent about half our time there, with Paris only about four and a half hours away by bus and train.

First we were in Balazuc for all of our vacations, and then for almost two years when I had a sabbatical year from Yale and was teaching at Université Lumière, Lyon-2. We became permanent residents of Ardèche in 1991, with sparkling French identity cards and working papers.

Residing in a small village (except when the tourist hordes arrive in July and August) raises the question of identity. Like everyone not originally from the village, we are both "from here" and "not from here." A good many residents of Balazuc have their origins in the north of France, especially the Nord and the Pas-de-Calais, as their accents make clear. But there is more than an accent at work. A southern accent or even a specifically Ardéchois one does not make one *un(e) balazacain(ne)*. A woman from an adjacent village married someone from Balazuc about fifty years ago, settling in our village. One of our friends asked her kiddingly if she missed the village of her origins. She admitted seriously that "sometimes I get homesick." She will always be considered *une étrangère* by many people born in Balazuc. This is the case for us as well, although our participation in village activities and events makes us considered honorary folks "from here," in a sense. We are thus differentiated from the many people (Lyonnais, a few Parisians, and others, including Dutch, Belgians, Britons, and even a Norwegian family) with a secondary residence here. But we will never really *be* from here. I guess that sometimes bothers me, because I have often had the feeling in the past of not really fitting in, of being marginal. Moreover, although arguably my family and I do indeed have a "second identity," because we have been here so many decades, and I have spent much of that time researching and writing about France, as well as exploring most everywhere in the country, I realize full well that I will never really be French.

I did not go to Balazuc with any intention of writing a book about the village. I was then working on two separate projects, *The Margins of City Life* and the first edition of *A History of Modern Europe*. Balazuc seemed irrelevant to the former and only a tiny part of the latter. Yet as I sat on our terrace across from the *église romane*, walked through the village on the way to take the kids up to their one-room schoolhouse, or ran on the rocky, arid, and rugged Jurassic plateau (the *gras*) that lies beyond and above the Ardèche River, I tried to imagine how people managed to scrape a living out of what was called, reasonably enough, the "ungrateful" rocky terrain. I also wondered what difference the "great events" of past centuries—the Wars of Religion during three different centuries, the French Revolution, the Revolution of 1848, and, above all, the two world wars—-had made in Balazuc.

On September 22, 1992, a tremendous storm began with lightning about three in the morning. It rained and rained and the river rose rapidly, coming within a few feet of the top of the bridge that had been constructed in 1884 as a political pay-off for the conservative village voting for the Republic. The storm killed three people in the Ardèche, although none in Balazuc; it took about 150 lives in Vaison-la-Romaine in Vaucluse and in a village in the Drôme. For more than two decades after the storm, a photo hung in the café *Chez Paulette* in Balazuc of the school kids with their teacher, Jacques Imbertèche, and me standing on the bridge, strangely confident that we would not be swept away. (When a friend gave up the café, he gave me the photo.) These *grandes crues* had come before. People had done what they could to repair the damage, and then they had gone back to work. I was struck by the sense of inevitability with which the dramatic storm had been greeted, and I wanted to know how people, whose lives depended on extracting a living from rocky soil, some of whom had homes near the river, had managed to bounce back after catastrophes that were described as periodic but that invariably left a mark on collective memory and in stories told before the fire in the evening.

I knew that the list of grievances (*le cahier de doléances*) that had been drawn up in Balazuc during the spring of 1789 had been signed in the medieval church across the small square below our terrace. I went over to the archives in Privas to read about what the men of Balazuc had to say about their isolation, their poverty, and their hopes. I was amazed to find that of the twenty-eight men who had signed the document (or had marked it with an "X"), the families of seventeen of them still lived in Balazuc. It was an astonishing continuity in a medieval village whose population had risen from four or five hundred in the eighteenth century to nine hundred in 1851 (swollen by the modest possibilities offered by the production of raw silk), before falling to barely two hundred after World War II. Some of the same names, not surprisingly, are etched on the *monument aux morts* outside the "new" church (built in 1896) honoring those killed in the Great War.

One evening, the parents of Balazuc's schoolchildren were asked to meet in the schoolroom. The topic to be discussed was the creation of a school *cantine*, or lunchroom, in order to discourage a few mothers from putting their kids in school in nearby towns in which they worked. We feared that the number of pupils in Balazuc had fallen so low that the school risked being closed. This was a meeting like many others in which Carol and I participated over the years, discussing kayak and canoe lessons or planning fund-raising activities to finance school outings or planning for "Nature's Classroom," the *la classe verte* (when the kids went to Paris, it became the *la classe grise*), which was a stay of four or five days in another *département*, thus well beyond the village. But this time the then-mayor, whom we barely knew at all, was going to attend. This lent a sense of formality to the occasion, unusual in gatherings that invariably ended around a bottle of Armagnac.

When we began to discuss ways to keep our school going, the importance of which virtually everyone in the village agreed upon, the mayor said something about how we might maintain an unofficial (and thus not approved by the regional school authorities) lunch service for children that would encourage mothers to put their children in our school. Our school risked being closed because the number of pupils in the *classe unique*—one-room school in which all grades may be represented—had fallen as low as nine. This made me wonder if the relationship between the state and France as a whole and our small village and its one-room schoolhouse had not been reversed since the nineteenth century. The French state had more often than not been viewed as an outsider, sometimes forcing unwanted changes on villages. For example, national school authorities insisted in the second half of the nineteenth century that the primary school pupils be taught in French, not in the Occitan patois (or elsewhere, whatever language, dialects, or patois were still common—thus Breton, German, Basque, Flemish, Provençal, Gascon, various Occitans, such as the Occitan spoken in southern Ardèche, and so on). This was, of course, not necessarily what actually occurred. Yet the state, in principle, called the shots. Now, the parents of the pupils were discussing how we could resist as long as possible the impingement of national and regional authorities on our school. Maintaining a school in Balazuc was, and still remains, essential to the village's ability to keepits identity and coherence as a community, and to not just become another beautiful site for the tourist hordes in the summer months.

I soon headed eagerly to the departmental archives in Privas and found precious documents that had been left in the *mairie*, where I could work pretty much whenever I wanted as the new mayor was a friend. I began another long and fruitful research journey. I explored the resourcefulness of peasants in Balazuc, contradicting the all too familiar image of rural people locked in routine until agents of "modernization" could come along to rescue them by teaching them French and taking them into the modern world. The "golden tree" in Ardèche, the Drôme, Gard, Vaucluse, and elsewhere in the region was the mulberry whose leaves fed silkworms from the eighteenth century (and even earlier) until the malady of *pébrine* that arrived in 1849, attacking silkworms and ending the halcyon days of raw silk production. I carried Balazuc's story into the present, when mass tourism— particularly during the summer months—emerged as the second "golden tree," benefitting some in the village, including friends, and annoying many others, including sometimes us.

When I started working on *The Stones of Balazuc*, Laura was asked what she thought of the village by a journalist from the *Chronicle of Higher Education* who had come to write a story about our lives in France. Laura, then very young, replied, "It's just a pile of rocks!" She could not understand why I was writing a book about the place. "Daddy, how many people will care how many goats there were in Balazuc in 1827?" she asked, reasonably enough. (Some folks in China appear to care, and *The Stones of Balazuc* appeared in Chinese translation after it was published in French and Dutch.) After a couple of years in school in Balazuc, Laura informed me that she had changed her mind about the village and, for that matter, *la belle France*. When I asked why, she replied, *"Je préfère la France, il y a des beaux mecs-là!"* She added that in Balazuc, "It's how you are, not what kind of car you drive." Laura got it right about the latter, and that's one reason among many why Balazuc became our real home and why our kids have spent half their lives in France. I guess because of this, *The Stones of Balazuc* was particularly fun to write.

The only real challenge of living in Balazuc is *haute saison* when tourist masses descend on the village. In July and August, the road through the village becomes one-way, with two municipal appointees turning back cars trying to head into the village from the principal route, pointing them instead toward increasingly vast parking lots with their modest fee of two euros. During the summer days, a constant procession of visitors walk toward the *église romane,* thus passing by our terrace. Fortunately this is not the Côte d'Azur, and the tourists are generally quiet and invariably polite. One hot afternoon I was sitting on our terrace in shorts and a t-shirt, as I often do during summer. Three elderly ladies suddenly walked up our seven steps, asking "It this the Romanesque church?" I cracked. "Yes, *Mesdames,"* I replied politely, "and I am the village priest and Mass will begin in forty minutes!" Shock—if not horror—hardly describes their reaction, as they retreated down the stairs, perhaps going on to relate to friends what a strange priest they had come upon in an Ardèchois village.

A one-room schoolhouse is a good way to grow up. Before Laura started CP (the equivalent of first grade in the United States), there were only nine pupils in the *école publique* of Balazuc (eight girls and one boy). The number jumped by a few the year she began CP and the next year CE1, second grade. The older pupils helped the teacher with the younger ones. A dog and sometimes a cat or two were invariably present. Before 4:30 p.m., the parents gathered outside the door, exchanging news and waiting for their offspring to finish the school day. One clear advantage of the *classe unique* is that if the teacher is terrific—certainly the case when our kids were in school there—the pupils can look forward to the next year with none of the uncertainty about what the teacher in the next class will be like. (Of course, when the teacher is not so good, dread can replace eager anticipation.) During the 1970s and 1980s, the government shut down thousands of one-room schoolhouses in France as an economy measure, frequently leaving kids with long bus rides to and from a school in another village or a nearby town. One test result demonstrated that kids who had been in one-room schoolhouses did slightly better than those who had not. In any case, our permanent connection to the village was solidified through the school. We met our best friends through Balazuc's little school.

Contemporary events can and do contribute to selecting topics for research. The fact that we are now living in an age of terrorism led me to write a book about Émile Henry, the anarchist who tossed a bomb into the crowded Café Terminus near gare Saint-Lazare in Paris in February 1894. I argued that by choosing ordinary bourgeois as targets to kill—people who were out drinking beer and listening to music—Émile Henry initiated the age of modern terror.[7] As in many of my other books, this one began with a story I tried to make gripping, and then circles back to analyze what was going on.

I originally became interested in anarchism in college when I read Barbara Tuchman's *The Proud Tower*. Having worked on topics related to the dynamic duo of industrial capitalism and the French state during the nineteenth century sharply increased my understanding of the emergence of anarchism. Unlike socialists, anarchists did not want to capture the state. They wanted to destroy it. The vast majority of anarchists were not violent. But I wanted to understand Émile Henry's hatred. As students, some of us had a similar (but not murderous) contempt for the U.S. government at the time of the war in Vietnam. Thus I followed Henry around for well more than two years, thanks to rich documentation in the Archives of the Prefecture of Police, newspaper accounts, and memoir literature. I guess if one is going to write a book in which a central character provides the focus and narrative, it made some sense to pick someone who only lived to be twenty-one years old—it made for a shorter book! Still, it was bizarre to have dined three or four times in the café-restaurant that the subject of my book blew up. On one occasion, I am quite sure that a colleague and I sat in the same location as Henry had when he ordered—and paid for—his beer before purchasing a cigar, which he used to ignite his small bomb. I went most everywhere Henry had been. Henry was an intellectual, thus not *marginaux* such as Ravachol or Auguste Vaillant, who tossed a tiny explosive device into the Chamber of Deputies in December 1893 to awaken people to the misery of the poor.

Following the deadly explosion of a bomb in the police station near the Palais-Royal, Henry was briefly a suspect. The boss for whom he worked near the gare du Nord had given him two errands to do, one of which was near the church of Madeleine and the other not far from the Arc de Triomphe. Between these two tasks, could Henry have returned to his room in Montmartre to pick up a bomb and returned to central Paris to place it in front of the door of the Carmaux Mining Company on avenue de l'Opéra within the time he was away from his place of work? It seemed unlikely that he could have covered so much ground in two hours and fifteen minutes. Émile was removed from the list of subjects. Later, when Henry was on trial for his life, a detective made the same trek and found that it was possible. I tried it myself in September 2005, replacing tramways and omnibuses with a bus and the métro and a carriage with a taxi. I subtracted the thirteen minutes when my taxi could not turn left onto the avenue de l'Opéra because of construction. I also subtracted seven minutes because I could not get into the building on the rue Véron (down the hill from what was for Henry the hated Sacré-Coeur basilica) and walk quickly up to his room on the top floor and then back down. I finished the same route in two hours and fifteen minutes. Parisian traffic congestion today keeps vehicles moving at the same pace as late nineteenth-century tramways and omnibuses.

I cannot imagine writing anything about the history of modern France without having seen and experienced the place, even if I was writing about things that had taken place more than a century before. While working on the French Revolution of 1848–51, I knew that some oaths to defend "*La Belle*"—the Second French Republic—had been taken in a rabbit warren in the canton of Toucy in the *département* of Yonne. And so on one very long afternoon, Carol and I drove through villages looking for something that seemed to fit the description provided by one of the arrested insurgents during the interrogation of a democratic-socialist prisoner in December 1851. We never did find it, but I had to try.

When writing *Dynamite Club,* I went out to Brévannes, southeast of Paris. Émile Henry had lived there with his mother and two brothers—and father, until he passed away in 1882—when the family moved back to France from Barcelona. I found the spot where his mother's modest auberge stood and looked without success in the cemetery for Émile's tomb. I had to try. When writing a book about Victor Kibaltchiche (later, Victor Serge), one of my heroes, I tried to get up to the top of the Palais-de-Justice in Bruxelles to see where Victor and his friend Raymond Callemin used to sit, discuss books, and look down on the two Bruxelles, one rich, one very poor. A policeman informed me that this was not a good idea. Back in Paris I went out to Choisy-le-Roi to find the location of the garage where legions of French police, gendarmes, and troops surrounded and killed Jules Bonnot. At that time—1912—the garage stood next to a sizable vacant lot. A friend and I found the exact location which was confirmed by the antique shop owner in the rebuilt garage. Looking at the building I could strip from my view the contemporary buildings that were not there the day of the famous siege in which Bonnot—firing pistols with both hands—met his fate. Having seen a good many contemporary images of the siege, some transformed into postcards, I could visualize what was left of the garage, which the "forces of order" had dynamited before rushing in to kill the awful Bonnot.

We also found in nearby Thiais the location of the house in which several "*illégalistes*" associated with Bonnot—"*la bande á Bonnot*"—bludgeoned to death an elderly man and his aged maid. Two of the gang perished in a shootout as they fired away from a modest "villa" beneath the viaduct of the Paris-Basle railroad in Nogent-sur-Marne. It was intriguing to photograph the location of the house and imagine soldiers dropping explosives on it from the viaduct above, while Bonnot's associates Octave Garnier and René Valet held off besieging gendarmes and troops until they were finally killed. Seeing places like that with my own eyes helps me write about them. Again, I think this is part of the historian's *métier.*

The idea of writing a book on Bloody Week during the Paris Commune of 1871 followed naturally. Émile Henry's father Fortuné had been a Communard, condemned to death in absentia by the Versailles government at the end of the tricolor terror that accompanied and followed the end of the Commune. Fortuné had seen state terror up close and had been very fortunate indeed to have survived.

I began to research a book on the *Life and Death of the Paris Commune,* focusing on "Bloody Week," in which somewhere around fifteen thousand Parisians were killed or executed by the troops of Versailles. The emphasis became basically: "*comment mourir pendant la semaine sanglante.*" To some extent, the Commune was the "*vengeance des expulsés,*" ordinary Parisians living in the *quartiers populaires* of the thirteenth, seventeenth, eighteenth, nineteenth, and twentieth arrondissements. Others had been forced out of their neighborhoods in central

Paris by Napoleon III and Baron Georges Haussmann's rebuilding of Paris, or forced out by rising prices during the Second Empire. This approach built upon my interest in the way that not belonging to or not being wanted by the center city helped to create a sense of solidarity among ordinary people on the margins of urban life. In the end, the Commune was a series of neighborhood actions. It began in Montmartre on March 18 when women up early, hoping against hope to find food to purchase at the market, saw the troops of Adolphe Thiers come to seize the cannons of the National Guard. It ended with desperate fighting among the tombs in Père Lachaise Cemetery where the *Mur des Fédérés* still attracts us.

I needed a strategy to create a compelling narrative that would clarify my bigger points about the varied support for the Paris Commune and its bloody demise. Whose lives and deaths should I follow through the dramatic events in Paris? Gustave Courbet was an obvious choice because of the Federation of Artists he founded, because he was later blamed for the decision to topple the Vendôme Column with the bust of Napoleon astride, and because most everybody has heard of the great, gloomy naturalist painter. Raoul Rigault, the Blanquist whose obsession with the police made him the obvious person to become prefect of police during the Commune, also seemed a logical choice. I admire Élie Reclus, the Protestant minister and anarchist. Moreover his accounts of life during the Commune and its fateful end are remarkable; the guy could write engaging prose. Louise Michel and Élisabeth Dmitrieff were obvious choices, along with Mélanie Le Mel, a working-class Bretonne who left her alcoholic husband and moved to Paris, about whom we still know too little.

On the Versaillais side, I wanted to know about the Gallican Archbishop Georges Darboy, taken as hostage by the Commune in early April in response to the beginnings of the waves of summary executions. He was shot on May 24 along with five others, including the *curé* of Madeleine. (I followed Darboy to Fayl-Billot in Haute-Marne, where he had been born and raised. I ended up being invited to give a lecture there after the parish picnic!) I came across Albert Hans, a member of the Volunteers of the Seine, who assisted the army of Versailles. His accounts of the fighting during Bloody Week told me much; moreover, he seemed quite different than many of Thiers' officers, who had ordered summary executions right and left. Hans had not. Finally, I found the memoirs of two bourgeois families that related what for them were the horrors of the Commune as they continued to eat very well while they fretted over their property. These lives and deaths helped me piece together an account of one of the most dramatic series of events of the long nineteenth century, and to argue that in some important ways, Bloody Week anticipated some of the demons of the twentieth century and beyond, when you could be killed simply for being who you were. In the case of the Commune, that meant anyone from a working-class person, someone from the *quartiers populaires*, a foreigner (Polish or Russian), or simply someone in the wrong place at the wrong time. In Paris, in the chilling words of a military prosecutor, "*tout le monde était coupable*," that is, everyone too poor to get out or who had nowhere else to go and who dreamed of a better life in a free city.

While working on my research projects, I have always continued to attend the professional meetings that are relevant to work in French history. The goal of such trips is to hear what other folks are working on, to listen to papers given by colleagues and my former graduate students, and to see old friends. I remain particularly loyal to the Western Society for French History. I presented a paper at its first annual meeting held in Flagstaff, Arizona in 1974. I often attend the Society of French Historical Studies annual meeting, although it has struck me as sometimes a bit stuffy, in contrast to the more laid-back Western. Thus I am a veteran of innumerable cash bars and invariably dreadful banquet food, an exception (by coincidence) being at the French Historical Studies meeting held at the magnificent Hôtel Frontenac in Québec Ville in 1986. I was fortunate enough to be the banquet speaker at that meeting. (During my talk I could not help but be distracted by wondering if Carol, back in New Haven, was about to give birth—I had agreed to be the speaker more than nine months before the banquet.) Above all at these conferences and at the Consortium on the Revolutionary Era I have had the pleasure of listening to fine papers and meeting terrific people, as well as hearing my many former graduate students present their work.

I guess my strangest memory of all my trips to conferences (the Western invariably meets in more interesting places) was the plane ride from the Twin Cities to distant Saskatoon for the 1997 WSFH meeting. The small plane was not only full of French historians but also carried a pack of hunters wearing camouflage outfits. They were obviously keen on slaying animals in the distant reaches of Saskatchewan. Across the aisle from me sat—rather uncomfortably—a French historian wearing a tie (thus striking a decided contrast with yours truly). He was intently reading a copy of *French Historical Studies*. In the seat next to him a man in army fatigues closely scrutinized the latest issue of *Militia Man*. Before we took off, a voice came over the loudspeaker asking if the owner of the dog "Killer" would kindly identify himself. The latter had broken loose on the tarmac. I could safely assume that the dog did not belong to one of the French historians on the plane.

Over the course of my career at Yale, I have seen enrollments in history courses decline. Back in the late 1970s, I was fortunate to have as many as 180 people in my lecture courses on French history (although my first lecture course had only nine students). History was the number-one major at Yale for forty-five straight years. Beginning around 2005, the numbers began to fall, at Yale and universities alike. In my view, three reasons seem responsible for this decline. First, the events of September 11, 2001 led to an increase in students studying political science and global affairs. Second, the economic crisis of 2008 raised the number of majors in economics and other "marketable" disciplines. Finally, at Yale the culture of "the lecture" began to fade with the retirement of such famous lecturers as David Montgomery, Edmund Morgan, John Blum, Jonathan Spence, Peter Gay, Glenda Gilmore, and others. There are still some terrific lecturers around Yale, but certainly not as many. Falling course enrollments in history in the United States are arguably one of the reasons that there has been much discussion of the "crisis in French history." This decline needs to be placed alongside the decline of French influence in the world, an increasing emphasis on globalization, more "world history" courses, and so on. With more retirements to come, it is likely that a good many French history slots in America will not be replaced. Moreover, graduate programs in modern European history have contracted.

At the same time, ironically, the reach of history as taught at Yale and some other places has expanded worldwide thanks to the Internet. Tens of thousands of people have followed my two courses online, reflecting not my influence but a continuing attraction to history in many places across the globe. I have answered well over a thousand e-mails from people who have followed one or both of the courses and have questions or want to tell me a story about the histories of their families. The United States, Great Britain, France, Hungary, Poland, and many other places have fallen prey to a dangerous populism that disdains and virtually celebrates ignorance of the past and, for that matter, of the world today. A knowledge of history is ever more important today.

Carol passed away suddenly in December 2016. We were together for almost forty years and married for thirty-six. Ours was a relationship in which history played a great role. We traveled everywhere in France, connecting the past with the present. She had been writing a novel about changes and continuities for generations of families in a southern French village. It was Balazuc, although that was not the name she chose for it. France had long since become her most cherished home. Messages of condolences that arrived at our house in North Haven, Connecticut, began with "*Balazuc pleure. . . .*" *Nous aussi.*

History on the Margins

ONE

The *Demoiselles* of the Ariège, 1829–1831

The Revolution of 1830 was part of a significant social, economic, and political crisis in France that lasted from 1827 to 1832. The popular protest of this economic depression included numerous grain riots, tax rebellions, forest disturbances, and possibly the mysterious series of fires in western France that still have not been adequately explained.[1] Such violence reflected more than just this particular economic crisis.[2] France was changing: the combination of a developing rural capitalism and a centralized, bureaucratic state, which protected and sponsored it, was winning its struggle with the French peasantry. The forcible integration of the peasantry into the national state and economy was not easy. The social and economic transformation of modern France in the nineteenth century came only at the expense of traditional peasant rights, local control over food supply and natural resources, and even the solidarity of the community itself.[3] In the spring of 1830, while the famous "221" deputies were opposing the intransigent Bourbon, Charles X, and his minister Polignac in the name of what they believed were their essential political liberties, peasant communities and the urban poor were resisting tax collectors, grain merchants, gendarmes, and forest guards.

The Revolution of July 1830 was precipitated by political issues that were of concern to only a small proportion of the population. Nevertheless, the revolution was not finished when Charles X had fled, the tricolor was flying, and a new administration began to carry out its duties to a new king. As the victors of the "Three Glorious Day" tried to consolidate their power won in the name of "liberty," the common people seized the opportunity afforded by the events in Paris and renewed their own struggle with vigor. They attacked customs barriers, ripped apart tax registers, rioted against the high price of grain, and devastated royal and privately owned forests.[4] This protest sometimes included an additional dimension, learned from the revolutionaries in Paris and seemingly legitimized by the tricolor and the official proclamations announcing the new regime—they often protested in the name of "liberty." The events of 1830 are an important indication of how France was changing economically and socially.

Far from Paris, in the mountainous department of the Ariège on the Spanish border, the struggle between the peasant communities and their antagonists, the revenue-hungry state and the local beneficiaries of a new economy, was waged in the forests. The most significant years of the peasants' organized resistance to these powerful "outsiders" were from 1929 to 1831, appropriately peaking in 1830. The "War of the Demoiselles," as it became known for reasons that will soon be apparent, lasted from 1828 until 1872. It has only recently been described in its entirety.[5] If we look closely at the two most important years of this "war," we will see a good example of how the traditional peasantry was affected by the impact of rural capitalism, which gradually transformed French society. We will also see that the Revolution of 1830 was part of this interrelated social, economic, and political transformation.

The Ariège is extremely heavily forested. In 1830 there were 175,000 hectares of forest in the department, often making up a considerable percentage of the area of communes. On the edges of the forests and in the valleys, a very poor subsistence agriculture was possible, particularly at the lower elevations. But many communities in the *arrondissements* of St. Girons and Foix were completely dependent upon access to the forests for survival. In these communes the peasants pastured cattle and sheep as a "cash crop" and sold them in the markets below the mountain elevations. But these peasants also depended on wood from the forests for use as fuel and for repairing their houses in order to survive the harsh Ariège winters. Until about the middle of the eighteenth century, the *seigneurs*, and the Crown, who owned most of the forests, had always freely granted rights of pasturage and of gleaning to the peasants. In some areas there was a traditional yearly allotment of wood for fuel and repairs of houses. But generally the peasants just took as much wood as they needed and pastured their flocks freely. There was certainly enough forest and wood plentiful enough so that there does not seem to have been any speculation. The forests were valuable only to the peasants. Ownership and use were two different things, and use was by far the most important. Collective peasant rights of usage had only been infrequently challenged, even if the actual deeds or the grants themselves often no longer existed. The conflict of interest between the owners, the Crown and the seigneurs, and the users, the peasants, was only latent.[6]

Beginning in the second half of the eighteenth century, this situation began to change. As France's metallurgical industry slowly developed, the number of forges increased in the department. The wealthy landowners could profit by using the wood from their forests to supply the forges. The price of wood soared, particularly in the 1820s. The departmental notables, whose number included many bourgeois who had purchased *"biens nationaux"* during the revolution (by 1830 only twelve of the forty-three forges in the Ariège still belonged to the seigneurial families—the others were owned by the bourgeois), began to challenge and oppose the peasants' use of their forests. Many contestations between the "owners" and the "users" ended up in the courts, where the local notables usually won.[7]

And for the first time, the Ariège began to be overpopulated.[8] There were now more peasants depending upon access to the forests for survival. Complaints of the devastation of the forests were frequent. As the price of wood rose, the local notables and the forest administration became more determined to keep the peasants and their meager flocks out of the forests. During the bad winter of 1816–1817, the peasants had difficulty finding enough wood for fuel and were put in the position, in the words of one mayor, of "dying from the cold and hunger or breaking the laws."[9]

In 1827 a new forest code of 225 articles was implemented in France. This code was both an attempt to prevent the diminution of France's forest resources and a major concession to commercial and industrial interests. The code put under the strict control of the forest administration all woods and forests belonging the state, and Crown, and "the woods and forests of the communes and of sections of communes." It created a complex and complete series of regulations covering all types of usage of the forests by peasant communes, even in forests that were communally owned, to be enforced by the forest administration, civil authorities, and the courts. From the point of view of the Ariège peasants, the most important articles forbade the pasturing of any "*bêtes à laine*," goats, lambs, or sheep, which the forest administration believed were eating their way through France's forest resources; established strict rules about the registration, marking, and pasturing of other animals; carefully regulated all other rights in the forests, such as, in the Ariège, the right to a yearly cut of wood for fuel and for repairing houses in each commune concerned; put one-fourth of the communal forest into reserve if the commune owned at least ten hectares as well as certain categories of fully grown and underwood areas; prevented any division of the communally owned forests among the inhabitants; and barred any clearing of forested land without specific authorization.[10]

The forest code also gave the sub-prefects the power to authorize the *propriétaires* of forested areas to hire private forest guards, who took an oath of service before the local court. They were to do the same thing as the royal forest guards did in the state, crown, and communal forests, that is, search the woods for peasants taking wood or grazing animals in violation of the forest code.

The tribunals were busy with an enormous number of prosecutions for violation of the forest code or of the private property of the notables. The latter were particularly vindictive. Even the local administration officials sometimes spoke of the "rapaciousness" of these fortunate few. Some peasants desperately searched for old deeds granting them rights of usage, checking the basements of deserted churches, and going as far to look as Montauban.[11] Many communes, already staggering under the onerous taxes that victimized the poor throughout France, were now faced with the loss of their most important, and in some cases only, resource. General Justin Laffite, the department's leading citizen, later aptly described the situation of "an indignant people and several oppressive families of this department; here as elsewhere everything was organized for the domination of some and the suffering of others."[12]

The peasants had no alternative but to resist. In February 1829 the Prefect, the Baron de Mortarieu, reported to the Minister of Interior that "for some time now, forest offenses have multiplied in a very alarming progression; there exists . . . principally in the arrondissement of St. Girons a spirit of resistance against the execution of the new code."[13] In May there were reports of "groups of armed men, disguised as women, and masked" in the royal forest of St. Lary, southwest of St. Girons.[14] Throughout the late spring and the summer violations of the forest code increased. Forest guards and *charbonniers* were attacked in what appeared to be an increasingly systematic fashion. A strange disguise was sometimes reported, even in the arrondissement of St. Gaudens in the neighboring department of Haute Garonne. Some of the incidents, which began to spread into new regions of the department after beginning in the canton of Castillon in 1829, are particularly revealing. They will serve as an introduction to a discussion of the nature of peasant resistance, in the months preceding the Revolution of 1830, to the loss of traditional rights in the forests.

In October 1829, Marrot, a wealthy property-owner and lawyer who lived in St. Girons, complained that the peasants were

taking wood from his forest every day and even selling it publicly in St. Girons, while local authorities looked the other way.
On October 14 he went into the woods with one of his guards.
They came upon a number of peasants taking wood. When the
peasants saw them, they sounded the alarm. The guard later
reported that "suddenly all of the fields of the gorge were filled
with peasants making the most menacing yells!" Marrot and
his guard were assailed with rocks. "My master fired at an individual dressed as a woman!" Marrot filed a formal complaint
for damages against the commune of Moulis.[15]

In Illartein, in the valley of Ballongue near St. Lary, a band
of peasants threatened an innkeeper suspected of lodging forest guards, shot into his house, warned him that they would
return in greater numbers, and continued their search for forest
guards in other houses and inns.[16] All of the peasants were disguised as women. In Aleu the mayor received notice "that if he
should present the slightest charge [against any forest offender],
his house and barns would be burned."[17] In the royal forest of
Buzan, the forest inspector and his guards found animals grazing illegally. When they attempted to seize the animals, they
were fired upon by peasants and driven away.[18]

Beginning in 1830, the incidents spread into the cantons southeast of St. Girons. Several wealthy landowners, principally M.
Laffont-Sentenac and M. Trinqué, dominated this area. On
January 26, 1830, forty peasants disarmed and threatened one
of Laffont-Sentenac's forest guards. The next day an imposing
crowd of between two hundred and four hundred peasants
came to Massat, the *chef-lieu* of the canton of that name, and
chanted, "Long live the King, Down with the Forest Administration!"[19] A month later, nearly eight hundred came to Massat, armed with hatchets, scythes, and guns, and warned that as
many as three thousand would return. The next day sixty peasants in nearby Boussenac burned down the house of a forest
guard.[20] On March 13 armed peasants devastated land belonging to Laffont-Sentenac and threatened to kill his sharecrop-

pers if they did not leave within eight days. The inhabitants of Boussenac were suspected of this attack.[21]

The difficulties of M. Trinqué are even more illustrative of the situation in the arrondissement of St. Girons. Trinqué bought the rights to the wood cut of 1829 in the forest forming part of the commune of Ustou, high in the mountains, quite close to Andorra. He paid four thousand francs, and his total investment would be twelve thousand francs, a considerable sum but easily returned with profit. On July 8, 1829, his charbonniers spent the day working in the forest. M. Trinqué tells us:

> At the moment of the completion of this work, when the *charbonniers* were to return to my forge toward two in the morning [!], a band of armed and disguised madmen appeared before my *charbonniers* and made them promise to abandon their work under the threat of death. Nevertheless, I was able to persuade them to stay in the forest, with the promise to obtain the protection of the authorities. Last Sunday, the 12th, toward four in the afternoon, a crowd of masked and armed men, who were without doubt the same who had appeared before, entered the work area, and firing rifle shots, chased away fourteen *charbonniers*. The people of Ustou, joyous spectators to this horrible scene, offered no help to the unfortunate *charbonniers*. The mayor of Ustou was sick in bed, and could not find anyone to represent and support him, not even the deputy mayor, who said that he could not go to the scene because he had to be away . . . everyone agrees, the justice of the peace, the mayor and the *charbonniers*, that the inhabitants of the commune themselves are the authors of similar attacks.[22]

The next spring, 1830, Trinqué again complained that the peasants were devastating his forests. On April 2 several armed and disguised peasants came to the nearby commune Rivérenert, led by a "Monsieur Laporte, captain of the Demoiselles." They gave the mayor a letter for Trinqué and announced that if Trinqué did not grant "to the inhabitants of the commune and to those of Massat the free exercise of pasturage, his forest would be ravaged on a daily basis and himself and his guards exposed to the most horrible treatment."[23] The mayor urged concession. Trinqué therefore went to the commune of Massat, where the peasants had gathered for an official function, and told the assembled villagers that he would give them pasturage for two years with the exception of certain areas of underwood, if they would guarantee no further destruction by the demoiselles. In nearby Rivèrenert, after unsuccessfully trying to persuade the mayor to call an assembly, Trinqué offered the peasants the same conditions offered in Massat. But when he said, "with the exception of the underbrush," the villagers cried out, "All or nothing." Trinqué's troubles were therefore not over; following this event, he "no longer dared to make any act of ownership in his own forest."[24]

By the end of 1829 there had been more than thirty separate incidents in the arrondissement of St. Girons, such as those described above. These incidents involved the participation of armed and disguised bands. These bands became known as the "demoiselles," because the peasants were disguised as women.

The disguise was first mentioned in St. Lary, in May 1829, when, as we have seen, "groups of armed men, disguised as women" were noted.[25] By July reports specifically mentioned the sighting of these "demoiselles."[26] One forest inspector described the disguise as leaving the "shirt out and darkening the face with red and black."[27] The disguise generally consisted of a white linen-cloth shirt, always left out and giving the impression of a woman's skirt or gown, some darkening of the face, and often some form of headwear. There were variations to the disguise, which seem to have corresponded to the extreme cultural, linguistic, and geographic compartmentalization of communes in the Ariège. Thus in one case, peasants from one commune were easily distinguished from others by local authorities because their disguise included a twig attached to their shirts, long a symbol of that particular commune.[28]

The similarity of the disguises contributed to the establishment of a collective identity of the demoiselles. A proclamation of the prefect of the Ariège on February 22, 1830, stated that:

Any person who, beginning the 24th of February, is found masked, face darkened, any sort of weapon in hand, shirt left hanging out, or dressed in any sort of disguise, will be immediately arrested and handed over to the Prosecuting Attorney of the *arrondissement*.[29]

This collective identity was fostered by the peasants themselves in order to give the impression of a well-organized, para-military structure that could not be defeated. Warnings, which threatened or preceded appearances of the demoiselles, were frequently signed by a "captain" or "chief" of the demoiselles. The warnings themselves were quite similar to the "Swing" letters at the same time in England, which usually preceded attacks upon threshing machines ("Revenge for thee is on the wing, from thy determined Captain Swing").[30] One warning in Massat, scene of numerous appearances of the demoiselles, read:

By order of the *superieur Demoiselles*, we advise the public of the town of Massat that the first person who furnishes lodging [to a forest guard will have] his house demolished [and], the penalty below [here was drawn a cross with the words *"A Mort"*] ... We warn the *clercs* of Massat that when the guards go into the forest, it will begin their own agony.[31]

The disguise served two important functions. First, it made each peasant anonymous while violating the forest code—taking wood from privately owned forests—or chasing away the "outsiders" from the forests, the forest guards and the charbonniers. Secondly, it expressed, and thereby reinforced, the solidarity of the communes involved in the struggle. The disguise, associated with the carnival in peasant communities, was an integral factor in communal behavior related to the community sense of justice and of traditional collective rights.[32]

The particular disguise of the demoiselles was neither unique nor novel to French peasants. As Natalie Zemon Davis has suggested, the link between the carnival and charivari forms of festivity and modes of collective communal protest is essential. Peasant carnivals and festivities "help explain how the peasant community defended its identity against the outside world."[33] It was quite logical that communities used traditional modes of group behavior, and particularly those festival modes expressing popular definitions of justice, when struggling to assert and defend those beliefs and values against those of "outsiders."[34]

In his recent study of the "War of the demoiselles," François Baby has even gone as far as to characterize this "war" as a "*révolte carnavalesque.*" Placing what he calls a "*jacquerie*" into the context of the region's traditional folklore, Baby sees the struggle as a "drama of social vengeance," a psychodrama mystic enough to be a "social exorcism," complete with the sexual overtones of the peasants, invariably male when disguised, attempting, as a cuckhold, to retake possession of the forest, to which is ascribed feminine characteristics, from the "outsiders," the forest guards and charbonniers who have violated it.[35] What is at least clear is that the peasant community found in the carnival-like disguises the solidarity against the powerful "outsider" who had disturbed and threatened the local sense of justice. Just as peasants often donned masks during festivals in early modern Europe to mock any inversion of the traditional, popular definition of justice or "misrule," so the Ariège peasants appropriately donned masks in seriousness to "do justice" to the outsiders impinging on their collective rights and customs.[36]

The outsiders were the representatives of the state and the forge owners and their guards and charbonniers. The guards and charbonniers were associated with the loss of traditional rights. They were strangers to the regions in which they worked, intruders who spoke and dressed differently. The forest guards were notoriously underpaid, uneducated, not above taking bribes, and, as a result, rather choosy about whom to turn in for violations of the forest code.[37] As outsiders, the guards and charbonniers were threatened by clumsily scrawled placards ("*Charbonniers,* if you work any more in this forest, your hours are numbered"), shot at, chased away, and often their worksheds were burned. It was virtually impossible for them to find lodging, because of the demoiselles' warnings to anyone who would give them

THE *DEMOISELLES* OF THE ARIÈGE

a place to stay. For example, "fifty masked and armed" peasants completely burned down a barn where charbonniers had been sleeping. Both the forest guards and the charbonniers were effectively prevented from doing their assigned tasks.[38]

Departmental authorities were faced with the extremely difficult task of repression. The villages stood solidly against the administration, which had few allies within any Ariège commune. Government usually came to the patois-speaking communities only when it wanted taxes or conscripts. When the gendarmes, forest officials, administrative officials, and troops came in search of information on the demoiselles, they found that, in the prefect's words, "Be it through fear, be it because of personal interest, be it through agreement, the inhabitants all maintain an obstinate silence."[39]

Most mayors were of little help to the administration. They were not just representatives of the government but members of the communities. At best they were deliberately or naturally inefficient. More often, they were silent observers or even themselves participants in the "illegal" pasturing and woodgathering. But if the mayors were revoked from their positions, who would replace them?[40] Furthermore, there was not an elite of citizens to be trusted as allies of the government. Calling out the National Guard of the insurrectionary communes was hardly a solution—many of its members were also "members" of the demoiselles. If there were members of the involved communes who sympathized with the notables and the administration, they dared not speak out. We have seen that measures were taken by the demoiselles to intimidate those who might be interested in lodging forest guards or charbonniers. Finally, the possible death penalty for any convicted demoiselle was probably an important deterrent against turning anyone in to the administration.[41]

Various normative appeals, such as proclamations by the prefect and Sunday morning pulpit denunciations of the demoiselles, only intensified community hostility against the guards, forest administration, notables, and curés. When the Bishop of

Pamiers ordered his *curés* to preach against the demoiselles, he received a letter, dated Masset, February 1, 1830, signed, "Jeanne Grané, *le chef des Demoiselles*":

> We insurgents, under the mask of the women called *Demoiselles*; Garchal, curé of Biert, and Séres, of Soulan, have had the imprudence to preach against us. The said parishes have written you several times. You are unrelenting, but we will know how to teach them . . . the lesson which was given to the clergy and to the nobility in 1793. Their residences will be torn down and burned, their properties pillaged and burned, their bodies torn to pieces, their limbs will be sent by the parishes of the *arrondissement* to better set an example.[42]

Whether these dire predictions would have come to pass is purely speculative, but there were no more reports of priests preaching against the demoiselles.[43]

Temporary concessions to the peasants in August of 1829 failed to halt the resistance to the new forest code. Despite the prefect's own hard-line stand that perhaps the best solution would be to eliminate all peasant rights of usage in royal forests, a royal decree of August 12, 1829, temporarily restored the right to pasture sheep in certain areas for a period of one year and allowed for possible appeals by communes for future extensions of these rights. But the incidents did not stop. The insurrectionary communes still perceived their rights as traditional and full rights of usage.[44]

Force was the only alternative to complete capitulation by both the forest administration and the local notables. In July of 1829, the Minister of War began to send troops into the department to support the harassed and undermanned gendarmes and forest guards. By August 21, 1829, there were 750 additional troops in the Ariège; by April 1830 there were more than 1200.[45] But the troops were ineffective, especially during the long winter, which took its toll in reduced efficiency and even deaths. The peasants who knew the woods so very well, could appear and disperse with astonishing ease. Many incidents occurred in villages with relatively large concentrations of troops. Furthermore, the quartering of troops in the communes, particularly in those only marginally involved in the struggle, only served to exacerbate local hostility against the administration.[46] And so, for all of the troops and forest guards, there were few warrants for arrest and even fewer actual arrests. For example, of eight warrants from an incident at Augirein, seven of the accused were listed as being "in flight."[47] There were two major trials, which were given the widest possible publicity throughout the department in order to intimidate the peasants.[48] But, in general, the demoiselles were not inhibited by the show of force by the Bourbon administration.

Finally, on March 15, 1830, the prefect announced that each commune would be made collectively responsible for violations of the forest code committed on its property, by virtue of a law that dated from the Empire. The twenty leading taxpayers, hardly an impressive fortune in many communes in the poor arrondissements of St. Girons and Foix, were to advance the sum to the commune in order to pay damages to the state or to the notables. It was clear that the demoiselles were the peasants from the communes struggling to maintain their rights of usage in the forests. This participation and responsibility was now legally acknowledged. The law itself was utilized by the courts several times, beginning with the assessment of 5875 francs in damages against the commune of Rivèrenert, to be paid to M. Trinqué, the state, and a small sum to two forest guards. Shortly thereafter, Boussenac was assessed the incredible sum of 20,000 francs.[49]

Throughout the spring, the demoiselles appeared frequently and over an increasingly wider area. The frequent appearances of the demoiselles in the commune of Saurat, who were easily recognizable as local people, led the mayor to write that "the people of Saurat only long for the moment when they can bring themselves justice and be assured of their rights of pasturage in the mountains."[50] But when July came, the demoiselles were not to be seen. The peasants needed less wood in the summer climate and, probably more important, many left the department to work the harvests at the lower elevations.[51]

During this same spring of 1830, a major political crisis mounted in Paris. But the confrontation between Charles X and the determined Chamber of Deputies had little noticeable impact in the Ariège. There was no organized political opposition or resistance against taxes, nor were there electoral associations.[52] It was only on August 3 that the prefect, the Baron de Montarieu, issued a proclamation that "Grave disorders trouble the capital of the Kingdom; the authority of the King has been ignored there—it will not be such in the department of the Ariège." By the fifth, as in numerous departmental *chef-lieux* in France, a provisional committee of administration had been formed. The prefect's announcement attributed this measure to "the request of several inhabitants of the Ariège for the creation of a commission with the powers to maintain order, public security, and law enforcement."[53] The next day the provisional committee of administration appointed the retired General Laffite to command the department, with the power to reorganize the National Guard.[54] A few local officials resigned. One regime passed to another. On August 9 it was reported that "the flag of liberty is flying in all of the communes of out department."[55]

At this point, so conventional histories would tell us, the revolution was over. But this sort of interpretation overlooks an essential point: the poor in France seized the opportunity provided by the events in Paris and asserted their economic grievances in renewing the struggle for power at the local level with determination.[56] This sustained the revolutionary situation in France, and the timing of the widespread social protest is indicative of the revolutionary process in general, as has been demonstrated by James Rule and Charles Tilly.[57] The new administration was confronted with a widely based challenge to its authority.

In examining the role of the peasants in the Revolution of 1830 in the Ariège, we will note two important aspects of their participation: Many communes became involved, and their collective protest covered a wider geographical area and had several objects. While the peasants' collective action maintained the sense of "doing justice" to the outsiders impinging upon traditional rights, a new dimension could be found—the poor began to claim to act and even petition in the name of "liberty" and this "legitimization" of protest made disguise unnecessary. The demoiselles temporarily disappeared.

If there was ever a moment for peasants to recapture ground they had lost, it was during the period immediately following the revolution. The local administration was disorganized; gendarmes, forest guards, tax collectors, and even soldiers were uncertain as to whom they were serving. In this first wave of violence, peasants attacked the châteaux and property of their antagonists, seigneurs and the bourgeoisie alike. They rebelled against the onerous taxes that made them even poorer, burned down a large forge, and, as we would suspect, renewed their struggle for the forests with collective enthusiasm. They saw themselves as "doing justice" to their antagonists, the outsiders. Generally, they were not disguised.

In early August, within days after the first sketchy news from Paris, the château of the unpopular Astrié de Gudanes was attacked by peasants who believed that he had usurped their forests. He had recently intensified the hate of the poor by taking to court numerous peasants for violations of the forest code, including some who were fined two francs for each animal they pastured even in "defensible" or permitted areas without attaching a small bell.[58] The population of the commune of Miglos, where the demoiselles had previously appeared in the bitterly contested forests, stormed to the home of a local notable and held him prisoner for four days.[59] Three communes assembled at the sound of the tocsin early in the morning and went together to pillage the château of Bélesta in the arrondissement of Foix.[60] The mayor of Rabat wrote the provisional administration in Foix that he believed that a leading property-owner would be harmed by the commune because "he represents for some of the people the former *seigneurs*."[61]

Forests in all three arrondissements were pillaged. Two hundred to three hundred people went into the previously tranquil forest of Camarade in the arrondissement of Pamiers. In the royal forest of Pradières, the mayor watched passively as two forest guards were threatened and driven away (possibly by demoiselles) while the local population cut down trees. Marrot, the lawyer from St. Girons, again wrote that his forests were being pillaged. In the commune of Prayols, all but five or six families participated as the guards were driven away and peasants took as much wood with them as they could carry.[62]

The most spectacular and perhaps most significant example of peasant revindication came on August 21. In the commune of Luzenac, near Ax, high in the arrondissement of St. Girons, four hundred to five hundred peasants announced that they were "doing justice" and burned the three buildings of the forge to the ground while fifty soldiers stood by helplessly. The peasants, who were not disguised, believed that the wood supplying the forge was in the domain of their traditional rights of usage. At the same time, an anonymous letter written to the major of Saurat said:

> The chief of the regiment of *Demoiselles* has the honor to tell you that the forges which are near the forests will be completely destroyed, and yours is in that number. Long live Liberty![63]

Popular revindications were not just limited to the battle for the forests, nor even to the forest communes. In the town of Pamiers, which was the *chef-lieu* of the arrondissement, townspeople participated in the type of tax "disturbance" that swept France after the revolution. A crowd knocked on the door of the customs-barrier tax office and demanded that the official hand over to the crowd the registration of the *boissons* tax. Knowing the burdensome tax structure all too well, they had an agenda, making three or four stops in town that afternoon and taking five tax registers with them. In the mountains, resistance against the taxes began almost immediately following the first news from Paris. A proclamation of the provisional committee of administration urged the people of the department to pay. Bu in Vicdessos, a warning from the demoiselles was followed by the arrival of people from the neighboring communes to "do justice" to the tax collectors there.[64]

However, the impact of the revolution on the peasants of the Ariège was more complex than simply creating the opportunity for the poor to "do justice" to their antagonists. First, some communes collectively attempted to wrest concessions from the notables who owned forests and often forges. Second, the peasants sometimes claimed to act in the name of "liberty," which, after all, was what the revolution in Paris was supposed to have been about. Third, they paused at that crucial stage when the new regime might have proven to be conciliatory. Temporarily, the demoiselles virtually disappeared and the peasant communities appeared as petitioners to the new administration for concessions. The response of the new government would be crucial in influencing the outcome of the struggle in the Ariège between the new economy and the new seigneurs and the peasant community and its sense of traditional rights.

Some communes took advantage of the confusion that followed the news of the revolution to the Ariège and attempted to wrest concessions from the property-holders. The inhabitants of Mongailhard, a commune adjacent to Foix, "assembled on the public place. . . . everyone manifested the firm resolution to claim the lands which were usurped from the commune." Only with "the greatest difficulty" was the mayor able to persuade the commune to refer the claim to the administration.[65] But further away from Foix, in the regions where the forests had recently been hotly contested, the peasants moved on their own. In at least ten cases, they were able to obtain concessions. One hundred peasants of Mirepoix went to the home of the Marquise de Portes, the mother of a member of the Chamber of Deputies, in order to force her "to give back to the inhabitants the rights of usage that they claim to have in the woods."[66] On August 26, "a great part" of the people of Freychenet went with the mayor and his deputy to neighboring St. Paul where they joined peasants from nearby Mercus. Together, they forced the "agents" of a property-owner to give them the right "to pasture in all of the woods of the said *Mademoiselle*, except those held in reserve by law." A number of communes were able to force concessions from Astrié de Gudanes after attacking his château. The peasants were reported as being satisfied with these concessions. "*Voilà la paix*," wrote General Laffite. News of the burning of the forge at Luzenac and of the concessions spread quickly and without doubt encouraged other communes to act.[67]

Before the revolution, cries of "Long live the King, down with the forest administration!" could be heard in the Ariège ("If the Czar only knew . . ."). After the events in Paris, popular protest became associated with the slogan "liberty." The peasants learned from the proclamation in each commune announcing the change in regime that "liberty" had been won in Paris. So the letter that warned the mayor of Saurat that the forge there would be burned was marked, "Long live liberty!" A cry of "Long live liberty" was heard in Luzenac as the forge went up in flames. The mayor of Ax noted that peasant demands for concessions had been part of "the outburst under the word, 'liberty.'" The mayor of Prayols, where the peasants from several villages were freely taking wood in the forests, wrote:

> The liberty which His Majesty Philippe I [*sic*] has just given the French nation has been misinterpreted by our mountain peasants, who now believe themselves authorized to violate the laws, in delivering themselves, without any limit, to all the disorders that they can commit against the forest administration.

The commander of the gendarmerie for the troubled arrondissement of St. Girons complained that "The public says resolutely that it has conquered liberty and that it wants to gain from its conquest; woe to him who would want to prevent it."[68] A good example of the convergence of social protest and the impact of the advent of political liberty occurred in the small town of Ax, almost literally as far as one could go from Paris and still be in continental France. In the words of the mayor, on August 22,

At three in the afternoon, I was with the deputy mayor and the secretary of the *mairie*, occupied with administrative affairs, when a numerous group invaded the town hall and demanded in the name of liberty that M. the Marquis d'Orgeix give them the use of his forests which they had fifty years ago; that the Monsieurs Astrié de Castellet give up their project of establishing the boundaries of the royal forests [which would be] prejudicial to their usage; that there be no more forest guards and that the taxes on beverages no longer be collected, all under the threat of death and fire. In this position, being unable to be supported by the National Guard, of which two-thirds participated in this uprising, having only twenty-five soldiers at my disposition, I did not think that I had any other choice than to be prudent.

After promising that "justice" would be done, the mayor sent a deputation to the Astrié family and the Marquis d'Orgeix. He then promised the peasants that the forest guards and the tax collectors would cease their functions, in returns for a guarantee of their safety. The satisfied peasants left the Town Hall well after midnight.[69]

At the same time, the mayor of Engomer, where there was a forge that the peasants particularly resented, wrote the new administration in Foix that the best way of calming the peasants would be to end the hated salt tax and to revise the forest code.[70] Of course, he was right. Liberty in the Ariège did not mean the "essential political liberties," the Constitutional Charter, or an extended electoral franchise. While it encompassed the general resistance to the burdensome indirect taxes that weighed so heavily on the poor in France, it primarily meant the return of traditional rights of usage in the forests.

The change in regime temporarily altered the response of both the peasants and the administration to the forest question. Once the initial wave of peasant violence subsided, the communes involved in the forest struggle became virtual petitioners to the new administration. And while the communes appealed to the new administration for "justice," the demoiselles were only rarely seen. The new administration seemed to offer some hope of conciliation.

The new government in Paris, faced with waves of disturbances across the country, increased militancy among the Paris workers, the threat of a major counterrevolution in the west, and the difficulties inherent in reorganizing the judicial, administrative, and military hierarchies, sometimes showed surprising conciliatory efforts in the early months of its rule because the discontent of the poor was so widespread and intense.[71] The fourteen hundred troops in the department of the Ariège in September 1830 were probably not any more likely to be able to put an end to the disorders in the department than the troops before the revolution.[72]

The appointment of the local hero General Laffite as commander of the department made conciliation seem possible. Laffite, who remained extremely influential even after the new prefect assumed authority, understood the situation clearly and tended to sympathize with the communes against the greedy local notables. He publicly expressed hope in the new government, urging the peasants to remain calm. His numerous reports to the Minister of War in Paris explained the local situation and indicated that conciliation would be advisable, particularly in that the previous "administration, tribunals and Gendarmerie had only one feeling, that of a brutal partiality" against the peasants.[73] Even the Minister of War agreed that the rights in the forests were necessary for the existence of the "mountain people" and that perhaps the Forest Code of 1827 should be reconsidered because it did not take into consideration "immemorial usage and perhaps some misunderstood rights." The military commander in Toulouse hoped that the "great property-holders" would "relent a little in their egotism" and that even the government, for the sake of peace in the Pyrénées region, would renounce some profit from the forests.[74]

In September small commissions were established for each department in the Pyrénées to check the validity of titles of ownership and usage in the forests and to see where additional concessions were needed. In the Ariège, where the difficulties were most extreme, a larger special commission as created to consider the claims of the property-holders and of the communes. This commission included six notables representing the large property holders and the forges, five representatives of the communes (four were mayors, the other a member of the Municipal Council of Foix), and eleven property-owners "representing the general interest of the department."[75]

A number of communes did formally petition the administration and this commission. The communes of the canton of Cabannes wrote that "rights of usage should be represented as the rights of property are represented." This petition noted that the reason for the somewhat deteriorating state of the commune's forests was not, as the owners alleged, because of use by the villages. Rather it was because "several of them [the *maîtres de forges*] have doubled their revenues. . . . all have indeed become extremely rich, and the *communes usagères* are in misery, their conduct has even made the seigneurial despotism be missed." The tiny (326 inhabitants) and impoverished commune of Montoulieu, surrounded by royal forests "in which it is rigorously forbidden to the inhabitants to cut a single branch," begged concessions, particularly for wood necessary for fuel as the winter approached.[76] The commune of Montgailhard, as we have seen, was persuaded by its mayor to forsake pillaging the wood and to turn their claim over to the new administration. The mayor petitioned on behalf of the commune.[77]

At the same time, two other conciliatory gestures were intended to limit disorders in the Ariège. A general amnesty was granted for those accused or convicted of violations of the forest code before the revolution. And, upon the recommendation of Laffite and others, an attempt was made to upgrade the personnel of the forest administration, especially the forest guards.[78]

The revolution had an important impact on the nature of the peasant's battle for the forests. The opportunity that the events in Paris gave the peasants, particularly by seeming to legitimize protest in the name of "liberty," and the first moves toward conciliation temporarily changed the form of peasant protest. Although the incidents of peasant mobilization increased in the two months following the change in administration, the disguise seemed virtually to disappear. The revolution legitimized protest and peasant action. Then, once the special commission had been organized in September as the most import of the conciliatory gestures, the Ariège was relatively calm.

Ultimately the new administration changed very little. The situation in the Ariège was not altered in any fundamental way. The commission, which reported in December 1830, offered only partial concessions. Although there was some modification of the forest code, such as the reestablishment of the right to pasture sheep, the forest administration still determined what were the "defensible" or permitted areas of pasturage.[79] The erosion of traditional communal rights continued. The forest administration itself was no more sympathetic to the peasants than before. A special report of the Forest Commissioner in Toulouse said that the peasants' claims were "without foundation." He recommended the confiscation of wood and the maintenance of garrisons of soldiers in communes where the peasants continued to resist in order to "stop the pretension that they should become the masters of the forests."[80] The "mountain bourgeoisie," which was being reorganized into an elite National Guard, had clearly won a decisive battle in the struggle for the forests.[81]

Some of the peasants saw this quite early. At the end of August 1830 a letter from a "captain" of the demoiselles warned the new officials and the clergy of an insurrection that would follow the example of Paris and conquer liberty: "This three colored flag is the only hope of our liberties, our beautiful hopes have been betrayed." A woman in Illartein said that if the forest guards returned at all, "it will be necessary for the white robes to return."[82] The forest guards did, of course, soon return, even to Ax, despite the mayor's proclaimed hiatus in that commune. The commune of Montgailhard found that it had waited in vain, after presenting their claim to the administration as their mayor suggested, and went back into the forest to take wood and dodge the forest guards of the July Monarchy. The mayor of one commune, elected after the revolution because he had led the peasants into the forest to take wood, was dismissed by the prefect, and his successor was only installed with the help of troops. When gendarmes came to a hamlet to search houses for wood, a crowd of peasants drove them away.[83]

The next spring the demoiselles were back in the forests in full disguise.[84] They appeared in the forests as late as 1872, but never again as frequently or in such large numbers. The squeeze on the peasants of the Ariège continued; the great depopulation of the Ariège began. Many peasants simply left, moving out of the mountains to find a livelihood elsewhere.[85]

The battle for the forests was very much a part of the Revolution of 1830. The revolution not only came during an important stage of the confrontation between rural capitalism and the peasant community, it widened and intensified the struggle. The peasants challenged the new administration; their claims were often formulated in the name of "liberty." The revolutionary situation, as James Rule and Charles Tilly have suggested, was perpetuated. The Revolution of 1830 did not end with the resumption of political power in the department by the new administration. It continued, involving the local issue—the forests, and who had rights to them. When the new administration demonstrated that it would perpetuate the policies of the forest administration and stood solidly with the local notables, peasant resistance continued.

The Revolution of 1830 marked a stage in the Ariège peasant community's losing fight for its traditional rights. The demoiselles represented the solidarity of the community against the powerful outsiders who were usurping the use of the forests. They were a colorful but tragic vestige of an old world and a different set of economic relations—in which use was communal and far more important than ownership. But the experience of the Ariège peasants was certainly not unique. In many regions of France the impact of rural capitalism was already apparent.[86] A fundamental conflict of interest divided the peasant community from the state and local notables—noble and bourgeois. The grain riots and forest disturbances of the 1827–1832 period illustrated the way in which this conflict was being resolved—against the peasants.

The communal solidarity of resisting the impingement of outside control over local resources, against both the bourgeois and the *fisc*, may go a long way toward explaining the evolution of rural radicalism during the Second Republic, as Maurice Agulhon has described for the Var.[87] The Revolution of 1830 was also an anticipation of the appearance of the common Frenchman as a contender for political power. The "liberty" of 1830, even if only the myth of a political elite, was a strong heritage, especially when it became rooted in the solidarity of the peasant community of equals. The era of "Long live the King, Down with the Forest Administration!" was just about over in France. The reaction of the poor, including those who remained in the Ariège and those who moved into the less mountainous regions of southern France, to the impact of state-protected capitalism would become more articulate, more organized. The communal solidarity of peasants fighting the fisc and the advance guard of rural capitalism soon gave way to a more modern age of protest.[88]

TWO

The Norman Fires of 1830

Incendiaries and Fear in Rural France

W hile France's elite feared the consequences of political division in the spring of 1830, ordinary Frenchmen in western France feared fire. The fear of fire was endemic in Europe, even in the best of times. Houses, barns, stables, and even entire villages, particularly those with straw roofs, could go up in flames quickly—when lightning struck, when people were careless with fire, sometimes in extreme heat waves, or when people deliberately set them ablaze. The French rural community feared "outsiders"—*malfaiteurs*—coming to steal, pillage, or make trouble. Rumor could accentuate the fear of brigands and incendiaries; rumor and the interplay of fear are recurring themes in French history—consider, for example, the Great Fear of 1789, the fear of the *petroleuses* of 1871, and the more recent "rumor of Orléans."[1] In the spring of 1830, when bands of incendiaries appeared to be operating in western France, a panic spread which, although not at all the same phenomenon, recalled the Fear of 1789.

Historians have thus far not gone beyond contemporaries' two principal explanations for these cases of arson. First, because the wave of fires came in the spring of 1830, it had important political overtones, as both liberals and Bourbons wildly accused each other. It is in this sense that the fires have been mentioned by historians of the period.[2] Others believed that the fires were attributable to machinations of insurance companies. The most widely held view, supported by Frederick Artz in 1929, was that the insurance agents themselves were responsible for the fires, trying to stoke up their business. We shall here examine some of the evidence and draw our own conclusions about the fires and, more important, about their significance.

The wave began in February, when a sixteen-year-old girl was accused of setting four fires in an eight-day period in the commune of Bremoy, in the *arrondissement* of Vire in the Calvados. Until about March 20 the other fires which followed were largely confined to that *arrondissement*. They then spread into that of Mortain in the Manche, reappeared in the Vire region, and spread further into both Calvados and the Manche, touching the Orne. By the end of June the blazes, and the fear that they inspired, had reached as far north as Cherbourg and included, in varying degrees, the departments of the Calvados, the Manche, the Orne, the Côtes-du-Nord, the Eure, the Mayenne, Maine-et-Loire, the Aisne, the Pas-de-Calais, the Somme, the Loire-Inférieure, the Sarthe, and the Nord. The wave was concentrated in the departments comprising the judicial district of the *Cour royale* of Caen (Calvados, Manche, and Orne), where at least 264 separate fires or attempts at arson were reported. Striking both rich and poor, some of the fires, most of which were unmistakably arson, did considerable damage; the most devastating burned fifty houses in Cauvicourt in the Calvados.[3]

One part of the series in the Manche included this sequence of events. On March 31 an "unknown" set fire to a bed in a house in Romagny, near Mortain; damage was limited because a passerby spotted the smoke. On that same day four fires occurred in two communes in the nearby canton of Saint-Pois. A few days later a farm was destroyed in Cuves, *arrondissement* of Avranches, while the villagers were at vespers. On April 8 two buildings in Boisyven, canton of Saint-Pois, were set ablaze. The next day, during the Good Friday services, several more buildings went up in the same canton, near Périers-en-Beauficel; it was believed that the *malfaiteurs* fled into the nearby woods. The same day a match was left to ignite a pile of leaves next to a stable in Sourdeval, *chef-lieu* of the canton of the same name.

The prefect of the Manche reported that "everyone is in readiness [*sur pied*]; the inhabitants stay awake day and night; patrols are organized in diverse communes." Gendarmes combed the region and arrested nine people on suspicion of arson.[4] Yet the fires continued.

Bands of incendiaries seemed to be operating over a wide region, centering on the *arrondissement* of Mortain. Peasants claimed that they had actually seen incendiaries and chased them into the woods. Many of the fires were clearly premeditated, because *boules*—some small and some "as big as hazel-nuts" filled with inflammatory liquids—were thrown onto straw roofs, where they ignited in the hot sunshine. Sulphuric phosphorous and wicks dipped in turpentine started some of the fires in straw or piles of hay. Outsiders were suspected, because the incendiary materials were unavailable locally and seemed to have been produced "by hands used to chemical operations."[5] In several cases young domestics or adolescents arrested for arson claimed that they had been paid to set fires; others reported that they had been approached by strangers who offered them money, which they had refused.[6] Rumors abounded concerning the suspected "bands." Peasants in the Mortain region believed that the incendiaries wore "blue frock-coats, top-hats or caps of blue cloth." Elsewhere "well-dressed" men on expensive horses were feared. Some left fancy handkerchiefs behind in the woods. Others saw men dressed in grey or black; still others searched for men *en blouses bleus*, a suspicion which perhaps reflected the fundamental tension between city and countryside. Twelve priests were "seen" running through the woods in the Orne; in the *arrondissement* of Domfront rumor spread that a fire in Antoigny had been set by strangers dressed in the costume of Trappist monks! A young domestic eventually confessed to setting the fire.[7]

All strangers became suspect as the fear of the incendiaries spread through the west. "The least sound, the least sound of a bell spreads terror everywhere," reported one official.[8] The *procureur général* of Caen complained that all outsiders, including officials and police, were suspected by the peasants and that "having one's papers in order is no longer any guarantee . . . it is time, they say, to do justice to all strangers." A police agent in the area discussed the difficulties of making any contacts within a village: "Their revolt against strangers is something odious. When I say strangers, I include even those from another village or residents of the town."[9] Another reported: "In every village armed peasants watch day and night . . . the sentence of death is pronounced in advance for any person who might be stopped. At the least appearance of a stranger, the population assembles, shots are fired, blows are given. They accuse the government, the priests, the Jesuits, others the Bonapartists, most of all, the English. The proximity of an English family has helped spread this latter idea."[10]

Some of the usual strangers passing through—hawkers, peddlers (especially *brocanteurs*), vagrants, traveling artisans and merchants—were beaten up by the locals. Even the *procureur* of Falaise, a town in the fire zone, was "mistreated" by peasants while conducting an investigation. One police agent in the *arrondissement* of Vire was fortunate to escape when surrounded by furious peasants, his identity papers of little help because none of his captors could read. Some villagers moved all of their furniture out of houses into the fields where it could be watched by armed guards around the clock.[11] In some places the church bells were not rung because the ring might be taken to be the sounding of the tocsin, the traditional sound of alarm in rural France. The fear of fire became so ingrained in the popular imagination that children, so it was told, were to be seen "playing at fire."[12]

Word of fires and rumors about their origins seemed to travel as fast as the blazes themselves. Descriptions of incendiary bands, whatever their location and dress, were whispered throughout the countryside. Word of a fire near Saumur in July quickly reached Bressuire in the Deux-Sèvres.[13] Anonymously scrawled threats of fire (*garde ou ne garde pas, tu seras brulé*) caused panic even in distant areas, as gendarmes, troops, secret police, and even the Royal Guard moved into the west.[14] Rumor attributed the conflagrations to a variety of sinister plots; each rumor increased the tendency to ascribe the fires to a single origin. As indicated above agents of insurance companies were sometimes blamed for the incendiaries. Another story was that the English, with an army of 100,000 and the cooperation of Charles X, were preparing to reconquer Brittany and Normandy. The presence of 500 English living in Avranches was considered proof of an insidious plot.[15] After a young woman incendiary accused a domestic of General Emmanuel de Grouchy of paying her to set a fire, a rumor spread that Bonapartist troops were operating in the west. An occasional nocturnal cry of "Long live Napoleon!" and stories of unemployed workers wandering through the countryside carrying the Napoleonic symbol of the eagle kept this particular version of conspiracy alive. It was rumored that the tricolor had been unfurled in Saint-Lô—in fact, this rumor started when a *cocarde*, stored in the corner of a *grenier*, accidentally fell into the street.[16] But even more often people seemed to blame the government[17] because France, in the spring of 1830, was caught up in a political crisis, which might have gone largely unnoticed among the poor in rural western France but for the fires.

In March 1830 221 deputies gave a vote of no confidence to the ministry of Prince Jules de Polignac, and the wave of fires became intertwined with the political crisis, leading to a series of contradictory and often absurd accusations. The liberal press hinted that the fires were a plot to keep opposition voters away from their electoral colleges. An issue of *L'Echo de la Manche* was confiscated by the prefect for such an allegation.[18] Writers made oblique references to the White Terror, which followed the Hundred Days, in the Midi. They recalled that a similar wave of fires in the Somme, the Pas-de-Calais, the Seine-Inférieure, and particularly in the Oise, had occurred in the spring of 1822, when electoral colleges were to be convened, and a time in which the Ultras were implicitly blaming all liberals for the assassination of the duc de Berri.[19] In fact, the property of two of the opposition deputies was damaged by fires in the spring of 1830.[20] At a minimum liberals accused the ministry of not taking sufficient measures to stop the fires and to arrest the guilty and of trying to create an excuse to re-establish the hated *cours prévotales* (which was indeed suggested by Guernon-Ranville at a meeting with Polignac and the king).[21]

The government press reversed the charges, accusing the liberal opposition of trying to unleash bands of incendiaries in an area of France which was traditionally devoted to the Bourbon cause. *La Gazette de France* claimed that "*La torche est allumée au foyer révolutionnaire.*"[22] The *procureur général* of Caen wrote that "civil war [was] inevitable." He cited several supporting facts: an anonymous placard declared it necessary to distribute arms to the people; a number of fires occurred in a canton in the Orne where there had been a political murder in 1793; and each time that local guards were organized it seemed that the leader was an old Jacobin sympathizer! Another magistrate was convinced of the liberals' responsibility by the fact, as he saw it, that "the incendiaries do not pillage, they do not steal. They burn for the sake of burning, to exasperate property owners, to raise them up, to push them toward rebellion." As a result "royalist" voters "trembled" when voting in June.[23]

Several incidents made it easy to believe that the fires were politically motivated. For example in June a man traveling with a woman and child was arrested for "saying the most injurious things about the King's government and religion." He was caught with a notebook on which was written, "*essence de thérébentine, huile de vitriol, pommade liquide et poudre à fusil,*" certainly an explosive mixture.[24] A domestic in the *arrondissement* of Le Havre was found setting fire to her master's house. She claimed that she had been induced to do it by a stranger who told her, "It is the King; it is the government who does this, and there will be many others, because France is too rich, everyone must be equal." When a man was arrested, the fires in that particular region stopped.[25]

The most bizarre case probably was that in Maine-et-Loire. After a number of blazes occurred near Saumur a fourteen-year-old boy named Jean Bonnière was found asleep in a barn in Les Rosiers by a patrol of villagers. The boy claimed to belong to a band led by a François Gaulthier, whom he met while traveling as a vagrant in the forest of Fontrevault near the Loire. The boy, who seemed exceptionally intelligent, told of a band of 100 incendiaries (mostly hawkers and peddlers) who were organized into three battalions subdivided into companies of ten each. He described how the band hid in the fields at night. The inflammatory *boules*, received from Paris, were hidden and ignited in stacks of hay or piles of straw on straw roofs after exposure to very hot air. The band would therefore never be in the immediate vicinity of a fire. Gaulthier, who told the boy that he was in the service of the English (corresponding to one rumor of a pay-off to an incendiary by a man "murmuring English"), had allegedly said that it was necessary "to burn the people because they could not be aroused." Gaulthier, who turned out to be an ex-convict named Ducos traveling with a false passport, was arrested. He denied everything but, while being taken as a prisoner to Angers, spat upon his guards and was later alleged to have said, "Vile *canaille*, in eight days you will see many others." The date was July 20, 1830, and eight days later Paris was again in revolution.[26]

Another gamin told authorities that he traveled with a handkerchief peddler, working as his "domestic." He set several fires at the time of the "events in Paris" and said that it "was the government who paid him to set the fires rather than to sell his merchandise." This might have been a scared and illiterate boy's imagination had he not been able to recall exactly the places and circumstances of fires a considerable distance from where he was arrested; he also precisely described the *boulettes* which ignited the fires.[27] And in the middle of July a *cultivateur peu aisé* was arrested with a sum of money after he returned from Paris and announced that the restoration of the *biens nationaux* to the Church was near. He was from a Vendéen village "completely closed off from civilization" and was considered a *valet du Parti* associated with a well-known former Chouan leader.[28]

Coincidences? Perhaps. But it is easy to understand why, after

the Revolution of 1830, the preparation of the case against Polignac and his former ministers included an investigation to determine if the fires had been part of the attacks by the Bourbons
upon the "essential liberties" of Frenchmen for it seemed in ret-
rospect that the blazes had begun "at the time of the first moves
of the administration against our citizens." However, as much
as they might have wanted to do so, a commission appointed
by the Chamber of Peers reported November 29 that it could
not tie the conflagrations to the Polignac ministry.[29] Possibly
national politics were responsible for a few of the fires by inten-
sifying local rivalries and hatreds. But none of the twenty-seven
trials before the *Cour royale* of alleged incendiaries turned up
real evidence of a political conspiracy which would have sub-
stantiated this most powerful rumor.[30]

Another popular rumor of conspiracy offers a more likely
explanation for the premeditated fires—that they were set or
paid for by the agents of competing insurance companies seeking to encourage people to buy insurance or attempting to drive
competitors from business. In the fires of 1822, which were particularly concentrated in the Aisne and the Oise, the rôle of competing insurance agents was beyond debate. Frederick Artz in a
short article published in 1929 argued that the "ambition without
scruple" of the insurance agents was responsible for the fires of
1830. As part of his evidence he cited the fact that only forty of
633 buildings set on fire were insured.[31] Indeed some local officials, including the *procureur général* of Amiens, would have
agreed with Artz. On the other hand some fires were apparently set in order to *collect* insurance. For example, an officer
of the Gendarmerie claimed that "the peasants are the scoun-
drels who burn their own houses," presumably to collect insurance, as in the case of a man who set fire to his own house "in
order to procure money . . . , and in order to remove all suspicions, he first set fire to the bakery of M. Gossard, his neighbor."[32] In the *arrondissement* of Vire, in the Calvados, a young
man was arrested for arson; before the fire he allegedly warned,
"You don't want to insure yourselves? You are wrong . . . your

house will be burned . . . within fifteen days, in the day or the night, because there are 200 dastardly brigands from Paris to add strength to the incendiaries." A tanner's apprentice in Cherbourg claimed that he was given money by insurance agents to set fires. An ex-convict from Paris was arrested with an itinerary leading to Saint-Malo and 640 francs in gold in his possession. More and more officials began to note in their reports whether or not the burned buildings were insured.[33] The *boules* seemed to be produced in Paris. And the normal flow of traffic to and from Paris—peddlers, wet nurses, vagrants, and traveling artisans—offered many ways for the *boules* to reach the west. For example, the canton of Sourdeval in the Manche, where several fires occurred, was the "commune of old clothes," and many inhabitants went to Paris each year to sell old clothes.[34]

But we cannot accept the thesis that insurance agents were responsible for the wave of fires or even for a major proportion of the fires in 1830. While it is probable that the fires in the Oise and the Pas-de-Calais were, as in 1822, set largely for insurance purposes, particularly in the *arrondissement* of Bethune in the latter department, clearly not more than half of the fires in the departments of the Manche, the Orne, and the Calvados fell into this category, and most of these were set by the *propriétaires* themselves. As one goes through the records of the hundreds of fires which were officially reported, it becomes obvious, as in fact it was to the prefects of the Manche and the Calvados, that neither political conflict nor competition of insurance companies, or indeed any single-cause interpretation, can explain the fires of 1830.[35]

Another kind of motive explains a high percentage—how high cannot be exactly determined—of the fires: the motive of vengeance. France in 1830 was still a traditional society, and ancient and new divisions ran deep within the peasant community. In any year, there were many fires traceable to family conflicts, hostility toward the *curé*, quarrels within the community, feuds with economic rivals, or revolts against economic superiors, and so on. In 1830, a year in which the economic situation was only slightly better than it had been in the catastrophic year of 1827–28, arson reflected this general crisis.

Among the accounts of hundreds of fires reported in the evidence collected by the commission of the Chamber of Peers are many which simply relate ordinary stories of petty hatreds and personal vengeance. A poor man burns down the barn of his enemy, whose complaint deprived him of something found on the communal lands. A fire wipes out a prosperous but unpopular former imperial mayor; the man has also impregnated a local favorite, Jeanne Cuevilli, *dite la Grosse*. A rejected suitor burns down the house of the father of his *petite amie*. An unsuccessful *cultivateur*, in a fit of jealous rage, burns down property he once sold to relatives, who have since prospered.[36] The prefect of the Calvados, reacting to the fires of March and April 1830, scoffed at the rumor that the fires were started or financed by the agents of insurance companies. The first wave of fires, in the *arrondissement* of Vire, were caused by local "malevolence" and *vengeance particulière*, that is, private vengeance, without the aid of the unusual incendiary devices. The second wave, which came in the *arrondissement* of Mortain in the Manche, seemed to him to have been caused by the rumored outsiders. He saw this wave as part of a political plot, with "sulfuric matches wrapped in white paper and thrown in an obvious place in order that they be discovered, in order to force the inhabitants of the commune to take up arms to protect themselves."[37] The first series was of little concern to him, because such arson was *normal* even in good years. This kind of fire of "revenge" accounted for many of the fires, even if rumor ascribed them to a plot. For example, a fire in the region of Nantes in early June was first believed to have been set by "unknown malefactors" operating in the area, but in fact the fire, set on the property of a former inspector of the postal service, was an "act of personal vengeance."[38] A match to a straw roof, to part of a harvest, or to a barn could destroy a rival or an enemy.

We can expand the notion of vengeance to include a particular group of causes involving "social vengeance," acts of social retribution by the very poor in rural France against their economic superiors, often those whom they did not personally know or have a personal reason to hate. For example, five fires in the Côtes-du-Nord almost destroyed an entire village. At first the people believed that God had sent them a plague; then they discovered that the blaze was obviously the work of a mere mortal. Attention focused on a down-and-out *sabotier*, an ex-imperial soldier mockingly called "General Sabot" by the villagers. When "General Sabot" originally moved to the commune in 1828, he tried unsuccessfully to borrow money from his neighbors. More requests led to more refusals and finally to a threat. Not long thereafter fire destroyed much of the village.[39] Fire also broke out at the home of a wealthy property owner in another commune shortly after two strangers, peddlers of cloth and handkerchiefs, had told one of the domestics, "All these people there are very happy to have châteaux while we sleep outside; but we will be there . . . it won't always be their turn."[40] A sixty-year-old day laborer has a grudge over a small debt and burns a stack of straw belonging to his more powerful enemy; a recently dismissed sharecropper starts a fire which destroys the farm of a wealthy *propriétaire*, his former employer; a domestic burns down the barn of his former master, and so on.[41] Anonymous threats sometimes captured the spirit of the hatred of the rich and even the moderately well off by the very poor: one, "Quinéville must be burned on the first of June, the château, Grous's mill, Jean le Long Ferrant's farm, Henry Osment, all will be burned the first of June"; another, even more straightforward, "Get the water, you are going to need it."[42]

Beyond this, vagrants, traveling alone or in the bands common in western France, traditionally used the threat of fire as a means of obtaining food, lodging, or small amounts of money. André Abbiateci was speaking of the ancient régime when he wrote: "Incendiary criminality is a form of this violent mendicity . . . the threat of fire, by the fear which it causes, is a means of economic pressure, of blackmail. It is the best weapon of the poorest category of rural society (artisans and small merchants, beggars)."[43]

Abbiateci could have been describing western France in 1830. Reports of local officials again and again mention the "astonishing number of mendicants who travel by band."[44] The wandering, begging poor were visible and troublesome; hawkers and peddlers were only slightly better off. This is why some of the first measures undertaken by local authorities were directed at the wandering poor. They were always suspect, such as the self-styled *aubergiste* arrested after one blaze who "ran the fairs" selling waffles. Some of the best evidence suggesting "incendiary bands" came from young boys who slept and ate where they could and who were willing to serve almost anyone and do almost anything for money. In numerous cases vagrants were directly implicated in cases of arson: in the Mayenne a mendicant was refused food and lodging, mumbled some threats, and returned to set a fire; in the Côtes-du-Nord a vagrant threatened a woman with a knife and fires followed.[45]

Of the few articles which have discussed the fires, perhaps the oldest, written in 1894, provides a useful analysis. H. Monin, writing in the eclectic *Revue de sociologie international*, one of the first journals of the social sciences, concluded that the fires were "an anarchist epidemic."[46] Influenced by the epidemic of anarchist attacks in France at the time in which he wrote, Monin's picture of an "anarchist epidemic," a kind of contagion by which "monomaniacs" followed the power of suggestion and set fires, is hard to accept. But there is something to the "suggestion" concept as an explanation for the wave of fires, their varied origins, and the way they spread. As the fires spread, they increased the possibility of "cover" for anyone who, for one reason or another, wanted to burn someone out. The idea of arson itself might have come from having heard about other fires or seeing the damage the blazes could do. A fire might be assumed by others to be the work of the rumored English invaders, the king's men, or insurance agents. The *procureur* of Vire worried that "it would be possible for individuals, desiring to avenge themselves, to profit from the moment when fires are multiplying in the vicinity."[47] The number of cases of arson, with several causes, perpetuated each other. Even accidental fires, of which there were very many, appeared to be part of the wave of fires believed to be of a single origin.[48] Fires made other fires possible; the domestic long mistreated by her or his master could profit from the occasion to get revenge, giving another meaning to the old French maxim, "*Il faut profiter.*" Scores could be settled, between rivals or enemies within the peasant community or by the wandering poor against those who refused to lodge or shelter them.

Paul Gonnet, among others, views the years 1828 to 1832 as a distinct period of economic and therefore social crisis. He correctly assumes that the fires are but another symbol of the crisis.[49] While the fires "peaked" in 1830, far more than the usual number of fires occurred in every year of this period. They were more visible in 1830 because their timing coincided with the political events and because some of the fires were systematically set with incendiary materials which seemed virtually to disappear after the revolution. But the unusual number of fires and rumors of incendiary bands lasted into 1832 and were not limited to the west.[50] While the equivalent of a Captain Swing "movement" did not exist in France in 1830, *le feu* became a primitive but effective weapon of social leveling in the hands of poor domestics, itinerant vagrants, and indigent hawkers and peddlers.[51] Placards warned: "Bread or fire, all will be burned, massacred and killed; the Great Revolution or bread—death to the rich who render the poor unhappy slavery!" and: "If in one month there are not fifty jobs, the château will be burned!" Threats of arson, particularly against the wealthy, were clearly tied to another familiar form of protest, the grain riot. A pack of matches was found with a note of the doorstep of a property owner believed to be hoarding grain. The note simply said, "Sell, sell, sell." A fire in a stable near Angers followed the refusal of lodging to a peddler and a coppersmith; before the blaze they warned that "this bourgeois rabble will not always have such nice quarters."[52]

The spring of 1830 was a difficult time for most Frenchmen, from Charles X to the most wretched vagrant. Tax riots, grain riots, and forest disturbances reflected the impact of the economic squeeze on the poorest strata of French society.[53] The wave of fires in 1830 may not be explained by any single cause. The existence of a political conspiracy still cannot be proved, yet some of the evidence is persuasive.[54] Insurance agents were probably responsible for some of the conflagrations, particularly those set with the relatively sophisticated incendiary devices; some of the fires were set by the *propriétaries* themselves in order to collect insurance. Others were accidental, but, like the rest, appeared to be part of a plot with a single origin. But most interestingly, a major proportion of the fires, particularly those outside of the departments of the Calvados, the Manche, the Orne, and the Pas-de-Calais, were caused by "private" and "social vengeance," the protests of the very poor against their economic superiors, against those whom they might have had a grudge, but not excluding those whom they did not even know.[55]

The timing of the Norman fires has made them intriguing. But their significance is that they were another reflection of a major economic and social crisis in France—one of the last of the traditional periods of difficulties beginning with an agricultural disaster, that of 1826–27. While French economic and social structures were gradually changing, French rural society was still traditional.[56] In ordinary times considerable tension existed within the village and between those of different economic strata; in rougher times these economic and social tensions within the community and fears of "evil doers" from the outside were exacerbated, moving the rural poor to settle scores, individually as well as collectively, in traditional ways. Fire was one of them.

BMW

THE
ALL-ELECT

MAGAZINE OF THE YEAR

GAZINE

31.07.21

THREE

Incident at the Statue of the Virgin Mary

The Conflict of Old and New in Nineteenth-Century Limoges

D uring the bitter and violent strikes in Limoges, France, during April 1905, the butchers of the city posted armed guards to defend their statue of the Virgin Mary, which had guarded their private chapel for more than four and a half centuries, against the porcelain workers from the city's industrial faubourgs. A generation earlier, there had been more than two hundred statues of Mary and the saints in Limoges, a city once known as "Holy Limoges." Almost all were in the central city and few or none in the working-class faubourgs that had spread along the main roads into the city. During this intense period of strikes in 1905, no violent confrontation between religious butchers and anticlerical porcelain workers took place—the energies and organization of the porcelain workers were directed against the patrons and the troops and police sent to keep order. The statue survived and is still there. But almost all of the others fell victim to the forces which brought Limoges a new reputation, that of *une ville rouge.*

Limoges's reputation in the nineteenth century as a radical city began as early as the end of the Restoration, when youthful bourgeois successfully challenged the Bourbon government. Some twenty years later, the workers of the city disarmed the bourgeois National Guard two months before the June Days exploded in Paris in 1848. In 1851, Limoges *démoc-socs* went into the countryside and succeeded in organizing some resistance to the coup d'état of Louis Napoleon Bonaparte.[1] When strikes were declared legal in 1864, workers organized work stoppages in several trades and industries. At each major social and political challenge to the French government in the nineteenth century, Limoges was in the forefront. The end of the empire was no exception. A series of strikes followed a revival of organization by Limoges porcelain workers early in 1870. The Limoges Commune was briefly proclaimed in April 1871, after workers prevented the departure of troops sent to repress the Paris Commune. The Confédération Générale du Travail (C.G.T.) was founded in Limoges in 1895. Ten years of labor militancy culminated in the 1905 strikes. And between 1910 and 1914, during the years of the Nationalist revival in France, Limoges had one of the highest rates of strikes in France.[2] During the war, the deputies of Haute Vienne, Limoges's *département*, issued the first organized wartime call for peace, in the antimilitarist tradition which had developed in the city over the years.

Why was Limoges at the crest of every wave of social and political conflict in France? Beneath nearly a century of conflict lay a fundamental urban transformation which saw a commercial town become an industrial city of expanded size and altered consciousness. The city's workers emerged as contenders for political power over the course of a century, first reflecting the impact of bourgeois tutelage, or what Maurice Agulhon has aptly called "democratic patronage," and then going it alone, but often finding a strong segment of radical bourgeois as allies.[3] Beginning with the Second French Republic, the politics of the city also became those of the countryside—with the exception of *l'année terrible* of 1870–71. The allegiances of class that developed in Limoges came to set the tone of political radicalism which marked the city's metamorphosis from "Holy Limoges" to "the Rome of Socialism."

This essay contrasts the communities of butchers and porcelain workers of Limoges to illustrate the process by which urbanization and industrialization fundamentally transformed the city, the consciousness of its inhabitants, the locus of social and political conflict, and even the politics of the city's region.

What factors accounted for the emergence of a relatively class-conscious community of workers which cut, to some extent, across occupational lines and which enjoyed some bourgeois support? How important was social geography in the organized quest of workers for political power in their city? How did traditional communities—like the city's butchers—with a corporate consciousness solidified by literally centuries of common experience fare in the face of rapid urban change? True, the relatively small group of butchers gathered on their own street were probably the most traditional trade in Limoges from any point of view and few comparable groups existed well into the nineteenth century. The porcelain workers, on the other hand, were the largest, most organized, militant, and geographically stable workers in the city. Yet such comparisons between social groups within the city over time may illuminate the evolution of nineteenth-century French cities, how, why, and in what ways were they reshaped, and what were the implications for urban politics and those of the city's hinterland.

The city itself—its configuration, neighborhoods, and relationship to its region—is often the neglected historical personage in the drama of social and political change when in fact it came to define and shape those changes. The impact of large-scale industrialization, the creation of a working class and the development of the labor movement cannot be divorced from its physical setting.

Emmanuel Leroy Ladurie once divided historians into parachutists and truffle hunters. We will need to be both, for the task at hand is far greater than the length and hopes of a short essay. As parachutists, we will first sketch the outlines of the city's growth as it might have been seen during a very slow descent of almost a century, beginning about 1815. We will then move from the broad outlines of the social, political, and geographic dimensions of the urbanizing experience of a single city to do some "truffle hunting," focusing on the experience of Limoges's butchers over the course of a century of life in a changing urban environment.

Limoges was one of France's fastest growing cities in the nineteenth century, with its population growing by 65 percent from 1846 to 1881, increasing from about 25,000 in 1821 to approximately 42,000 in 1851, 59,000 in 1876, 73,000 in 1891, and over 85,000 in 1911.[4] This rate of growth, while not terribly impressive by English standards, was considerable, particularly in that Limoges is the capital of the Limousin and the department of Haute Vienne, both of which were losing population. Old Limoges stood on one ban of the Vienne River, enclosing in an amphitheater-like setting in the valley of the Vienne, a plain broken by small hills that have always hindered traffic in the central city. Until the French Revolution, Limoges was really two separate walled cities that had been enemies upon occasion and once fought a war. During the One Hundred Years' War, the "*cité*" was destroyed by the English while the "*château*," the other city, survived and indeed prospered for having favored the enemy. During the Renaissance, Limoges was renowned for its enamels and began to emerge as a major commercial center, favored by its location as an axis for the roads from Paris to Toulouse and from Lyon to Bordeaux. As Limoges's three most important fairs, Bordeaux wines were traded for iron and textiles from the north, eau de vie, salt, and spices from the west, and hats made in the east. Even during the Restoration (1815–30), more tonnage of wines rattled through the city than its new product, porcelain. The 1768 discovery of kaolin, a fine white clay, near St. Yrieix, a relatively short distance from Limoges, changed the city and its region. During the course of the nineteenth century, Limoges became a major center for the production of porcelain, particularly after the arrival in 1842 of the American David Haviland, and in search of porcelain to market in the United States. By 1848 the number of workers employed in the industry had jumped to about 4,000; twenty years earlier there had been 800 or 900. The dispersed and languishing textile industry was replaced as the city's premier product.[5] By 1901, despite many severe crises and setbacks, the industry employed more than 8,000 workers, many of them women, such as the *decalqueuses*,

INCIDENT AT THE STATUE OF MARY

who put the decal designs on plates and had replaced many of the skilled *artistes en porcelaine* or decorators (Auguste Renoir began as one) who had hand painted the porcelain. Limoges's shoe industry expanded even more rapidly, but much later in the century. Mechanization imported from St. Louis allowed the expansion of shoemaking, which became the city's second industry during the Third Republic, but one in which the role of skilled artisans was diminished as unskilled migrants, particularly females, made up a large part of the work force.[6]

The growth of these industries altered the shape and life of Limoges. Until the Second Empire, the production of porcelain was dependent upon and largely situated near the river, where an insular community of river workers, whose wives frequently were the city's laundresses, floated the wood that fueled the fires for the *fours*. The shift to coal, which could be brought in plentiful quantities and cheaply after the railroad came to Limoges in 1856, permitted the expansion of porcelain production. At the same time, porcelain patrons ceased to be former skilled workers who had accumulated enough capital to begin a small operation. The new porcelain *patrons*, who required a considerable capital outlay and were more distant from the production process, were able to adopt techniques of mass production. While the *fabricant* François Alluaud earlier had constructed the first building designed as a porcelain factory near the Vienne River, the new larger factories were located in the faubourgs, relatively near the railway depots built in the 1850s.

The altered industrial geography of Limoges may be seen in the maps showing the city and particularly its northern edge in 1828, 1851, and 1892. This shift in the locus of industry and an expanding population encouraged population growth away from the saturated and cramped central city. Migrants, drawn from the Limousin's generally infertile land by the possibilities of work in the city, settled in the 1830s and 1840s along the roads that radiated like spokes from the center city. Most of this industrial expansion was to the north, away from the river and in the direction of the porcelain factories. The (Faubourg, then)

Rue de Paris had, by 1848, five porcelain factories and eleven fabricants de porcelain living on the street. This faubourg left the city at the Place Dauphine and began a gradual ascent away from Limoges. Like the nearby Faubourg Montmailler, its houses were often as crowded, poorly built, and unhealthy as those of the center city (which were justly renowned for their shocking condition); but they were considerably cheaper and sometimes offered the possibility of a small garden because of the spoke-like shape of the faubourg streets. The Rue de Paris eventually gave way to isolated houses, sometimes occupied by weavers and peasant workers, then to farms and grazing lands that came to prosper as the city grew, and finally to the chestnut groves that still contributed much to the diet of the poor in the Limousin.[7]

Horace Say, the secretary of the Paris chamber of commerce, once remarked with some surprise that as a result of the rebuilding of Paris undertaken by Louis Napoleon Bonaparte and Baron Haussmann (whom Richard Cobb once called the "Alsatian Attila") "one did not find bourgeois families" in the suburbs where those forced from Paris by expropriation and high prices had fled.[8] The same was only somewhat less true of Limoges's northern faubourgs although they were populated as much by *campagnards* settling in Limoges as by people fleeing the inner city. As early as 1848 the faubourgs were occupied by workers of the large-scale industries. On the Rue and Faubourg de Paris (48 percent) in 1848, and the Faubourg Montmailler (46 percent) porcelain workers and day laborers, most of whom worked in the porcelain industry, were by far the two largest occupational groups living on those streets. By 1905, the weavers and peasant workers who once lived at the far end of the street, had disappeared. There were now many small shops to cater to the large population (almost two-thirds of all buildings in Limoges had some sort of workshop or store on the ground floor); but porcelain workers, shoemakers and other workers predominated. Settlement became, with organization and class consciousness, linked to the organization and relative militance of the Limoges workers. By the middle of the century, the center of the city, roughly corresponding to the limits of the city at the beginning of the July Monarchy, had retained much of the classical vertical structure described in many of Balzac's novels. Working people, primarily artisans in traditional crafts and day laborers, lived in the top floors while the bottom, larger apartments were occupied by more prosperous shopkeepers and professional people. There were some important exceptions to this pattern, as several specialized quartiers survived. A number of streets were exclusively occupied by Limoges's wealthiest bourgeois, their families and servants (such as the Rues Andeix Manigne, Montant Manigne, and the relatively new quarters of the Champs de Juillet and the Rue Pétiniaud-Beaupeyrat), and the tottering remnants of the city's small group of nobles, some of whom had had to borrow money from their neighbors, the butchers, in order to emigrate during the French Revolution; and other "specialized" quarters, first, that of the butchers themselves, centering on the Rue de la Boucherie; the Naveix quartier of river workers (*flotteurs de bois*) and laundresses at the edge of the Vienne and the *ponticauds* across the river; and several streets devoted to prostitution. The differences between the faubourgs and the center city, while in no way absolute, were nonetheless important.[9]

Limoges's boundaries expanded as its population grew. Where did this new population, particularly that of the faubourgs, originate? We know that the growth of the city was due to migration, which is not surprising, as deaths exceeded births in most early and mid-nineteenth-century industrial cities.[10] For example, between 1823 and 1834, births outnumbered deaths only in 1831 and the pattern continued throughout much of the century. Limoges's range of migration was relatively short, as demonstrated by a remarkable unofficial census apparently ordered by the provisional administration just after the 1848 Revolution and discovered in the dusty attic of the town hall. Work with the census of 1906 indicates that, if anything, the range of migration became even narrower as the nineteenth century progressed and the porcelain industry developed; skilled workers, particularly the *artistes en porcelaine* and the turners and moulders, had previously included many workers from other porcelain towns in France, particularly Villedieu (Indre), Vierzon, Paris, and Bourganeuf in the Creuse. In time, some of these skills were developed in Limoges; the artistes en porcelain themselves were reduced in number and importance because of the shift to lithographed decals as the decoration for porcelain and because plain white porcelain which was mass produced required no decoration. By 1906, porcelain workers had by far the highest percentage of workers born in Limoges. But almost half of the population as a whole continued to be immigrants; and these mostly came from Limoges's relatively impoverished department of Haute Vienne, particularly from the southern region.[11] Unable to be supported by the land or by rural industry, they came to Limoges in search of work. The drying up of porcelain production in the small Haute Vienne towns of St. Yrieix, nearby Solignac, St. Brice, and St. Léonard also gave migrants from those regions with some skills in the industry cause to come to Limoges. Some of these migrants lived with kin or with others from their native villages, and relied upon them for information about jobs and assistance, a sensible arrangement demonstrated for other regions. The *montée à Limoges* was thus easier, and by no means as exciting, as the trek to the capital undertaken by migrants from the northern part of the department who went north, especially to Paris, where they worked in the building trades like their Limousin confrères.

Limoges's short range of migration may have had some consequences for the growth of the city and development of a relatively organized working class which may cause us to rethink the relationship between town and country. Alain Corbin's careful study of the Limousin stresses some fundamental tensions between Limoges and the Limousin countryside before 1885; it is echoed by Eugen Weber's stimulating book, which relies heavily on the Limousin and several similar regions to support his general argument.[12] The *villauds* hated the mythical wealthy peasant (indeed a myth in the Limousin) who hoarded his grain and drove a hard bargain when he finally did decide to market

INCIDENT AT THE STATUE OF MARY

his produce. At the same time, country people feared the city, its officials, bourgeoisie, and unruly workers; French rural folk embraced Bonapartism during the Second Empire, sidestepping the influence of the *notables* and protecting themselves against the political agitations and disruptions of the city.

Within Limoges, there were tensions between the villauds and the newly arrived peasant workers, called *bicanards*. The villauds, who considered themselves the "real workers," teased their rustic coworkers about their lack of a sense of humor and joked that they still listened for the call of the rooster which could be easily heard in the morning, and not the bell of the factory.[13] Rural migrants may have sometimes been seen as competitors for jobs, unwelcome refugees from the archaic countryside. Migrants pouring into the cities should, in any case, be expected to hinder and perhaps even challenge the solidarity of the workers already in the city, particularly those who were city born. Edward Shorter and Charles Tilly have stated that "urban growth impedes solidarity and reduces the ability to act together," an argument which is anything but a restatement of the uprooting hypothesis, but one which implies that recent arrivals will not have the organizational resources or shared work experience to become organized contenders for political power.[14] Indeed a recent study shows that shoemakers, who were less organized and militant than porcelain workers in Limoges, had a much higher proportion of rural migrants.[15] But Limoges's narrow range of migration may have contributed to the broad base of support enjoyed by national, departmental, and municipal socialist leaders as well as the giant cooperative association L'Union and the Bourse du Travail by making more likely the assimilation of migrants into a community that shared a relatively similar Limousin culture. Furthermore, it certainly helps explain the marked political impact of Limoges on its hinterland.

We should not exaggerate the antagonism between town and country even before the Third Republic at the expense of understanding some essential relationships between them. The population of Limoges was linked to the countryside in several important ways. The relative proximity of the natal villages of a good number of first- and second-generation migrants enhanced contacts between the city and its region. Consider one example. During the revolutionary months of 1848 in Limoges, the porcelain workers went into the countryside to convert the rural population, first to militant republicanism and then, in 1849, to democratic socialism. They failed in 1848, and a slate of moderate and conservative candidates for the Constitutional Assembly were elected from Haute Vienne. But a year later they succeeded; the Haute Vienne returned all Montagnard representatives, establishing an electoral geography which has varied little in the region since that time. I once described this contact between urban workers and campagnards as if reporting the meeting of two totally alien worlds; as if the market place, where relations were not always happy, or the annual fair where countrywomen came to the city to sell their hair, were the sole links between town and country. My simplistic account was misleading, because relations between town and country were much more complex, subtle, and intense than I had realized.[16] Limoges's workers had many ties to the countryside, the *pays natal* for many of them. For example, many porcelain workers were originally from the small towns manufacturing the product in rural Haute Vienne, such as St. Yrieix and nearby Solignac, where they had learned some skills which served them well in Limoges. When these workers went out in 1848 carrying a political message, many were going home.

The complex relations between town and country in Limoges and elsewhere have scarcely been discussed in the literature on cities and social change. But it may not be too far fetched to suggest that Limoges's faubourgs were psychologically as well as physically contiguous. This sounds like common sense, but has frequently been ignored. Most migrants had families somewhere in the hinterland, who shared their vigorous anticlericalism. They returned home when it was possible, or necessary; they spoke the same language. Newcomers who passed the customs barrier and entered the faubourgs found people very much like themselves. If one looks closely, signs of this closeness are visible: striking or unemployed workers returning to their villages for food and work—for example to work the meager harvests; porcelain workers attempting to organize resistance to the onerous salt tax in 1860; the comings and goings of ordinary people to marriages and funerals, including their own; workers returning to the countryside, as they do today, for their favorite leisure activities—hunting, fishing, and gathering mushrooms (*cèpes*). Indeed as one historian noted in an article on the 1905 strikes, "the links between the working population of the city and the rural population were numerous, and exchanges incessant."[17] Until World War I, many workers continued to speak a patois characteristic of Limoges's region, particularly the southern part of the department. Limoges and its workers maintained an important political influence on the region which went beyond the expected relationship with the small industrial town of St. Junien. The political clash between the countryside and Limoges during the Franco-Prussian War and the Paris Commune seems to have been an aberration related to the willingness of Limoges republicans to carry the war forward, which would have necessitated military conscription from an area with a tradition of repugnance for such service, and to a number of pillaging forays of unemployed workers into the countryside. The narrow range of migration almost certainly accentuated the political influence of Limoges, its radical bourgeois element, and its growing working-class population.

At the same time, over the decades of the city's industrial growth, it is likely that Limoges's range of migration facilitated the creation of a community of workers in the faubourgs which cut, to a certain extent, across occupational lines. Although the porcelain workers were the most geographically stable group in the Limoges working class (having a significantly higher percentage born in Limoges both in 1848 and 1906 than other groups of workers) as well as the most organized and militant, they relied upon the support of other occupational groups, as did Limoges's Socialist and trade-union leaders. It seems that non-Limoges-born migrants were relatively integrated into the working-class community and the organizations that provided a framework for the emergence of workers as contenders for economic and political power, particularly the Bourse du Travail, the cooperative L'Union, and the socialist political groups. At the local level the lines between "political" and syndicalist contention were blurred by the reality of municipal politics and working-class strikes. Migrants participated in this contest for power, supporting those more organized and established groups. The fact that many still spoke patois in 1905 as in 1848 does not seem to have prevented them from participating in the politics and culture of community. Some Limoges workers protested the military conscription law on the eve of World War I in patois. *Bicanards* and *villauds* often spoke the same language of work and community, as well as patois. Work experience and residential geography were instrumental in the development of their consciousness as workers, but so too were their common geographic origins and participation in a Limousin culture which retained some of its "archaic" nature.[18]

I will cautiously suggest that by the 1880s, if not before, the customs barrier was a less significant dividing line than that between the faubourgs and the core city. One of the major markets and the Place Dauphine stood between or near where the faubourgs to the north began. The Place Dauphine, where the *diligences* once deposited weary travelers during the Restoration and the July Monarchy when Limoges extended little further than the place, was renamed the Place Denis Dussoubs during the Third Republic, in honor of the Limousin radical killed in Paris during the heroic but abbreviated resistance in the capital to the coup d'état of December 2, 1851. The statue seems to have been appropriately placed, almost guarding the entrance to the faubourgs; it was destroyed by the Germans during the occupation. The Third Republic developed in its own self-conscious and didactic iconography. Social conflict assumed a geography of its own in Limoges, as in Paris, Lyon, Rouen, and other cities, although this phenomenon was less marked in Limoges than in many cities. However, striking differences in voting patterns may be seen in the municipal elections held during the years that voting by section was imposed on the city. Emile Labussière, Limoges's socialist mayor and deputy, once called the second electoral district, which corresponded to the northern faubourgs, "Limoges's Belleville." The second section, together with the fourth and fifth toward the river, stood in sharp contrast to the first and third sections, which corresponded to the old central city and several new bourgeois quarters. Indeed, the second section met the first and third precisely at the Place Denis Dussoubs. Even given the location of an army barracks between the Rue de Paris and the Faubourg Montmailler, could not have the placement of the workers' barricade on the latter street in April 1905 have had symbolic as well as tactical meaning? The working-class community in Limoges centered in the faubourgs, particularly, as we have seen, those to the north. When workers came en masse to the center city on May 1, it was as contenders for power to march to the Bourse du Travail after presenting petitions at the seats of national, departmental, and municipal authority, or to the large halls found only in the center city to listen to rousing speeches by Jules Guesde, Jean Jaurès, their respective lieutenants, to local labor leaders such as Edouard Treich and Jean Rougerie, or to political bosses such as Emile Labussière, or, later, Léon Betoulle. And was it more than coincidence that when the long-neglected and terribly sordid Viraclaud quarter was demolished at the turn of the century and a new prefecture built, the office for *assistance publique* faced the direction of the faubourgs?

Politics in Limoges, which were closely if not inextricably tied to the labor movement, were hardly ever triggered by wrangling party congresses or automatic imitations of events and issues in Paris. Control of the city was at stake, and despite the strength of the Guesdists, the working-class political party, a reformist municipal socialism predominated and worked in Limoges. After the violence and disappointments of 1905 led to a Radical takeover of the town hall, the socialists were once again victorious in 1912. The issues at stake set much of one class against another, but perhaps also the faubourgs and the relatively recently formed community of workers and their bourgeois allies against the traditional city.

This takes us back to the butchers and the symbolic confrontation which took place under the beatific gaze of the Virgin Mary in front of the chapel of St. Aurelien on the Rue de la Boucherie. No community was more firmly identified with the traditional city than the butchers. Their primary allegiances were to their trade and the families of their trade, their neighborhood, saints, and to a hierarchical and vertical system of political and moral authority based upon the power of father, priest, and king. In this way they resembled a good many trades in traditional French cities. In Limoges, they were perhaps most analogous to the flotteurs de bois and laundresses of the Naveix quartier along the Vienne River. Urban growth and large-scale industrialization brought, as we have seen elsewhere in this volume, a shift in solidarities and consciousness. This transformation may be traced—where it perhaps may most usefully be studied and seen today—in the stones of the city. How did the butchers fare in nineteenth-century Limoges? On that day in 1905, two communities, one old and one relatively new, with different solidarities, allegiances, and priorities, but both defined by their own work experiences and a strong sense of neighborhood, momentarily confronted each other.

In 1854, a Bordeaux visitor to Limoges had recalled his visit:

> I suddenly found myself in a street forming a horseshoe, humid, and closed tightly by relatively tall houses, which tried to hide their decay with a rather offensive whitewash. There I found only the exhalations of sweat and blood, a chaos of buildings, of muffled animal groans, and the hoarse moos of cattle; in the somber interior of the shops, nothing but ropes, hooks, and the dank smell of dead flesh . . . *C'est la rue de la Boucherie.*[19]

In 1828, an army lieutenant, ordered to prepare an imaginary defense of the city, described the butchers as follows:

[They] form a type of corporation . . . [and] have nothing in common with the rest of the city; their clothes, their habits, the saints who protect them, their church, their language, indeed everything is unique to them. They delight in the most excessive filth. Under no circumstances will they change their clothes . . . showing up at every gathering and public festival as though they were going off to the most disgusting tasks of their profession . . . even those people not ordinarily repelled stay far away.[20]

Thus the butchers were, during the Restoration, left alone to organize their own National Guard unit. The butchers of Limoges, first mentioned as a corporation in 1322, had received an absolute monopoly on meat slaughtered in the city in 1535; over three hundred years later that monopoly was essentially intact. Unlike any other trade or occupation, the butchers paid their customs taxes on goods brought into the city by subscription, or *abonnement*, and divided the tax among themselves. They waged war against the itinerant sellers of meat, protecting their privileges.

The center of their closed community was on the Rue de la Boucherie, where only butchers and their families lived. There were only six butcher clans, as there had been at the end of the seventeenth century: Plainemaison (who dated as far back as 1344), Cibot (1362), Parot (1535), Pouret (1536), Malinvaud (1561), and Juge (1575). Virtually all marriages were arranged within the families. The Revolution had only nominally ended the tradition of primogeniture on the Rue de la Boucherie, where the absolute authority of the father was passed on to the eldest son. This was a weighty charge in that many of the butchers had extremely large families: one Cibot had twenty-three children and another sent sixteen into the crowded street; there were fourteen Malinvaud children in one family and fifteen in another. No one even bothered to count the cousins; and ten Plainemaison offspring lived in the same house. The butchers retained their traditional nicknames throughout the nineteenth century, as in the sixteenth. These were even listed in the departmental almanachs as late as 1914. These names, which were necessary to differentiate the various Léonards, Martials, and Jeans (all extremely common Limousin names), had their origins in personal habits (Martial Pouret *dit* l'abbé, who was pious; Francois Cibot, *dit* le Pape, who was pious and perhaps bossy; Parot-Cherant, whose prices were high); physical characteristics (Parot-the-flat-nose, Eloi Cibot Père *dit boiteux*, the lame, whose son inherited the name but presumably not the limp); or experiences (Cibot *dit* Maisonneuve, who built a new house, Plainemaison *dit* Louis XVIII, because he had once cried out "Long live Louis XVIII!" which would have been fine except that it was at the height of the First Empire); for others we can simply guess the origins of Jean Pouret *dit* le dragon; Barthélémy Pouret *dit* Jambon; Barthélémy Cibot *dit* Sans-quartier, and so on. The patriarchs gathered each night on the corner to discuss (or rather to fix) prices, do business, and prepare for the next day's foray thirty to forty kilometers in their wagons to the markets of the region. Their dogs terrorized the adjoining streets, it was noted, "an imposing battalion like their masters, when united."[21]

The butchers were fervently religious. One visitor recalled, with horror, that on the Rue de la Boucherie, among the "hacked and hanging pieces of meat, the glistening livers and salted hams and the blue heads of dead cattle . . . punctuated with large spots of blood were niches sheltering pretty statues of saints or rich madonnas with azure coats starred with gold, before which burned religious lamps."[22] The life of the community centered, as it had for literally centuries, on the small chapel of Saint Aurelien, which had been preserved during the Revolution when two of the wealthiest butchers bought it secretly as a *bien national*, or national property, on behalf of the corporation of butchers. "Woe to those who would be bold enough to violate the sanctuary which sheltered the venerated relics of Saint Aurelien," was advice given at the Jacobin Club of Limoges, which included only one butcher, *le citoyen* Audoin Malivaud *dit let Petit*, who, it was assumed, was sent by the Corporation of Butchers to gather information. In 1827 the chapel legally became the property of the corporation.

The butchers' confraternity celebrated Limoges's annual religious festivals, particularly that of their patron saint, Aurelien, and of St. Martial, the protector of the city. The butchers maintained their ceremonial rôle in the Ostensions (begun in 1515) every seven years, during which the remains of St. Martial and other saints were paraded about town in a procession which involved a total of 230 relics, in 92 reliquaries and 8 *grandes chasses*, one of which cost 45,000 francs and was made in Lyon during the July Monarchy. The butchers auctioned off the right to carry the most precious relics of St. Aurelien to one of their own, escorted the relics and the bishop who, during the Restoration and the July Monarchy, was a bit of a relic himself. They fired off their muskets during the final procession as many Limogeauds cringed and entertained the clergy at a subsequent banquet.[23] The butchers' wives maintained their own confraternity, Notre Dame-des-Sept-Douleurs, and celebrated the feast day known locally as Notre Dame-des-Petits-Ventres by preparing steaming plates of special tripes.

Deeply religious, the butchers were devoted monarchists throughout the nineteenth century and into the twentieth. Having suffered during the Revolution, they had little use for the Orleanists and none for Bonapartists or Republicans. They insisted on their traditional right to escort princes of royal blood into the city in 1815 and 1828; in 1845 they had to outrace the less sturdy sons of finance to greet the duke de Nemours at the entrance to the city. But soon there were no princes or princesses to escort officially. Henceforth they corresponded with royal pretenders, and even the pope, who became an honorary member of their confraternity and blessed their flag in 1887. They responded unenthusiastically when the municipal council tried to present them as a folkloric remnant to two presidents of the Republic. Marshall Pétain ultimately proved more to their taste, and it was they who offered him the keys to the city in 1942.[24] But during the Third Republic, they celebrated the feast of Jeanne d'Arc with pomp, occasionally turned out for royalist meetings, were arrested for defacing the tricolore with religious emblems, and were still mocked as "the princes of blood."

But as Limoges grew, the butchers first began to run afoul of the municipal authorities in the name of public health. The lax municipal government of the Restoration period, ostensibly run by an incapable nobleman who preferred his countryside residence and the breeding and racing of horses to his Limoges apartment and the tedious tasks of the mairie, had tolerated an occasional dead cow floating in the Vienne River, much to the horror of the customers of the new and profitable public baths. Subsequent administrations did not. And although the butchers refused to provide meat for ten days in protest, they were forced into a municipal slaughterhouse in 1832 and could no longer slaughter in the street, as was originally required by law to protect the customers who could see, more than they probably wanted, that they were getting fresh meat.

During the Second Empire, the city's limited municipal pride was stung by the barb of a slick Parisian journalist, who, sent to visit Limoges's rather modest "Exposition du Centre" in 1858, sniffed around the city and, when asked his opinion, haughtily announced, "Limoges is a sewer!"[25] Another journalist, writing in *La Presse*, claimed that a visit to the butchers' street was enough to make even a Frenchman a vegetarian. An extensive and hurried program of public-works projects and rebuilding, as in Paris, Lyon, Marseilles, and other cities, followed. The old town hall came down, replaced by one which looked suspiciously like that in the capital. But although the butchers accepted street lamps, they tried to resist the advent of public latrines on the street that another observer called "without question the most disgusting street in France." The butchers' neighbors sometimes exclaimed that "*pour arranger la boucherie, il faudrait y mettre le feu.*" This seemed a realistic possibility in that the city, whose houses were built of wood above the ground floor, had burned to the ground several times in its history and had other serious fires. But when flames threatened the Rue de la Boucherie during the disastrous fire of 1864, the officers of the confraternity hauled out the relics of St. Martial, and the wind, so it was said, shifted as it had during the 1790 fire, sparing the ancient quarter.[26]

Unwilling to change the way they lived and thus far spared an act of God, the butchers, like the river workers and laundresses and even the prostitutes, ran into more gradual forces for change which were related to the growth and expansion of the city.

The religiosity of the butchers had been the rule in traditional Limoges. At the time of the French Revolution, Limoges had a cathedral, thirteen parish churches, two seminaries and a total of twenty-three abbeys and convents. One-tenth of the population of twenty-four thousand served as some sort of religious personnel. Many of these churches, convents, and abbeys did not survive the Revolution; the uses of some of these other buildings were drastically altered, such as one former convent whose purchaser outraged religious traditionalists by dividing the space between a masonic lodge, a café, and a public bath. But organized religion continued to be an important part of life in Limoges during the Restoration and the July Monarchy, a fact particularly noted by the military officer describing the city in 1828. The majority of the population celebrated an astonishing number of religious holidays with verve. A good number of religious confraternities were thriving, having been reconstituted during the First Empire. The most important of these were the six groups of penitents whose origins may be traced to 1598; in 1806 they had almost four thousand members and were a major force in the city during the Restoration and the July Monarchy. Nowhere outside of the Midi could one still find such a "multitude" of confraternities and regularly see, as described by the 1828 military observer, "these long lines of poorly aligned men, processional crosses covered with banderoles made from the richest cloth, lanterns placed on the end of sticks, this fantastic procession, an almost barbaric sight, this garb recalling the classic costume of magicians emerging from the shadows in China."[27] The purple penitents still accompanied the condemned to their execution, as they had for centuries, having survived the inevitable disapproval which followed what perhaps was their most charitable act, helping a condemned man escape during the 1740s. The penitents participated actively in the ostensions, which was the most significant public event in the entire region.

Signs of religious attachment were easy to spot in Limoges. Stone crosses stood at several carrefours in the city, hindering the passage of traffic. Statues of the Virgin Mary and of saints could be found in niches at almost every corner of the central city; some were the object of special quartier festivals and processions. The cult of the saints and of the magic fountains continued strong through the first half of the nineteenth century. And the poor, as they had for centuries, still could be seen going from house to house on the Fête Dieu, asking for *"le part de Dieu, s'il vous plaît,"* their piece of the special cakes baked for the occasion.

But as the nineteenth century progressed, signs of this traditional attachment to religion gradually disappeared. The penitents declined in devotion and in number and did not survive the beginning of the Third Republic. The bourgeoisie began to turn their backs on many of the trappings of organized religion. Anticlericalism was an important theme in the growth of the political opposition to the Bourbons before the Revolution of 1830; Limoges's young bourgeois liberals protested the political power of the bishop and the arrival of the traditionalist missions. The theme of "Jesus the Montagnard" seems strikingly absent from the radical political mobilization in the city in the Second Republic, although it formed an essential part of democratic-socialist propaganda in some other regions of France. The waning of religious practice in nineteenth century French cities among both the bourgeoisie and the working classes is of course well known. Large-scale industrialization, political liberalism, and ultimately the advent of socialist, anarchist, and syndicalist ideology were incompatible with the maintenance of traditional social, political, and religious allegiances.

But it is worth noting that one important reason for the decline of traditional religious adherence in Limoges may have been the character of the migrant population which accounted for the growth of the city. Those moving to Limoges seem to have been already indifferent and openly hostile to organized religion and prepared to follow municipal political leaders who shared and capitalized on their attitudes. Radicals and Socialists in France could agree on issues of religion. Limoges's hinterland, the source of much of its population, was already "dechristianized"—assuming it had *ever* been Christianized as tales of wild superstitions were common—and Haute Vienne was considered to be a missionary region by the church. Both significant delays in the baptism of the newborn and an exceptionally low level of religious vocations in rural Haute Vienne indicated a growing indifference to organized religion. The region was the despair of Limoges's bishops and the department's aged priesthood.[28] The value of the faubourgs of Limoges and, increasingly, the central city became secular, and militantly so. By the 1890s the workers' "processions"—which were not really processions but *manifestations politiques* and sometimes *cortèges révolutionnaires*—took different routes and had a significantly different agenda of stops than the city's traditional processions.[29] The organizational world of the workers came to center, after 1895, on the Bourse du Travail and the cooperative association L'Union, which grouped five thousand families of workers, and not on Limoges's rather ungraceful cathedral, which overlooked the river and around which the first settlements had been built.[30]

The changing structure and shape of the city confronted the butchers, and the symbols of their community and traditional religion. The butchers had some allies during the anticlerical heyday of the Third Republic Royalists and Social Catholics praised their corporate, familiar, and religious traditions as a social glue which could counter the disintegrating impact of godlessness. They claimed to have discovered in the butchers a "pearl of the middle ages." One Royalist compared their quarter to the faubourgs, generally feared in French cities in the nineteenth century, "populated with factories which stretch out without end."[31] Another wrote,

If one does not go to the butchers' *quartier* to find lessons in grammar or delicate language, one does find honest work. Confined to a special quartier, they have until this time resisted the invasion of modern ideas. At the time when the existence of society is universally threatened, where the question of work is posed as the most terrible problem, would it not be useful to establish, by the example which we have under our very eyes, the condition absolutely essential to social peace?

The butchers, he went on to argue, "have shown themselves wise by abstaining from certain novelties," such as the department store.[32] He held up the butchers, these pearls of the middle ages, as models for the community of workers to imitate. But the workers, whose numerical predominance assured a tradition of socialist municipal governments after 1890 (the only exception being the tenure of Doctor Francois Chénieux, a Radical), wanted to live in their own era. The butchers' wealth (which, while widely exaggerated, was considerable) and their avarice (which apparently could not be exaggerated) were resented. No one had ever enjoyed coming all the way to the Rue de la Boucherie for expensive meat which, it was often argued, was not always correctly weighed. As workers broke many of the statues, symbols of religious fidelity,[33] radical and then socialist municipal councils, elected by the workers, changed the name of many of the city's streets around them. The Avenue de la Crucifix became the Avenue Garibaldi in 1883; and today a large number of nineteenth-century socialists are still commemorated by street names. A municipal decree in 1876 banned the firing of muskets during religious processions; and in 1880, the municipal council dealt a mortal blow to the butchers' traditional religious life when it banned all religious processions in the city, citing the complaints against butchers as one of the reasons.[34] The "princes of blood" protested against what for them was unthinkable—the elimination of the ostensions from the streets of Limoges. At least once they disobeyed the law, taunting a police commissioner and nearly initiating a riot.

INCIDENT AT THE STATUE OF MARY

They continued to illuminate their street on the holy days or on the feast days of their saints, but the lights were gradually going out on the streets around them. In 1883, a nearby *calvaire* was knocked down to expedite the circulation of traffic while the butchers and their dogs were on the alert to protect their statue in front of the chapel of St. Aurelien. Finally, during the mid-1880s, the butchers were compelled by law to transform their corporation into a legal association, while retaining ownership of the chapel, in order to conform to the law on associations. Their *syndicat* officially recognized by the government in 1891, was thereafter listed in the *Almanach Limousin* with all the other voluntary associations of the city. They had to wait in line to file their statutes at the prefecture like every other association or leisure group.

By the 1890s, there were even some signs of change within the butchers' community. The appalling filth seemed to be subsiding a little in the quarter, where, in 1887, there were still fifty butcher shops. A few second sons moved away and set up shot outside of the Rue de la Boucherie, such as Parot, whose store may be seen in pictures of workers following the coffin of their slain comrade at the Place Carnot in the heart of the faubourgs in 1905. Some sons and daughters, having more education than previously would have been possible, married outside of the community; there were other signs of the decline in the absolute authority of the father, a change sadly noted by the Social Catholic writers. And very gradually the butchers began to lose the de facto monopoly they had had for centuries, as new butchers set up shop in the faubourgs. In 1860, only four of the sixty butchers in Limoges were not members of the original clans. But during the next forty years the names of other butchers appeared in the annual *Almanach Limousin*: nine in the 1860s, seven in the 1870s, fifteen in the 1880s and eighteen in the 1890s. And in 1887 there were six new names listed as members of the butchers' corporation. But in all, the butchers had changed remarkably little, while the city and its population, work, consciousnesses, social organizations, and politics had changed around them.

The insular community of butchers had, all in all, survived remarkably well in a city whose life and very face had been altered by large-scale industrialization and relatively rapid population growth. Limoges in 1905 had long ceased to be a city based upon corporate and religious allegiances; over the course of more than fifty years, a community of workers developed as contenders for political power. Their allegiances were those of class. Social and political conflict developed both a geography and an iconography. As the statues of the Virgin Mary watched over the old city, the statue of the Limousin Socialist Denis Dussoubs pointed the way to the new city, its factories, and its workers. Rapid urban growth forged a community based upon work experience, class consciousness, residential patterns, and even common geographic origins. Each of these factors was important, and together they tell the story of the development of a predominantly working-class city whose politics were for the most part socialist and practical, based upon an appreciation of the local contest for power. The religiosity, craft, social and cultural values of the butchers were of a different time and a different city. If one had asked those butchers to comment upon Professor Weber's engaging argument about a single urban culture conquering the countryside between 1870 and 1914, might they not have turned the argument on its head and asked, relative to their experience and those of other traditional groups within the city, who conquered whom?

FOUR

The Language of Social Stigmatization and Urban Space in Nineteenth-Century France

As language can embody and reflect power, so can it express subordination and accentuate relative powerlessness. With the growth of French cities in the nineteenth- and twentieth centuries, a discourse of spatial stigmatization developed in response to the economic and social evolution of the peripheral spaces of urban life: faubourg, *banlieue, bidonville, la zone.* . . . Such stigmatization began gradually when the terms faubourg and banlieue lost their neutral senses (although one can find the stigmatization of the former in the Old Régime, and that of the latter is essentially a twentieth-century phenomenon), with the growing identification of peripheral spaces with activities and people unwanted by the center.

In this short article, two aspects of the question deserve particular consideration within the context of a discussion of les mots de la ville. First, to repeat, it was principally during the middle decades of the nineteenth century that this language of stigmatization developed. And second, and considerably more difficult to assess, we will want to ask when, and to what extent, did terms of stigmatization become self-referential descriptions that helped empower the people of the periphery? What follows, then, is directed toward these questions, in the context of some earlier work I undertook on the margins of urban life in nineteenth-century France.[1]

Such a discussion takes us into the realm of marginality, relations of power, with particular attention to the role language. To be sure, the concept of marginality over the centuries took on a geographic as well as a social meaning: "La marginalité, tout comme la centralité, recouvrent à la fois un état social et une position géographique."[2] Faubourgs felt unevenly the authority of government, the power of capital, and the domination of urban elites, and they sometimes resisted. Even if social marginality was not necessarily confined to the edge of the city, during the nineteenth century, the perimeter of urban life in France was increasingly identified with social marginality, associated with recent migration, a lack of skills, uncertain employment, and vulnerability to economic crisis. The term marginal itself has undergone a more recent change in meaning. Bernard Vincent has described its evolution from an adjective in French to a noun, an important step in the stigmatization of the people of the periphery.[3]

To be sure, the association of the faubourgs (at least of large cities) with poverty, immorality, and vice goes back a long way. Bronislaw Geremek's study on fourteenth- and fifteenth-century Paris suggested the development of a dichotomy between center and periphery in the late medieval period. Geremek notes that "L'infamie et la marginalité sociale sont aussi liées dans l'espace ... D'une manière générale, la misère et le crime atteint de pair dans l'espace urbain, plutôt en dehors du centre de la ville, vers les faubourgs," the dumping grounds for "des immondices physiques et moraux."[4] Despite the difficulties of accurately establishing the social geography of poverty, the northern edge of Paris, along the ramparts, was already suspect, the realm of the poorest of the poor.[5]

One can find an excellent example of the stigmatization of the faubourg in the eighteenth century, in the remarkable faubourg Saint-Antoine. As Steven Kaplan has documented, the "faux ouvriers" of the "faux bourg" of Saint-Antoine in Paris during the eighteenth century provide an interesting example of "negative integration" and the emergence of what may well have been a provocative self-identity feared by urban elites of the center.[6] In that faubourg, the "bastion d'indépendance, noyau du travail sauvage, retraite de fugitifs de toutes espèces, pépinière de garnis discrets, sancuaire d'assemblées illicites," lived the "usurpers," workers "without skill," working "without limit or discipline." They created a world of parallel work in their neighborhood beyond the Bastille. Their "illegal" work and lower wage demands challenged the monopoly of the recognized corporations, benefiting from the size and complexity of the neighborhood and the complicity of those who depended upon their work or shared their status as outsiders. Stigmatized by the corporations they resisted, the "faux ouvriers" successfully resisted various campaigns by the corporations and the state to break their defiance. "L'étendue même du faubourg" seemed alarming, "cette sorte de frontière interminable, infiniment extensible qui semble s'élever contre Paris pour détruire à la fin la ville même." In the faubourg, everyone was not equal, but not having a title could not bring exclusion. Small wonder that demands for improved policing of the faubourg Saint-Antoine were heard, as Kaplan relates: "Visiter sans prévenir, visiter sans restriction, visiter pour inspecter la qualité de l'ouvrage et la qualité de l'ouvrier. Ceci équivaudrait à la reconquête du faubourg par la ville, à sa quasi-incorporation, à la fin de son extra-territorialité." However, the looming nearby presence of the Bastille notwithstanding, nothing could prevent either the arrival of faubourg-produced goods into Paris or of Parisian workers to the wide-open world of the faubourg Saint-Antoine. Turgot's famous Edict of 1776, then, seemed to the enemies of the faubourg to represent nothing less than "la réhabilitation et le triomphe des faux ouvriers . . . Paris y perdrait son integrité: toute la ville risquait de devenir un faux bourg, une fausse ville, pleine de faux ouvriers, produisant de fausses marchandises."[7]

The stigmatization and, to a certain extent, fear of the faubourg continued. The wealthy Jean-Baptiste Réveillon, who in 1763 had moved his booming wallpaper business to "Titonville," the site of the Folie Titon, was among those who had reason to be afraid. The destruction of this factory in April, 1789 by crowds largely drawn from the faubourg Saint-Antoine, joined by compatriots from the faubourg Saint-Marcel, only added to the turbulent reputation of the faubourgs of the capital.[8]

With the Revolution, the fear of the seemingly uncontrollable faubourg Saint-Antoine took on an increasingly political dimension. The events of the Revolution, beginning with the storming of the Bastille and the decapitation of its commander, Delaunay, certainly seemed to confirm that. An indictment of the Revolution published in 1817 was also an indictment of the faubourg Saint-Antoine:

> Au commencement de nos troubles politiques, où les factieux allaient-ils chercher leurs auxiliaires? . . . c'était dans les faubourgs, où ces corporations n'existaient pas: au milieu d'une indiscipline de prolétaires, aveugles artisans de tous les désordres et tous les crimes . . . (et les) plus déplorables excès de la Révolution."[9]

In all, Jean-Claude Perrot's comment on the significance of town walls for bourgeois urban dwellers in the eighteenth century echoes even more for the period of the great growth of the faubourgs in the nineteenth: "The ramparts . . . retain in the landscape an eminent place . . . when they lose all military value, the barrière still protects the bourgeoisie from the riff-raff of the faubourgs."[10]

As the faubourg increasingly became a space identified with people and activities largely unwanted by the center, the space faubourg and its residents came to be castigated by writers and arguably by elite public opinion. Sébastien Mercier wrote with some exaggeration that "Il y a plus d'argent dans une seule maison du faubourg Saint-Honoré que dans tout le faubourg Saint-Marcel." He described the inhabitants of the latter as a race apart in virtual hiding: "Les hommes ruinés, les misanthropes, les alchimistes, les maniaques, les rentiers bornés, et aussi quelques sages studieux qui cherchent réellement la solitude et qui veulent vivre absolument ignorés et séparés des quartiers bruyants des spectacles." He was quick to add: "Si l'on fait un voyage dans ce pays-là, c'est par curiosité. C'est un peuple qui n'a aucun rapport avec les Parisiens polis des bords de la Seine. C'est ce

Faubourg qui, le dimanche, peuple Vaugirard et ses nombreux cabarets . . . Le peuple boit pour huit jours. Il est dans ce faubourg plus méchant, plus inflammable, plus querelleur et plus disposé à la mutinerie que dans les autres quartiers. La police craint de pousser à bout cette populace: on la ménage parce qu'elle est capable de se porter aux plus grands excès." The police, he insisted, were afraid of men like the infamous gagnedeniers and other toughs who worked in the Halles, and who returned at night to their peripheral domain.[11]

"Vous soupçonnez à peine l'existence d'une autre moitié de Paris," proclaims a young man of means in Voyage aux faubourgs Saint-Marcel et Saint-Jacques par deux habitants de la Chaussée-d'Antin in 1806, "Vous sentez-vous assez de courage pour entreprendre un voyage dans les rues sales et enfumées des faubourgs? Pour moi, j'aime les contrastes et il me semble que j'aurais quelque plaisir à considérer les allures de ce peuple presque sauvage."[12]

However, the stigmatization of "faubourg" was a slow, uneven process, the account of which must be nuanced. For example, in Louis-René Villermé's description of the laboring classes, published in two volumes in 1840, the edge of the city is for the most part (but not entirely, as in the case of Reims) strikingly absent. Most of his descriptions emphasize the burgeoning industrial city, and villages that are the locus of rural industry, or communities sending labor to the urban world.[13] Likewise, Eugène Buret's *De la misère des classes laborieuses en Angleterre et en France* (also published in 1840) gives scant attention to the urban periphery in France. His comparative account emphasizes that "Chaque grande cité industrielle a son Ghetto, ses quartiers maudits où le voyageur ne pénètre pas, et que l'homme riche ou l'habitant aisé connaissent à peine de nom, et qu'ils ne visitant jamais." Locating the quartiers of the la population pauvre "ordinairement situés dans les parties les plus anciennes des grandes villes," he asserts that "à la gloire de notre pays et de notre temps, que sur tous les points de la France les autorités municipals rivalisent avec les particuliers pour faire disparaître peu à peuces foyers d'insalubrité et de misère. À Paris, la Cité a changé d'aspect depuis quelques années, et les vieux quartiers malsains de la rive droite de la Seine, où est entassée la population ouvrière, cèdent peu à peu la place à une ville nouvelle." However, leaving aside the question of where workers displaced by these modest changes were to go, he draws on Villermé to focus the reader's attention on, among other places, the notorious caves of Lille (which, from the point of view of "l'ivrognerie . . . le fléau des ouvriers de l'industrie," he concludes is the only city that could be compared to what horrors he has witnessed in England). Buret thus continued to identify "l'extrême misère" in France with the urban center, dividing workers of large cities into those who worked alone or with their families at home or in workshops, and those working in factories.[14]

Losing its descriptive function, the term "faubourg" thus began to take on a pejorative, even threatening meaning for urban elites and other contemporary observers. Clearly in the early 1830s some stigmatization of the peripheral space can be seen in accounts emphasizing working-class unrest. No more powerful image of fear of the peripheral could be found than that shared by the wealthy merchants of central Lyon, in the quarters of the hôtel de ville and the Place Bellecour. They confronted the hatred of the silkworkers of the Croix-Rousse—it was still called "faubourg"—who came charging down to attack the beaux quartiers, behind a banner that shouted, "Live free or die fighting," in April, 1834, as they had in November, 1831. Their organization made them doubly threatening. Indeed, an army officer in 1841 described the Croix-Rousse as if he were describing a foreign land with which he was at war: "The morals there are coarse and one can easily understand why. Situated near a completely corrupted large city, populated by people whose precarious position relegates them to the very lowest class of society and who receive little education, the Croix Rousse is a place that can only be considered a receptacle for a sizable, impoverished population. Civilization is barely to be found there."[15] Lyon reached out to annex its three troubling faubourgs in 1852: the Croix Rousse, Vaïse, and

La Guillotière, the latter, in particular, representing a wide-open, festive, and sometimes turbulent space across the Rhône, for the most part beyond the authority of the Lyon police.

Contemporary bourgeois opinion lies at the heart of Louis Chevalier's famous *Classes dangereuses et classes laborieuses à Paris dans la première moitié du dix-neuvième siècle*. To be sure, Chevalier's classic tome has been sharply criticized over the decades since its publication in 1958.[16] The spate of studies of the various "crowds" in the revolutions of 1830 and 1848, as well as in other uprisings during the period, has demonstrated that, despite bourgeois perceptions, those who rebelled were not the uprooted, "dangerous" classes, nor the poorest workers, marginaux on the edge of organized society, but artisans defending their way of life against large-scale economic changes over which they no longer seemed to have any control.[17] Trade solidarities and organizations led to the barricades; the "dangerous" classes represented a minority of industrial workers.[18]

However, the real value of Chevalier's volume is its presentation of the view that the upper classes had of ordinary people, of the "sick" other race, unequal before death (as the cholera epidemics of 1832 and 1849 would demonstrate). The language of contemporary bourgeois opinion marshalled by Chevalier is one stigmatization. It is noteworthy that the pejorative view of ordinary people he presents particularly extends to the urban periphery, presenting a terrifying picture of the world of what Richard Cobb called "professional strangers"[19] and the links between deprivation and crime. Thus, Chevalier argues that by a simple kind of "détermination" that Sue's *Les Mystères de Paris* begins in Cité and ends at the Barrière St. Jacques, the most suitable place "pour rassembler aussi sur le plus petit espace possible toutes les violances et tous les plaisirs populaires, des joies du carnival aux voluptés de l'exécution."[20]

Indeed, Victor Hugo specifically identified criminality with the barrières, including the Boulevard and Barrière of Saint-Jacques and the Barrières of Italie, Croulebarbe, Oursine, the aptly name Enfer, and the Faubourg Saint-Marcel. The latter was stigmatized, above all, as "sick," because of the image that infection, illness, and death seemed more rampant than anywhere else in and around Paris. During the Ancien Régime, it had been known as the "sick faubourg" of Paris, with its piles of rotting corpses, animal and human. Chevalier reminds us that Jean Valjean "did not enter Paris by one of the barriers, but he went there at once . . . the characters in *Les Misérables*, try as they may to move into other districts, fall back to the barrière as if weighted towards it by a species of gravity."[21] It was at or beyond the barrières that the compagnons fought it out. Poverty and criminality went hand in hand to the barrière. It was to the barrière Saint-Jacques that the guillotine moved near the desolate landscape of Montfaucon. The faubourg Saint-Jacques, a dumping ground for garbage and even corpses in the eighteenth century, retained its identity as the refuge of the pitifully poor, the unwanted, the unemployed, including ill prostitutes and others no longer even able to afford the garnis, or rooming houses, of the center. It became, appropriately enough for those who viewed fringe of urban life with disdain, the site of some public executions, at the Barrière Saint-Jacques, until 1870.[22]

Hugo pounds home a negative view of the faubourgs. On Gavroche, "C'est surtout dans le faubourg, insistons-y, que la race parisienne apparaît; là est le pur sang; là est la vraie physionomie; là ce peuple travaille et souffre, et la souffrance et le travail sont les deux figures de l'homme." Then he warned the upper classes not to be reassured by the relatively small size of the average Parisian who lived in misery, "Prenez garde . . . Si l'heure sonne, ce faubourien va grandir, ce petit homme va se lever, et il regardera d'une facon terrible, et son souffle deviendra tempête, et il sortira de cette pauvre poitrine grêle assez de vent pour déranger les plis des Alpes."[23]

The urban periphery was increasingly stigmatized as being beyond the law, policing, even beyond understanding. Even some workers referred to the new exterior boulevards of Paris as "the shores of the New World."[24] Prostitutes may have been common sights in the "consumer society" of the central city; but "the worst" sort of prostitute, down and out, often took refuge on the periphery. There she might avoid the degrading weekly or monthly check-ups for venereal disease. Near the end of her own sad life in Zola's *L'Assommoir*, Gervaise prostitutes herself on the exterior boulevards. Zola did not select the rue de la Goutte d'or at random. It was not the most miserable peripheral neighborhood—he might have picked Lower Belleville or Ménil-montant. Nor did he select the poorest of the poor—the workers in *L'Assommoir* could be relatively well paid when things were going well. These falls were thus made even more dramatic, none more so than that of Gervaise. These points needed no explanation to the mid-nineteenth century French reader.[25]

In December, 1844, the brutal murder of three people—an aged café owner and his two domestics on the edge of Blois, with the owner of an adjacent building critically injured—sent shivers throughout much of France.[26] For weeks anyone passing through or returning home to the faubourgs, particularly in Blois or anywhere in the valley of the Loire, and in other cities as well, must have jumped at the shadows of trees moving in the wind. Yet the very fact the minister of interior sent a circular to every department describing the murders does suggest how rare such events were, even in the faubourgs.

At least two killers had entered the building through the café. Little was learned of the suspects, except that the three victims had been dispatched with a burin, a pick used to pierce rock. Stone-breakers fell under suspicion. The café stood near the construction site for the railway to Tours. Here we can observe three components of the changing nature of fear of the periphery. First, large-scale industrialization—the railway as an often terrifying symbol of a new age that in some ways seemed out of control: the frightening crash, symbolic and real, in Zola's *La bête humaine*. Second, the "dangerous classes," attracted by such work—even if often skilled, or semi-skilled—by definition nomadic, required such attention that during the Second Republic special police commissioners were named to oversee the policing of the construction sites—this was the origins of the special police commissioners (*commissaires spéciaux*) attached to the railway stations in the Third Republic. As the tracks drove far into the countryside, the work areas offered a strange juxtaposition of modern industrialization in a rural context, without the intermediary of rural industry. Third, the plebeian cabaret, a symbol of uncontrolled disorder for the bourgeoisie, particularly when such rural taverns were located beyond the octroi.[27]

Such incidents, however rare (at least in the case of the murderous violence cited above), caused no small degree of apprehension among urban elites. During the middle decades of the nineteenth century, the notion of what caused anxiety and even fear changed in elite discourse: prostitutes, beggars, criminals and other outcasts became at least partially identified with the edge of cities. But not only "outsiders" provoked uncertainty and anxiety. Workers, who seemed now almost "dangerous" by definition, were increasingly identified with the periphery of the city. As is oft quoted, the *Journal des Débats* memorably stated in 1832, in the wake of the protests and insurrections that had marked the early July Monarchy: "Les ouvriers sont hors de la société moderne . . . qui doivent donc entrer dans cette société, mais qu'il faut y admettre après qu'ils auront passé par le noviciat de la propriété."[28] In this famous stigmatization, assez provocatrice, workers, marginal by virtue of being property-less and poor, are placed beyond the gates of the city.

But it is interesting to note how this stigmatization changed. For during the July Monarchy, the essence of *what* frightened the bourgeois about faubourgs and suburbs began to be nuanced in an important way. Shortly after Louis-Philippe became the first—and last—Orleanist King of the French, his prefect Chabrol warned him, as noted above, that the factories on the edge of the city could "be the cord that will strangle us one day." What had changed was the upsurge of militancy in Paris, and the fairly rapid growth, even during the Restoration, of the urban periphery. And, St. Marc Girardin, deputy from the Creuse, the department that sent thousands of seasonal migrants to work in the building trades in Paris each year, sounded his famous alert at the same time. He warned that "the barbarians who threaten society are in the faubourgs of our manufacturing towns, not in the Tartary in Russia."[29]

Popular republicanism after the Revolution of 1830 took on for the urban elite of Louis-Philippe's juste milieu the combined images of social and physical marginality. Countless examples can be found in provincial towns, as well. During the protests against bread prices and taxes in Strasbourg in 1832, the prevailing rumor was that the faubourgs would rise, as young republicans circulated through the cafés and the garrison of the frontier city was put on alert.[30] In Blois, a petition in favor of electoral reform in 1838 found no favor among the "reasonable inhabitants of this town." However, it won support "in a part of the suburbs called Les Granges, the inhabitants of which are in general not very enlightened and almost all busy with agricultural work." Since 1830, they had fallen under the influence of "men hostile to the government."[31]

A song circulated by frustrated supporters of the Bourbons in 1832 stigmatized the faubourgs for having risen up in 1830 (although there is little evidence to support such an interpretation):

Et vous braves gens des faubourgs
Dont Paris dans ses trois jours
A vu l'infatigable audace
Croyez que nous vous rendons grâce
De ne pas nous avoir pillés
Tout autant que vous le vouliez
(…)
Vous surtout, braves ouvriers,
Qui viviez tous de vos métiers
Pour vous soustraire à l'esclavage
Vous avez perdu votre ouvrage
Mais aussi vous êtes enfin
Bien libres de mourir de faim.

Here we have a revealing combination of grudging admiration for and fear of the workers of the faubourgs, who had driven the Bourbons from the throne, but who now shared a common enemy with the legitimists—the Orleanist monarchy.[32]

As strikes became more prevalent in the Restoration, rumors of brigands, beggars, and arsonists had given way to fears of "workers" banding together to plan strikes or other mischief on the edge of town. For example, in May, 1829, the story circulated in Cholet that the workers of the five nearby parishes were going to meet together and then come into town to demand work from the merchants. Given the dispersion of industrial work in the hinterland of Cholet, this comes as no surprise, but provides another example of the pervasive fear of the semi-skilled industrial proletariat on the frontier of urban life.[33] Here, too, social stigmatization gradually took on a political face.

During the July Monarchy, strikes increasingly were planned and sustained by meetings in the faubourgs or beyond, away from police. Workers could discuss, debate, and organize in the relative freedom of auberges or even open spaces, sometimes posting guards to spot the arrival of gendarmes. For example, a strike by shoemakers was planned by leaders such as "Le Nantais" in a cabaret in Flacé in 1840, a small village outside Mâcon; in April, 1845, police arrested striking bakers, who were meeting at the Tour de l'évêque outside Nîmes, where they had placed sentinels.[34]

During the Second Republic, fearful descriptions of the faubourgs abounded. Lord Palmerston, closely following events across the Channel, proclaimed that he was not afraid of "the scum of the faubourgs of Paris." Although most of the fighting in Paris during the February Revolution occurred in the central districts, de Tocqueville observed passing of revolution from the center of Paris to the eastern faubourgs; on May 21, he had noted that during the Festival of Concorde on the Champs de Mars, "the bouquets of the sturdy young women from the industrial faubourgs . . . fell on the assembled Deputies like hailstones, reminding the authorities that concord was somewhat less than perfect."[35] Fear of the faubourgs and of the edge of the city had been a recurrent theme in the repression that followed insurrections in Rouen and Limoges after the April elections. And, yet again, a good deal of the fighting during the June days took place in and around the Faubourg Saint-Antoine. Residents of Belleville, with its Club des Montagnards 1,200 strong and 5,000 laborers in the National Workshops, took an active part in the insurrection of June, 1848.[36] One of the liberty trees planted in the enthusiasm of the spring of 1848 in Belfort, then a small town of not much more than 5,000, was placed between the town center and its faubourg (the other near the church), as if to establish harmony between the two. Neither liberty trees, nor the harmony, lasted long.[37]

By the late 1860s, the potential threat to the social elites of the central neighborhoods of Paris seemed to have settled on the edge of the city, in Montmartre and Belleville.[38] Of the Second Empire, Jeanne Gaillard could write "The fear of the faubourgs replaced the fear of the sick quarters of the center."[39] Gérard Jacquemet describes the rapid transformation of Belleville during the last years of the Second Empire, from a site where workers, ordinary people, children, and soldiers enjoyed simple pleasures to a place which "ne respire plus la joie, mais une sinister odeur de crime suinte de partout. Des ouvertures d'une hauteur prodigieuses servent de gueules à ces fours, qui, désertés par les travailleurs, deviennent souvent les oubliettes de la grande bohème parisienne. [Le quarter de] l'Amérique et ses carrières ont été de tout temps l'asile du vagabondage, du vol et du crime." A school inspector did not mince his words in 1856: "Dès qu'on a traverse le boulevard extérieur, on se trouve au milieu d'une population à peu près uniformément ignorante et féroce ... Il y a d'abord l'écume de Paris, les gens de barrière et des mauvais lieux que le vice a conduits à la misère et à l'abrutissement. Il y a ensuite je ne sais quels barbares venus des deux rives du Rhine, de grands enfants de trente à quarante ans, qui n'ont pas fait leur première communion (on n'est même pas sûr qu'ils soient baptisés) et qui ... montrent une brutalité, un groissier égoïsme, bientôt une perversité qu'ils n'avaient pas sur le sol natal. Tous ces sauvages sont plongés dans une effroyable dégradation mentale."[40]

The Paris Commune, of course, added more fear to the stigmatization of faubourg and nascent banlieue. The Commune has been described as the revenge of those expelled by Haussmannization, for whom the decision of the provisional government to allow landlords, despite desperately hard times, to demand immediate payment of back rent was an outrage and a disaster.[41] Appropriately, particularly given Belleville's active role during the Commune, among the last barricades to fall during bloody week, May, 1871, were those in Belleville and near the cemetery of Père Lachaise.[42]

As the world of peripheral work moved further out with the growth of Paris, that of stigmatization followed. Over the long run of the Third Republic, the stigmatization of the urban periphery continued, identified with, among others, the *chifonniers* who had begun to move further away from the center in the 1840s, a displacement accentuated by Haussmannization,[43] and, during the "Belle Époque," the "*Apaches*," bands of thugs who came in from the suburbs—"the Band of the Four Paths of Aubervilliers," "the Wolves of the Butte," and so on, marauders from the edge of urban life.[44] And, to be sure, the post-World War I era further merged stigmatization and fear. Paris seemed encircled by "la ceinture rouge," symbolized by Saint-Denis.[45]

Such stigmatization was common enough that it can readily be found in nineteenth-century dictionaries, where neutral descriptions of peripheral urban spaces went by the wayside. "Faubourg" derives from the Roman foris burgus or furis burgum (1478)—from de furis, outside, and burgus, bourg, that which is outside the bourg, outside the town walls, by way of old French fursborc or forborc (from the late twelfth century) or furbours (1260),[46] as seen in the Picard forbourg or forbou and the Burgundian faubor.[47] However, the etymology of "faubourg" has sometimes been given as the medieval Latin falsus burgus or faux bourg, "false city," an alternative etymology that

THE LANGUAGE OF SOCIAL STIGMATIZATION

seems particularly appropriate.[48] Gradually, the definition of faubourg came to include "by extension, the working-class population of the faubourgs," as the "'sulfuring' faubourg, the name that Parisians gave facetiously to the quarter of Saint-Marceau, by double allusion to the numerous factories making sulfuric matches there before the invention of chemical matches, and to the wretchedness of the inhabitants of this quartier."[49]

Dictionaries evoked contemporary writers to present a pejorative image of "faubourg." Balzac is invoked to describe the resident of a faubourg in a neutral sense: a faubourien became "a simple worker, one of the joyous residents of the faubourgs . . . a gay fellow."[50] Maupassant, drawn on by the Grand Larousse for an example of "inhabited space on the periphery of a large city," chose Rouen's dreary Saint-Sever, "the faubourg of manufacturers, pointing its thousand smoking chimneys toward the heavens," again, a somewhat neutral description.[51]

But, gradually, stigmatization took over dictionary definitions, and began to include reference to the assumed revolutionary tradition and potential of the faubourgs. Thus, the *Littré* (1863) offered one of the meanings of faubourg as "to raise up the faubourgs." The *Complément du Dictionnaire de l'Académie française* (1862), "Les faubourgs (Hist.): Se dit absolument de la populace de Paris, surtout dans l'histoire de notre révolution. Armer, soulever les faubourgs . . . particulièrement du faubourg Saint-Antoine et du faubourg Saint-Marceau. Il s'est employé en parlant des soulèvements populaires." The *Trésor de la Langue Francaise* (1980) provides three examples, the first of which, passed down from a history written in 1870, suggests the dichotomy between center and periphery: "He (Bonaparte) armed the residents of the faubourgs immediately, thinking that they would have an old score to settle with the gentlemen of the Lepelletier section and its vicinity"; the second "in speaking of a physical trait, of comportment; generally implying an unfavorable impression," as "his faubourg-like verve, his vocabulary of a thug"; the third, "The workers of the factory passed by . . . with silk caps on their faubourg heads, mean and corrupt"; and, finally, the image of criminality: "'You won't take me,' he cried, 'dirty bourgeois.'" In uttering this exclamation of the faubourgs with a dreadful irony . . . he fell into the arms of the guards, seized by convulsions that stopped almost immediately. He was dead." Becherelle's *Nouveau dictionnaire national* (1887) selected the following as examples: "Plunged completely into the feelings of the moment, no thought of the future ever entered the mind of a faubourien. He is indifferent to duties, love for one's family, all that joins and links other men; he exists only to amuse himself (St. Prosper)"; "Those who have still not arrived at wisdom, but are lodged in the faubourgs (Malherbe)." Following Bescherelle, the *Grand Larousse* (1985) drew on old definitions shaped by later nineteenth-century views: faubourien is "pejorative. That which relates to the plebeian faubourg and its inhabitants. 'Under the parasol waiting for us was the little laundress in her Sunday best. I was surprised; she was truly nice, although pale, and gracious, although with an allure that was somewhat faubourienne'" (Maupassant). As an adjective, faubourien/enne gradually became pejorative, describing habits and language. It became insulting to say someone had "faubourg-like manners," or spoke a "faubourg-like language," or had been unable or unwilling to overcome a "very faubourg accent."[52]

Let us suggest that the stigmatization of terms describing the spaces of the urban periphery followed most closely from the awareness by the elites of the center of the political challenge posed by faubourg and, ultimately, banlieue. Again, if such a view may be accepted, this once again points us toward the crucial decades of the mid-nineteenth century.

If the timing of the stigmatization of the periphery, in particular, the faubourg, followed by banlieue, seems relatively straightforward, it is more difficult to determine how and where the terms of stigmatization themselves encouraged a sense of belonging perhaps contributing to the social and political challenge of the people of the periphery. In the case of the faubourg Saint-Antoine, it seems almost certain stigmatization contributed to a sense of collective self-identity and solidarity that helped generate the faubourg's role in the Revolution. If the Commune, to repeat, may be considered to at least some extent the "le vengeance des expulsés," those ordinary people forced by higher rents or urban demolition during the Empire into the periphery of Paris, some of whom packed the hangars of the outer arrondissements,[53] did a sense of common rejection by the center contribute to collective identify and defiance? Certainly, the precocious role of Bellevillois in the Commune has been frequently noted. Certainly one is tempted to view the working-class families, among others, who walked to the Place Vendôme to watch the toppling of the statue of Napoleon (at the suggestion of Gustave Courbet) as coming to occupy the "beaux quartiers" of the center which many of them had never seen before. Indeed the campaign by the Church during the Republic of the Moral Order to build churches in working-class faubourgs and suburbs reflected the sense that the stigmatized periphery needed churches to provide social organization and instill morality. The basilica of Sacré Coeur itself represented both penance and conquest.[54]

More research is necessary before more than the vaguest assertions about the construction of a "sense of belonging" and a sense of collective identity (since the two are not quite the same, and collective action far more likely to be linked to the second) on the periphery of urban life can be made, at least until the post-World War I period. Yet, I have elsewhere tried to suggest that this sense of not-belonging may have contributed to a sense of solidarity and even to class-consciousness in the faubourgs of Reims during the Second Republic, although I did so cautiously, and would not push the argument too far.

However, it is clear that during the Second Republic, the faubourgs of the textile town (and ecclesiastic center) of Reims, which had about 15,000 woolens workers in 1846, came alive. The faubourgs, particularly that of Fléchambault in the shadow of the basilica of St. Remi and the faubourg Cérès, became overwhelmingly the locus of the woolens industry. And it was on the edge of the city that woolens workers gathered to plan their strike in 1834, at the Place Saint-Nicaise that workers demonstrated and sang the Marseillaise in 1844, and at the porte de Fléchambault that workers met before marching around the exterior boulevards to the faubourg de Cérès, and at the Esplanade that provided the intersection between old Reims and the faubourg de Cérès that they continued to meet during the harsh winter of 1846–47. No more dramatic assertion of the contest between faubourg and center could be found in Reims than when, during a brief strike, groups of workers met in a cemetery beyond the northern gates of the city, where they began their march into the center of Reims, behind a black flag. Driven back from several factories, they attached their flag to the statue of Louis xv in the center of the Place Royale. Then, during the Second Republic, the faubourgs of Reims were certainly the most militant and organized in northern and eastern France, and perhaps in the entire country. The provocative descent of the workers from the faubourg into the central city became common. The Association Rémoise, a very ambitious and temporarily successful consumers' cooperative, drew upon the existing mutual aid societies and cafés. The Montagnards of Reims challenged the central town from the periphery and feeling the weight of the repression, before the coup d'état overwhelmed the faubourgs, though not without a demonstration at the place Saint-Nicaise.[55] It is difficult to say to what extent the sense of not-belonging to the center accentuated the solidarities of Reim's Montagnards in the faubourgs. But without question center and periphery eyed either other warily, and their respective coalescence may well have drawn on solidarities and identities of space.

During the same period, it is clear that in Nîmes the sense of not belong to the center probably helped affirm ties of loyalty among poor Catholic workers in the Catholic faubourg the Enclos de Rey in a town in which Protestants, who made up only about a third of the population, largely called the shots.[56] And in Perpignan, where the Catalan quarters of Saint-Mathieu and Saint-Jacques were characterized by different levels of religious practice and, above all, by radically different political allegiances—"quartier rouge, quartier blanc"—the sense of living in what were considered to be "faubourgs," although both neighborhoods were within the walls, contributed to perpetuate the bitter rivalry between the two and, at least during the Second Republic, arguably of both toward the relatively beaux quartiers of Perpignan, the locus of support for the Bonapartist authorities.[57]

Moving to the turn of the century, Limoges would seem to provide an example of where the stigmatization of the industrial faubourgs contributed to a sense of not belonging to the center, and helped generate and sustain the social and political challenge to the center city. Again, what follows is drawn research undertaken some time ago, but here viewed with a somewhat different eye, emphasizing the power of words.[58]

With the rapid development of porcelain manufacturing, Limoges' faubourgs to the north of the city grew rapidly (see chap. 3). They attracted a working population largely drawn from the southern half of the Haute-Vienne. Living in the small houses that stretched along the two principal roads into Limoges, they developed an identity as bicanards, rural folk, as differentiated from the citadins. To be sure, the demarcation between faubourg and central city (identified with the city's modest social elite and traditional trades, the most well-known and controversial of which were the butchers, a trade concentrated on a single street and had been dominated for centuries by five extremely religious families organized into a corporation) was not absolute, but contemporary impressions reaffirmed this dichotomy. The statue of Denis Dussoubs, a local Montagnard shot to death on the barricade of the Petit Carreau during the resistance in Paris to Louis Napoleon's coup d'état in 1851, stood on a place that marked the beginning of the faubourgs. The large Haviland factories lay in the faubourgs, and the world of industrial work in Limoges centered on those large structures, policed by foremen.

The development of clearly identified industrial faubourgs that provided a base for remarkable Socialist strength in Limoges, leading to the socialist (of an essentially reformist variety) municipality of Emile Labussière at the turn of the century, and encouraging the waves of strikes that propelled Limoges into the national spotlight off and on during the 1895–1905 period. The Bourse du Travail, centered in the faubourgs, provided a base of operations for working-class militancy, and maintained close ties with the socialist municipality. The widespread strikes of 1905 brought troops, violence, and death (the shooting of a young porcelain worker in April of that year), as the faubourgs of Limoges—with barricades blocking the principal narrow street that stretched northward—defied the patronat and state authorities.

Although it is difficult to make a concrete connection between a language of stigmatization and the social and political coalescence of the faubourgs, some degree of self-identity within the faubourgs certainly existed. For one thing, the electoral districts into which the city was divided left the faubourgs as basically two separate electoral sections. Socialist leader and candidate Labussière directed his appeals for support to the faubourgs, although he needed the support of some other districts in order to defeat the Opportunists. He pointed out, in the case of the 1896 elections, which were essentially a referendum on his first year, that the election of the Opportunists would lead to urban projects that would benefit the bourgeois neighborhoods, not the faubourgs. *Bref,* municipal elections reaffirmed the self-identity of Limoges' working-class, peripheral spaces, the world of the faubourgs. In the 1900 municipal elections, socialist candidates in the second electoral district proudly proclaimed their section's identity as "the Belleville de Limoges." The tilting of politics in Limoges toward the faubourgs thus helped the city earn its reputation as Limoges, ville rouge.

The massive strikes of 1905 culminated Limoges' reputation as a center of socialist and syndicalist militancy. Contemporary postcards captured the defiance of the workers of the faubourgs, marching through Limoges with red and black flags and standing proudly before barricades outside factories. Workers destroyed the automobile of Theodore Haviland in the courtyard of his factory. The way in which the strikes took place reflected the spatial concomitants of industrial growth and self-identity in the faubourgs of Limoges. In one telling incident, a group of workers temporarily left the barricades and went into the center of Limoges in an attempt to destroy the statue of Notre-Dame-la-Pitié that stands outside of the small chapel of the butchers on the Rue de la Boucherie. This sortie failed, as they found the statue guarded by the butchers. Limoges' two cities clashed, represented by two very different collective identities. A picture taken shortly thereafter, however, shows the remains of a crucifix destroyed during the strike on a nearby avenue, the head of Christ almost intact, not far from a porcelain factory and the barricades.

These examples suggest that further attention to the question of language and self-identity in the changing world of urban life may lead us to a greater understanding and appreciation of the power of language. Yet, at the same time, such work may also make clear that the power of language and the impact of words and terms of stigmatization follow from economic and social changes that create disfavored urban spaces, the locus of activities and people unwanted by the center. Words stigmatize, and they can accentuate a sense of belonging (and counter sense of not belonging, that is, to the center) and of collective identity, but they do not create the spaces in the first place.

Finally, the contrast, while in no way absolute, between the sense of "suburbs" that developed in the United States, and that of faubourg/banlieue in France is particularly intriguing, particularly when one considers "the problem of the suburbs" in France in our time. The differences between the reality of suburban life in France and in the United States are important, and revealing. A systematic comparative study of the evolution of the use of the term "suburb" (which is unfortunately the most common English translation of both faubourg and banlieue) would focus on the social realities behind the mirror images of suburban spaces, and on the development of a language of stigmatization within the context of contemporary perceptions.

FIVE

On the Loose

The Impact of Rumors and Mouchards *in the Ardèche during the Second Republic*

More than merely an occasional force in history, rumor has perhaps been an inherent part of the political process itself. The intersection between rumor and the evolution of public opinion, and the impact of rumors on the shaping of government policies, largely remains to be studied. Yet, the history of France in the Ancien Régime, during the Revolution, and in the nineteenth and twentieth centuries offers fascinating glimpses of the role of rumor. Rumors that King Louis XVI was profiting from the hoarding of grain before the Revolution may well have helped prepare the French Revolution; certainly, the impact of the Great Fear on the night of 4 August 1789 is beyond dispute, or at least should be. Richard Cobb frequently returns to the role of rumor during the waxing and waning of popular movements during the Revolution and Empire.[1] More recently, Bronislaw Baczko has considered the significance of wild rumors about Robespierre-the-king sweeping Paris, which he argues influenced the fall of the Incorruptible One on the Ninth of Thermidor.[2]

I have in this volume tried to demonstrate the power of rumor in France in 1829 and 1830, when, before the July Revolution of 1830, a frightening and sometimes devastating series of arson attacks in Normandy sparked widely believed rumors.[3] To liberals, bands of brigands armed with matches were trying to frighten *censitaires* into voting for the candidates of the Polignac ministry; to conservatives, the fires were the work of those in the pay of liberals, trying to frighten electors into joining the rapidly expanding liberal forces challenging the Restoration politics. Alain Corbin has splendidly evoked the role of rumor in the atrocious murder of a Poitevin noble during the Franco-Prussian War in 1870, even if subsequent rumors had it wrong that the latter had been eaten by his murderers.[4]

During *la semaine sanglante* in May 1871, rumors spread rapidly on the Versaillais side that *les pétroleuses* were torching buildings, including the Bank of France. Rumors of German atrocities, including rapes and murder, against civilians during World War I probably contributed to the firm resolve with which the French home front held on in 1914 and thereafter.[5] The impact of powerful rumors—even the most bizarre— did not end in France with the era of the mass press, nor were they confined to the country's rural world. In 1969, the "rumor of Orléans" had it that Jewish shopkeepers were kidnapping girls and selling them into slavery.[6] This particular rumor generated a boycott against Jewish shopkeepers.

We do not have a general study of rumor—*les on-dit, les rumeurs, les bruits*—in modern French history. I will here expand the consideration of rumor to include not only *"les on-dit"* that began in small, distant villages, or in cabarets in small towns, or at the octroi of larger ones, but also briefly consider what one might call "official rumors"—some of it simply misinformation, or what Cobb calls "political rumors," set running by politicians. Rumors became "official" when they reached sub-prefectures, prefectures, and the corridors of the ministries of interior, justice, and war in Paris. There, manipulated at different levels of the administrative, judicial, and military hierarchies, they helped shape the government's contention that the Montagnards stood on the verge of insurrection in 1852. Both kinds of rumors, which were easily conflated by officials looking to confirm their worst fears and determined to destroy the Republic, helped shape government policy in 1850 and 1851. They thus contributed to move conservative public opinion toward acceptance of, indeed eagerness for, the destruction of the Republic. Thus, Louis Napoleon Bonaparte's regime would later insist that the coup d'état had been necessary to save France from socialist-inspired civil war.

I also want to consider the role that *mouchards*, or police spies, played in propagating rumor during the Second Republic, in shaping the confrontation between the government of Louis Napoleon Bonaparte and the Montagnards. To be sure, the French monarchy had frequently relied on police spies during the Ancien Régime, including none other than Brissot himself.[7] For these particular *mouchards*, convinced that what they were doing was extremely important and would be therefore pleasing to those who employed them, accentuated the diffusion of official rumors. Thus, it is possible, I think, to pluck rumors from the air in which they seemed to float, and place them squarely in the context of the social and political reality of the Second Republic. In this *ballon d'essai*, I can only scratch the surface, drawing on some examples I have recently marshalled from the Ardèche, where rumors, Montagnard secret societies, and police spies abounded, and whose archives include some extremely rich reports from three police spies.

First, what do we mean by rumor? A rumor can be defined as "a common talk or opinion, a widely disseminated belief having no discernible foundation or source," or "a statement or report current without any known authority for its truth," which, however distorted, may have some foundation in reality. Thus, a rumor is news that is diffused and widely believed, whether true or false.[8] Rumors are not, then, the same thing as oral communication, which, at the time of the Second Republic, still remained the principal source of news for most people. Nor are they necessarily the same thing as misinformation, though misinformation, diffused directly or indirectly by state authorities, could itself be a source or rumors and, in turn, be shaped by them.

Certainly, we need to know much more about the language, representation, and receptivity of rumor, for example about the relationship between French and patois in regions in which the latter greatly held sway among ordinary people. Historians might also want to determine to what extent the role of rumor declined with the emergence of more institutionalized mass political life (mass circulation newspapers, political parties, universal manhood suffrage, then universal suffrage, and so on) during the French Third Republic.[9]

To be sure, several of major studies of the Revolution of 1848 and the Second Republic in France have noted the importance of rumor, notably Ted Margadant's study of the resistance to the coup d'état, and that of Peter McPhee on Roussillon.[10] At a minimum, we can say that one of the results of rumors during the Second French Republic was to increase social conflict during the period and to encourage supporters of the government to anticipate and accept a violent end to the republic, as well as to keep Montagnards in a state of anxious readiness. Thus, both "official" rumor and popular rumor served to drive Montagnards and the regime and its supporters further apart as the destruction of the Second Republic loomed near.

Rumors thus operated as a powerful force by helping define the "view of the other" for the two principal political forces of the Second Republic: the démoc-socs, or Montagnards, of the left, and the government of Louis Napoleon Bonaparte, backed by many conservatives who would welcome his coup d'état with a sense of relief. Long ago, J. Dagnan noted that although the Bonapartist state had at its disposal the most technologically advanced means of communication—the telegraph—it fell back on the power of rumor.[11] Rumors convinced many conservatives that Montagnards were blood-thirsty fanatics posed to launch a major insurrection throughout much of France, after which they would turn against property and social hierarchy. By mid-1850, many administrators and magistrates believed that a massive plot existed to seize power, and in 1851, the year "1852" was whispered fearfully as promising a Montagnard takeover, whether by the ballot-box or through insurrection.

Rumors spread in provincial France during the Second Republic by the familiar conduits that traditionally carried news of all kinds along valley routes, upland footpaths, *chemins vicinaux,* on upgraded departmental and national roads, and by steamboats and, then, railroads. They were carried by commercial travelers, journeymen, peddlers, and seasonal migrants leaving and returning to the Massif Central, the Limousin, the Pyrénées, and the Alpine region, among others. They were related by and to peddlers working fairs and markets, and selling door to door in the countryside. Rumors accompanied journeymen on the tour de France; *colporteurs* brought not only published material with them to be read, but songs to be sung, *les images d'Épinal,* viewed and discussed. Yet, it is far more difficult to assess the number of people who believed rumors, or to chart the path of rumors with anything like the accuracy of Georges Lefebvre's study of the Great Fear.

The role of rumor after the Revolution of 1848 should be placed in the context of—and indeed was part of—the massive political mobilization that followed the revolution.[12] Rumors themselves reflected the degree of social and political conflict intensified by the revolution of 1848, accentuated by the economic crisis of 1846–47 that the revolution re-ignited following the brief recovery. The violence of the June Days, the subsequent attempted insurrections in 1849, and the heated rhetoric of the left contributed to this social polarization, expanding the power of rumor.

Nowhere did rumors—both "official rumors" and popular rumors—run more rampant than in an increasing number of prefectures of southern France. And yet, while convincing themselves that each arrest, discovery of Montagnard propaganda, and, sometimes, a cache of powder revealed a plot being secretly organized, prefects, subprefects, and *procureurs* themselves accentuated the power of rumor. Rumors surrounded and helped invent the "Complot de Lyon" of 1850, and various other "uncovered," largely imaginary plots large and small to overthrow the regime, such as those of the Southeast, Béziers, Perpignan, and perhaps the most pathetic invention of all, the "plot" surrounding a banquet in the Ardèchois village of Laurac in October 1851, which helped provide an excuse for the government to declare a state of siege in the Ardèche, along with five other departments. Prefects and magistrates thus elevated rumor to the status of fact, and then shaped policy accordingly, preparing the way for the coup d'état less than two months later.

However, some rumors aided the Montagnard cause, none more powerful (and ultimately accurate) than that picturing the regime as posed in 1851 to overthrow the republic. The Montagnards viewed officials of the centralized state as ruthless plotters against the great hopes of the republic who were fully capable of turning France back over to the great hopes of the republic who were fully capable of turning France back over to the great property-owners and to the hierarchy of the Catholic Church. McPhee considers rumors that the victory of the Montagnards and the establishment of a "democratic and social republic" was not far away to have been an important part of the *démoc-socs'* "language of justice and retribution," one greatly informed by rural life.[13] These rumors may have manifested a millenarian quality. Furthermore, some rumors probably added to the ranks of the left, for example convincing some peasants that under a "social" republic, only the rich would have to pay taxes. In the final attempt to defend hope for the "democratic and social republic," rumor would play a role in swelling the ranks of the insurgents in early December 1851.

The power of rumor was immediately apparent in the wake of the February Revolution, among great political uncertainty, as *commissaires* named by the new revolutionary authority assumed power and delegates from the Club of Clubs arrived in some regions to attempt to mobilize support for the republican left as the elections of April 23 approached. Rumors of leftist alleged misdeeds and plots quickly mobilized conservatives of all persuasions, probably contributing no small amount to the coalescence of France's notables, frightened by the potential move of the revolution to the left.[14]

From the beginning of the republic, the collective memory of the French Revolution and its accompanying violence remained closely linked to rumors among conservatives. Certainly, the claim by some radical republicans that the emerging Montagnard party had inherited the mantle of 1793 contributed to rumors that a violent insurrection of the left was not far away, even before the June Days. Shouts of "*Vive la guillotine!*" and "*Vive '93!*" were taken to augur a return of the scaffold, as in Bédarieux—where three gendarmes would be killed during the insurrection following the coup d'état—when an electoral meeting in April 1848 "cheered the memory of 1793 and called for a red flag."[15]

Such shouts and revolutionary songs such as *Le Chant du départ* and *Ça ira* were easily transformed by rumor into real acts of violence, or into certain projects for the future. Rumors accompanying news of the June Days had something of the impact of the Great Fear of 1789 in some places. Reports by *commissaires de police*, gendarmes, and secret police were, of course, not always very reliable; senior authorities did not just simply believe *anything* they heard. But by the last months of 1851, virtually any rumor seems to have been routinely taken as fact, or at least treated as such to encourage support from public opinion and to justify continued systematic political repression. For example, in 1850 the subprefect of Tournon assured the prefect of the Ardèche that a banquet of 3,000 people was being organized to celebrate the anniversary of the February Revolution. In fact, the eighty people picnicking at Crussol were outnumbered by the 100 troops sent from Valence to disperse them. Officials took "the smallest excursion among friends [*camarades*]," to be part of a massive conspiracy.[16]

Later that year, another banquet was rumored but never held near the vineyard town of St. Péray on the Rhône. Another "*on me dit que*" had a small banquet having taken place in remote St. Romain de Lerps, and yet another planned for the following weeks. The subprefect concluded, "I scarcely believe these meetings in the fields. People could have been mistaking hunters for socialists." Even the prefect knew that the very location of St. Romain de Lerps made any such gathering highly unlikely:

"You have to climb for an hour to reach St. Romain de Lerps, which consists of a church, the rectory, an inn and the house of the mayor who is a blacksmith. What effect would a banquet in such a place have? My arrondissement is perfectly calm."[17] A year later, such rumors were taken to be fact that a massive Montagnard conspiracy was afoot.

Officially orchestrated rumors of Montagnard conspiracy were something of a self-fulfilling prophesy. The centralized repression may have cut apart the radical apparatus in much of France, but it also forced Montagnards in much of the Midi and some parts of the Center to organize secret societies.[18] Increasingly, many of the rumors that swept regions focused on these Montagnard organizations and particularly on the belief that their insurrection was near, if not a hand. In April, 1850, Minister of the Interior Baroche summarized the "numerous warnings," however vague, imprecise, and, in some cases, already known, that had arrived in his ministry, which "lead one to believe in the existence of plots for insurrection in the departments of the East and the Midi," which awaited only the orders [*mot d'ordre*] from Marseille, Toulon, Lyon, and other major Montagnard centers."[19]

Such rumors that Montagnard leaders had given the password for an armed uprising to be prepared drew on fears among high officials and local elites that *démoc-socs* were stocking gunpowder and bullets and forging knives. The *Commissaire extraordinaire* of the sixth military division commanding the state of siege in the Lyon region went so far as to claim that from August 1850 to the end of March 1851, "from St. Étienne there have been sent to the department of the Ardèche alone 20,000 firearms, rifles and especially pistols."[20] In August 1850, a denunciation offered by three members of a so-called "society of order," reached the prefect of the Ardèche. Based on rumors that a Montagnard insurrection was in the works, it warned that "To prevent an imminent armed uprising and to strike a salutary terror against anarchy, it is necessary to proceed immediately to search the house of Meyssat." Specifically, they promised that a search would turn up under the counter on the first floor or in a room up the stairs the seal of the secret society and "an extensive correspondence setting in motion a vast conspiracy." As for the *cave*, the "men of order" advised that what appeared to be an empty barrel contained munitions. After listing leaders of the secret society who should be arrested immediately, the letter warned that if "no measure is taken within three days, we will take our concerns higher up, and we will be heard. Our safety demands it." However, a thorough police search turned up nothing suspicious.[21]

In June, 1850, officials in the Ardèche were tipped off that many leaders of the Montagnard secret societies had met in Montélimar in the Drôme, including about twenty from the department. Since this meeting, he could assert that there had been "considerable movement in the villages, meetings on Saturdays, [and] new affiliations." Members thereafter let their mustaches grow. Beards and mustaches were, at least in the Bas Vivarais, sometimes taken to indicate that he who sported one was a Montagnard and so was the gesture of tugging at one's ear with the thumb and index fingers of the right hand.[22] According to a police informant, the insurrection had been set for June 10, "at nightfall, the *tocsin* will everywhere be sounded, [the insurgents] will meet, take the arms of the national guard, and those in public storehouses, then depart, march all night to arrive the next morning in Privas, to the number of twelve to fifteen thousand men. There, they will seize the administration of the department and the public treasury, dispatch the prefect or take him hostage . . . and subsequently, in concert with other departments, proclaim Ledru Rollin president, and after this president has been installed in Paris, take, under his direction, great measures of public safety."[23]

In the hills above Aubenas and Vals, Antraigues had become a minor center of *démoc-soc* activity. In November, 1850, a police *confidente* related that "I have received a confidential report that there exists a conspiracy to set fire to the prefecture and the barracks on the night of the 19–20 or 20–21 and to liberate the prisoners." Even as he wrote, it appeared that a "large number of socialists" from other corners of the department were heading toward Antraigues and other places preparing for "some sort of surprise attack,—the result of the extraordinary intrigues of the secret societies, who, as you know, are infiltrating all our villages."[24]

The postman from Vernoux who delivered mail to the village of Bouffres had bragged that he had distributed more than forty pounds of gunpowder to Montagnards on his rounds, and that they were many *servatines* [*chevrotines*: small bullets for hunting game] in Vernoux. In Privas, Bouvier, a tinsmith, had called for calm, and patience: "When the time comes, we will make them dance a famous dance [hanging from a pole]; we have guns and we have ammunition, if you need some, we will pass some along."[25] The quest for the goods on Montagnards could, however, lead to some fairly elementary mistakes. In November, 1849, the commissaire de police of Annonay reported that some of the glove makers were wearing the *bonnet rouge* of the sans-culottes of the Revolution. It then had to be pointed out that such woolen red caps produced in Annonay were normal winter headwear for mountain people. Likewise, rumor transformed gunpowder being prepared for the Ardèchois passion of hunting into preparation for bloody insurrection.[26]

In February, 1850, at the time of the anniversary of the 1848 Revolution, an outing by about twenty workers from Vallon led to "*le bruit*" that near the famous natural bridge Pont d'Arc itself "they had sworn to remain faithful to their cause." The workers, when interrogated, insisted that they had gone out on a Sunday "for a pleasant outing, and not with other intentions," although, to be sure, such initiations almost certainly did occur, even if not necessarily that particular day.[27] Large gatherings of Montagnard leaders from the Ardèche, Haute-Loire, and Drôme were rumored on several occasions during that same year. In September, a rumor circulated that the prefect had asked that the Ardèche be put under the state of siege, but that the departmental *Conseil Général* had refused to permit this (as if that body would have had any such leverage). Again, such a *bruit*, no matter what its origins, probably helped propagate the belief among people of means that only by a strong, authoritarian move could the Montagnards be defeated.[28] And when a rumor had Annonay becoming the center of insurrection in November, the commander of the Gendarmerie claimed that such rumors "are only disseminated for the purpose of sowing unrest."[29]

In June, in the hills of the Ardèche "an individual, an outsider, had come to the village of St. Étienne de Boulogne and had harangued the public as people were leaving mass, calling on '*le peuple*' to remain ready to soon take up arms, and overthrow the government." An investigation failed to verify this event, but, in any case, the rumor was launched. A brief investigation revealed that a man from Ucel, across the Ardèche River from Aubenas, had indeed been in St. Étienne-de-Boulogne on 9 June 1850; he had stood in the middle of the village square drinking *eau de vie* and handing out swigs to those whom he met, but no more than this.[30] Similarly, in September a police report arrived in Privas that "assured" the prefect that in Pouzin in the Rhône Valley a woman—*la crieuse public*, appropriately enough—had shouted a warning that all those who had gunpowder and weapons should hide them, because the police were undertaking house searches. When asked who had told her to shout out such a message, she had replied that "a man had paid her to do so." Gendarmes who went by asked her who had her shout that and she said that she did not know him, that was the end of the investigation, but probably not the rumors of Montagnard mobilization that followed the incident.[31]

Even the absence of apparent Montagnard activity sparked rumors among conservatives that an underground plot was in the works.[32] And when Montagnard activity seemed to rise again between June and December 1850: "It is difficult not to see in this the work of a master plan, if not a conspiracy." The "discovery" of the "complot de Lyon" in October, 1850 centered on the political activities of Alphonse Gent, a former member of the National Assembly, who spent a great deal of time in Lyon, making many trips to see other Montagnards in various towns in the Southeast.[33] The idea of giving or receiving a "password" in cafés, *chambrées* [private male drinking and social clubs in parts of the Midi], or at the market or fair, or in other "permanent centers of disorder," "disguised [political] clubs, dens of demagogy," and so on, remained the core of plot hypotheses.[34]

And when the local Montagnard leader Mazon was arrested and taken away with a heavy chain around his neck that same month amid considerable "agitation," rumor had emissaries going out from Largentière to organize a mobilization to free him: "The rumors of a rescue of the prisoners have been verified in such a serious way that I have had to take all necessary precautions to guard against such an eventuality, whose realization, if not probable seems at least possible."[35] A day later, the *procureur* ordered Mazon freed (at which point he went into hiding somewhere between Thueyts and Prades above Aubenas), fearing precisely such an eventuality. In this case, too, authorities accused the Montagnards of starting rumors that they believed served their interests: "The reds have circulated the rumor that the local authorities have been frightened by the obvious movement of armed men in the hills, and that they gave up Mazon in order to prevent Largentière from being burned down and its inhabitants massacred."[36]

In late 1851, the justice of the peace of the canton of Aubenas related a series of "*on me dit que*": that secret gatherings were being held all over the department, "where letters are being read that incite this agitation. It has been claimed for some time now that the triumph of socialism is imminent. Since people are sure that general Changarnier will vigorously crush the rebellion, they want the departments to take the initiative, and seven generals have been designated in advance as the leaders of the movement to inspire confidence," including, absurdly enough, General Cavaignac.[37]

Several incidents in the Ardèche of Montagnard resistance to gendarmes accentuated official certainty and elite fears that a popular insurrection lay not far away. Gendarmes raiding a

Montagnard gathering in the largely Protestant village of Sala-vas led to the freeing of prisoners and the flight of a number of "suspects" into the hills, where they were protected by the population, and the inevitable attempts of authorities to link this "conspiracy" with the "complot de Lyon."[38] Yet, the *procureur général* of Nîmes complained of the incomplete and vague nature of the reports coming out of the Bas Vivarais.[39]

The aggressive presence of gendarmes at *fêtes votives* [festivals celebrating patron saints] in the Ardèche generated two cases of popular resistance that further convinced authorities that secret societies were organized and ready for 1852. When gendarmes tried to break up a brawl in the Protestant village of Labastide-de-Virac on 3 August, "Protestant democrats" chased them away and, as in the Salavas incident, "suspects" disappeared into the hills. A week later, in Laurac, just off the road from Aubenas to Alès and only a few kilometers from Largentière, two brigades of gendarmes moved in to break up a Montagnard "banquet" organized by local activists, at which fifty or sixty people challenged prefectoral decrees by singing "demagogic songs." A crowd then moved against the gendarmes, hurling bottles and rocks, to which the gendarmes replied with swords and guns, but had to be rescued by the arrival of the subprefect with loyal national guardsmen from Largentière. On 31 August at Vinezac, a few kilometers up the road toward Aubenas, villagers assailed gendarmes who prevented their *fête* from even beginning. Troops rescued the gendarmes, firing shots, and arresting several people.[40]

Two weeks earlier, a Montagnard supposedly *had* confessed that a *démoc-soc* plot existed to storm Largentière, put to death various officials, and pillage the place. After admitting in a letter that it would be difficult legally to prove that a plot actually existed before the banquet at Laurac, the seizure of letters in rural communes seemed to provide proof that secret societies existed. Only a sizable military presence could help the authorities turn the corner, reassuring the "men of order."[41] When the *procureur-général* of Nîmes expressed doubts that sheer military force could overwhelm political opposition and suggested that the proliferation of such incidents as had occurred in Laurac and Vinezac could be counter-productive because they acclimated the local population to resist the forces of order, the Minister of Justice insisted that the wide-spread organization of secret societies in the district necessitated such an aggressive show of force.[42]

Thus, in order to get the goods on the Montagnard secret societies, three police spies were sent into the Ardèche, one for each arrondissement, but while they apparently had no contact with each other, they knew of each others' existence. Sent to the Bas Vivarais by orders of unspecified Parisian authorities, each was put in contact with the prefect ("I belong to you, body and soul") and two subprefects of the department. Yet, they had no "official" authority. "I am in no way an agent with official standing," wrote one of them, "Arnaud," traveling as a wine merchant, "I must be and remain foreign to all authority, and if the occasion is sufficiently urgent, the authorities may treat me like the other criminals caught red handed . . . we must have recourse to the ruse."[43] Letters from the prefect and subprefects were to be sent care of the hotels in which they were staying, or *poste restante*, or even to neighboring localities.

When they were not writing to ask for more money, the three *mouchards* planted themselves in cafés, where they spent their time in idle chatter. They seem to have knowingly treated the rumors they heard as fact, and threats and playful pleasantries as one and the same. They did so, in part, because (as Richard Cobb insisted in the case of the *commissaires de police* of the Revolutionary and Napoleonic eras[44]) they tended to report what they believed their superiors wanted to hear. In the Second Republic, *commissaires de police* tended to be more cautious and accurate in their reporting, because they had to limit their investigations to the town to which they were assigned. "Arnaud" claimed that in Annonay a Montagnard hairdresser had told other socialists in the glove-making town, that "if we take action, we will make those famous gloves with the skin of the prefect. It was said to him, is this a joke? He replied: no, this is very serious; he will not leave Privas alive. We don't ever want to be caught." In the arrondissement of Largentière, the *mouchard* Vigier traveled with a passport in the name of Antoine Ballard, thirty-six years of age, commercial bookkeeper [*comptable d'une maison de commerce*]. In the meantime, another agent, a former café proprietor from Avignon, had been posted in Annonay. Vigier's trek took him from Thueyts above Aubenas on the road to Le Puy to the predominantly Protestant communes in the cantons of Le Vans, Joyeuse, and Vallon in the Bas Vivarais. The subprefect hoped to link the secret societies directly to the Laurac affair, construed to have been part of a specific Montagnard plot. Compounding the difficulties of Vigier's assignment was the fact that the secret agent on the loose in Privas and its region had been totally compromised by his own foolish comportment, and was widely considered to be a *mouchard*.[45]

How was Vigier to become a well-informed informant, after receiving a quick crash course from the subprefect on the Montagnards of the Bas Vivarais? The subprefect knew that it would take at least some time for him to be able to pass on useful information to the subprefect on the Montagnards of the Bas Vivarais? The subprefect knew that it would take at least some time for him to be able to pass on useful information to the subprefect, who would, in turn, send it to Privas: "If he endeavors to acquire little by little the confidence of the reds, and he will accomplish this, I do not doubt, if he works at it seriously."[46]

The local gendarmerie and police *commissaires* were not let in on Vigier's mission. Thus, Vigier encountered an occupational hazard of his métier—a gendarme arrested him in the village of Mayras. He stood accused of being a Montagnard propagandist. After all, he had with him a list of local "demagogues" and their addresses, and pamphlets like "The People Will Take Revenge," as well as a list of his expenses. But Vigier could not hide his indignity at being arrested, nor his sense of self-importance in working for higher authorities than the gendarme who arrested him. Even his description to the subprefect of his arrest could not have been complete without the comment that he had been thrown in the jail because he was taken to be "a very dangerous man, inciting the masses to rebellion." Thus, Vigier told the gendarme taking him to Aubenas that he had been sent from Paris: "I let him know that I had business in Jaujac, on the orders of authorities, but he did not want to believe any of it." After being freed by orders of authorities, but he did not want to believe any of it." After being freed by order of the subprefect, Vigier did not want to be turned loose in Aubenas, fearing that the Montagnards would find him out, and was packed off in a coach to Largentière.[47]

After this episode, Vigier began a tour that took him to Montréal, Laurac, Rosières, Joyeuse, Lablachère, Les Assions, Les Vans, Berrias, and St. André-de-Crozières; all of the stops were to be completed by the time he was to meet with the subprefect in eight days.[48] From Laurac, one of his first stops, Vigier reported that the "party" of Montagnards "is not extinguished, but there are men who are not well intentioned," a significant minority of the population, including a certain Dussère "known as *le penitent blanc*," who, although not a radical, had twenty-three bullets and two "little packets of hunting powder," in a drawer in his armoire. As for gunpowder, all the Montagnards, he claimed, were in perfect agreement that it could be produced so quickly that it was perhaps not wise to stock up, since it could be seized in searches. In the wake of the state of siege, Vigier believed that "a kind of secret society has existed in principle, but since the state of siege was imposed, it no longer exists, or at least no longer appears to exits." The Montagnards appeared somewhat demoralized, frozen in their tracks—"everyone is afraid"—with a couple of their leaders in hiding.[49] In and around Privas, republicans and *démoc-socs* believed that the effect of the siege would be to "democratize the Ardèche even more by annoying it. They expect that the peasants will be furious and that they vote in the elections for whomever they please."[50]

But rumors that Vigier was a police spy circulated. Furthermore, the subprefect complained that his reports "tell us nothing new, and only repeat what I have already said to him myself. [Yet] his evaluations are, in general, accurate enough," but of the relations that he has with the demagogues, "those are boasts that he has attempted to exaggerate." For example, some of the stories he passed along at the time of a Montagnard banquet to celebrate the anniversary of the February Revolution could be dismissed as "pure invention." The *mouchard* had exaggerated the number of members of the Montagnard secret society to be 900, while the subprefect held to an also inflated total of "five or six hundred, of whom only three hundred could be counted on." His passing on rumors of alleged Montagnard plans for insurrection including a fanciful account of the execution of the prefect on the *place* de L'Airette in Aubenas (which would have, for one thing, entailed bringing him over the difficult Col d'Escrinet from Privas simply to be hung in Aubenas).[51]

Vigier's downfall came after his return from the canton of Vallon, as well as a quick trip to Montpellier for family matters. After his report that several gendarmes in the canton of Aubenas had been publicly singing Montagnard songs could not be verified by their commanders, he asked to be put at the disposition of the prefect in Privas or elsewhere, however not in the arrondissement of Largentière. Furthermore, the subprefect criticized Vigier's "lack of caution"; the *mouchard* had apparently related his arrest to gendarmes in Vallon, where he had no reason to do so, and had revealed his identity as a secret agent to the *commissaire de police* there. By then, "the reds are stating openly that he is a government agent," telling him this to his face. "People are talking openly about this matter, and Vigier is strolling in public with the *commissaire de police*, which discredits him even more." In the opinion of the subprefect, Vigier was intelligent, yet very lazy. Vigier, however, continued to boast of his energy on behalf of the Bonapartist cause: "I have had intimate relations with the mistress of Lemairoux, I am going to resume these and attempt to find out, via this intermediary, where the fugitives have their lair." He could keep a secret, but only up to a point. Again, Vigier's need to be important got the best of him; he had proudly revealed his mission to gendarmes in order to learn information about the Montagnards in the villages he was supposed to be infiltrating; he did so in order to avoid the expense and bother of more traveling to new places, and of hobnobbing with people to whom he believed himself superior, and whom he disparagingly referred to as the "vile multitude."[52]

It must be said that Vigier was educated: few French speaking Ardèchois and certainly precious few police spies used words like "the coryphaeus" to describe a leader of the Montagnards of Largentière. However, Vigier had gone to Montpellier against the wishes of the subprefect, while insisting that his purpose was to learn more about the Montagnards in and around in the *chef-lieu* [departmental capital] of the Hérault. While the subprefect had kept "the silence of death about this man and his mission," now even a modest *commissaire de police* stepped forward to complain about Vigier. The subprefect concluded that it was necessary to send Vigier out of the arrondissement: "He cannot do any more good here . . . he is too compromised." That, as far as we know, was the end of the Vigier's mission in the Ardèche.[53]

What had Vigier accomplished? Despite his obvious incompetence, the essence of his reports reached Paris, through the intermediary of the prefect, helping confirm the image that the Ardèche was on the verge of a Montagnard insurrection. His reports confirmed what was already known about Montagnard strength in the Bas Vivaais. He identified Montagnards, leaders and followers, adding some new names, complete with detailed descriptions, to the growing list in secret files in Largentière and in Privas. He assessed their degree of radicalization (for example, carefully noting those who could be defined, rightly or wrongly, as "*partageux*," and those who remained fully respectful of property). Village by village, Vigier estimated the percentage of *démoc-soc* among the population: three-fifths in Salavas, three-quarters in Vallon, at least two-thirds in lovely Balazuc, half in Ruoms, and so on. These were good guesses. Vigier recognized that the state of siege had indeed driven Montagnard activity further underground in the Ardèche, and believed that the arrondissement of Largentière might well rise up if an insurrection occurred in Paris or Lyon. In October, Vigier reported that the Montagnards of Largentière "are convinced that the decisive crisis will occur before January 1, and that a violation of the constitution will bring about an uprising [that] must open the doors of prisons to those accused or condemned of political crimes in the Ardèche and everywhere else."[54]

But, in the end, Vigier added little that was new, sometimes simply repeating information that the subprefect had provided him at the outset of his small adventure, and he even got some things flat wrong. The subprefect did not share his optimistic assessment of Joyeuse, nor his pessimistic view of Les Vans, at least from the point of view of the authorities concerned with such things. His reports nonetheless added to the willingness of the administration to convey to Paris the continued existence of secret societies—though he greatly exaggerated the number of members—to which authorities responded by attributing secret preparations, including the stocking of gunpowder in Vallon and other places to plans for armed insurrection in 1852. Rumor helped determine and later justify official policy.

In Privas, "Arnaud" did not do much better, and seemed almost obsessed with providing careful physical descriptions of Montagnards. He thus described the long-haired man accompanying a Montagnard at the "republican café" as "[wearing] bourgeois clothing that is shabby, and talking politics with the goal of bring others into a general conversation, probably in order to get me to participate and to learn who I am." This preoccupation with physical descriptions at a time when police depended on *signalements* [written descriptions of features] is to be expected. When, in the early days of his stay in Privas, the *mouchard* maintained the discretion of attentive silence so as to avoid suspicion while seeking acceptance as a politically reliable *habitué*, a peasant on market day who was a little drunk chastised him for using a white handkerchief for his cold, repeating several times, "*A bas les blancs! Vivent les rouges!*" Integrating himself into the small world of Montagnards took time: "Yesterday was a good one for increasing my popularity, which I do with extreme moderation at the end complete confidence will be obtained." His attendance at a nearby rural festival helped build confidence—a confidence, of course, that was completely misplaced—among "*les rouges*." In September 1851, Arnauld left Privas with two or three printshop workers and spent some hours there. "I played *boules* with the peasants; at times we addressed each other familiarly [nous nous tutoyâmes parfois], and we drank, danced and sang with a primitive independence." Ever playing the role of a bourgeois socialist, Arnaud could not resist cautioning the young workers to help keep the *fête* on a reasonable, restrained track, as a vigorous water game led to a fight and to the intervention of several gendarmes.

He then naively claimed that his attendance at the *fête* had demonstrated to all that he was a Montagnard, not a *mouchard*. Police spies, after all, had to be actors (and, as such, risked having the same status as actors, if even that). Excluded from citizenship (or rather subjectship, as it were) until the French Revolution because they were reviled as dishonest and untrustworthy for their facility in adopting different personnae, the *mouchards* were in the end trusted neither by the Montagnards upon whom they spied, nor, by virtue of their failures, by those to whom they reported.[55]

Flushed with excitement and emboldened by some sense of triumph, Arnaud wrote, "It seems to me that I constantly have a demagogue on my shoulders, I will continue to write you about this kind of terror in our department." He then fell ill with a fever, which he was unsure whether to blame on the air, the water, or the heat of the Ardèche; in any case, he soon found himself covered with red splotches. Sick or not, in a letter to the prefect he unctuously expressed pleasure at the harsh measures taken by the government: "Arbitrariness itself loses its name when confronted by the orgies and the criminal designs of the demagogues." A prefectorial wall poster underlining the illegality of wearing the color red (Arnaud's red splotches did not count)—identified with the Montagnards—gave Arnaud the chance to report to the prefect more conversations, including one *rouge* who boasted, "As for me, I will wear my red robe to have this kid [*chevreau*, also the name of the prefect] hobbled."[56]

Yet though he took care to grow a Montagnard beard, Arnaud was increasingly assumed to be a police spy. In mid-September, Montagnards informed him that the *commissaire de police*—whom Arnaud believed was jealous of him—had identified him as "an agent of the government [*pouvoir*]," and he had to talk his way out again. For one thing, as he pointed out himself, he may have attracted attention because a wine merchant—his purported profession—did not usually stay in one place for such a long time. How would he deal with the leading *démagogues* who suspected him, besides conspicuously reading *La Feuille du village*, which had been banned by decree? He would really put on a show: "Let me as well fear the *mouchards*! . . . From that time on, I will crush with my republican pride those who raise doubts . . . It is something like an actor's role that I am developing, with an aplomb and an accent of conviction that will persuade them!" After such bravado, Arnaud's moment came in the Café Meyssac (where he apparently limited himself to drinking *sirop* with water) when a well-dressed man with two other Montagnards in tow entered, announcing, "I have come because I was told that there is a *mouchard* here. I would be very happy to see his face." To which Arnaud claimed to have replied, "In Paris we are accustomed to see thieves be the first to shout 'Stop thief!' Everyone knows this and the insolent fellow lets his head fall and remains silent."[57]

As for the *mouchard* sent to the arrondissement of Tournon, his reports "tell us nothing new, and only say what I myself, have already said to the agent." Local authorities already suspected the various mutual aid societies among the glove-workers of Annonay of helping to mobilize Montagnards, whom he counted at about five to six hundred. His embellished reports on his relations with local Montagnards in order to make him look good.[58]

The rare and sometimes fascinating letters from the Ardèche's three *mouchards* do not help us resolve one interesting problem, that of accent and, for that matter, language. It was difficult enough finding some degree of acceptance—at least for a time—as a Montagnard. In the Ardèche, a strong Languedocien accent was prevalent among the upper classes in the Bas-Vivarais, and patois almost universally spoken among ordinary people, particularly in the countryside. In the mountains of the Ardèche toward the Haute-Loire, another accent and another (Auvergnat) patois could be heard, while the accent of the arrondissement of Tournon was somewhat different still.[59] At a minimum, the *mouchards'* urban references (Arnaud's quote about thieves in Paris, for example) attracted no small degree of suspicion that even claims of holding positions as commercial travelers could not allay. In short, to repeat, we need to know more about language.

The Ardèche was certainly not alone in being awash with rumors and fear in late 1851. By March of that year, the Gers "has been taken over by fear of the reds: this fear leads to the most childish alarms, people constantly believing they are on the brink of the most serious trouble," amid discussion of a possible revision of the constitution to allow Louis Napoleon to stand for another term as president. At the time of the return of the National Assembly in November, rumors of a coup d'état were rampant in the Gers, contributing to a growing anxiety among people of means and fear that perhaps, as *l'Opinion* editorialized, "we need to resign ourselves to legality, as to the inflictions that God sends us," and that 1852 would be the year of Montagnard "revenge, expropriations, and pillage."[60] In Roussillon, the "men of order informed their apocalyptic vision of 1852 with symbols of a natural world in chaos."[61] Amid such panic, *Le Constitutionnel* publicly called into question the need for new elections. "Legality" would require elections in 1852 "in the face of terrifying organization of all the forces of socialism." On 27 August it suggested that any solution which crushed the left would be preferable to "the dangers of that sort of legality." Auguste Romieu in *Le Spectre rouge de 1852* proposed such a solution:

The social order has as its sole and real support, not your ridiculous collection of law codes, but the strong ramparts where authority remains with its flag, ramparts alive with strong hearts, bristling with bayonets and artillery . . . Do not despair. Blood and tears will flow . . . As for the soldiers' leader, his task is simple. He must resolutely make himself a total dictator.[62]

Writing eighteen years after the coup d'état, Eugène Ténot's two books on the resistance to the coup—written to rehabilitate the insurgents pictured by official Bonapartist accounts and propaganda as blood-thirsty monsters—recalled both the pervasive fear of "1852" and mounting rumors reaching into other European states that a coup d'état was imminent: "At the moment when the National Assembly was about to resume its labors, there was no noise but that about the Coup d'État, which had failed to occur during the prorogation. The newspapers entertained their readers with it; in political circles it was the subject of every conversation . . . The singularly violent language of the Napoleonic press against the Assembly and against the Constitution, at the same time as against the Republican party, was not of a nature to allay the general apprehensions."[63]

The coup d'état of December 2, of course, generated massive resistance in which well over 100,000 people took arms in France. The secret societies, as Margadant has clearly demonstrated, lay behind the widespread resistance to the coup in the Midi. The secret societies of the Bas Vivarais, based in perhaps as many as fifty communes, spearheaded the local insurrection in defense of the republic. The Montagnard secret societies in the Ardèche rose up to defend the republic, particularly but not exclusively from communes (notably Salavas and Chomerac) where there were many Protestant families for whom the history of the wars of religion remained alive.[64] A column of several thousand Montagnards from the canton of Vallon marched on Largentière, their numbers drawn from Lablachère, Lagorce, Balazuc, and other beautiful but impoverished villages. In the darkness before dawn on the morning of 7 December, they turned back in panic when confronting a small armed infantry regiment on the outskirts of the subprefecture.[65]

On the side of the Montagnards, early rumors of insurgent successes certainly encouraged continued resistance in the Bas Vivarais, as well as some other regions of the Midi.[66] Rumors in some places convinced people that armed defense of the "democratic and social republic" was sweeping the entire nation, or exaggerated the number and success of insurgents in neighboring departments, or in the same department. In one village in the Drôme, insurgents confidently told a local notary that "Crest, Valence, and Lyon were in the power of the insurgents." Likewise, a political fugitive in another village predicted that "before dawn [on the eighth] 50,000 people would reach Loriol from the departments of the Drôme and the Ardèche."[67]

However, the most salient legacy of the role of rumors during and after the insurrection was to provide an official interpretation of the coup d'état as having been necessary to save France from social armageddon in 1852. The aggressive rhetoric of the Montagnards certainly played a part in the propagation of rumors about the threat they posed to social order. Alain Corbin cites an example from the Haute-Vienne, where an insurgent in Saint-Auvent "proposed to re-establish the guillotine for the rich and the government officials: they would catch the 'whites'; once again the movement would take the form of a *fête* in the course of which they would command that food and drink brought to them."[68] For administrators and the upper classes, armed resistance, leading to the death of several gendarmes in Bédarieux, were taken to demonstrate what would have been in store for France's social and political elite had not Louis Napoleon Bonaparte intervened. Baroche, giving a speech as the results of the (first) plebiscite were announced to Louis Napoleon on 31 December, summarized the Bonapartist canon shaped by officially orchestrated rumors: "Let France be at last delivered for those men always ready for murder and pillage; from those men who, in the nineteenth century, bring horror into civilization, and seem, while awakening the saddest remembrances, to carry us back five hundred years into the past."[69]

We return to the Ardèche to conclude. In the period following the coup d'état, officials assessing the political situation in the Ardèche blamed rumors and "false news" for the mobilization in the countryside of early December 1851. The prefect claimed that Ardèchois peasants had been "misled" as to the goals of the government before the coup. "Poorly enlightened, in addition, and having no easy and habitual communication with the centers of population from where real news originals . . . they let themselves be led into the most glaring error. The false news propagated by the leaders of the secret societies, with the help of the taverns and the bad press, has misled the ignorant, made them believe in the infallibility of [their] success, and led them into an armed uprising."[70] All of this was quite ironic, in that rumor had itself been a weapon of the government in the Ardèche, as other departments.

In August 1852, the prefect decided to grant freedom to a *démoc-soc* implicated in the resistance to the coup—under the supervision of a priest from his mountain village—in exchange for information that would lead to the arrest of several Montagnards. The one-time *démoc-soc* had attracted the prefect's attention by informing him that several of those implicated in the resistance were still in the uplands of the Ardèche, preparing and distributing gunpowder in preparation for a new insurrection that had been commanded in Paris, and that was to occur by the end of August. The soldiers of this insurrection would be drawn among peasants, especially Protestants. An amnesty for some insurgents anticipated for August 15, "the rumor of which has been spread," was to swell the ranks of the insurgents: "Should it occur, the secret societies will make one final attempt."[71] A friend of the newly proclaimed Second Empire, the schoolteacher of St. Just, wrote "In my village, I combat these rumors, with all my strength, but my duties as teacher leave me with little time to chat and scarcely permit me to work against them in the café, I am powerless against them."[72]

A certain irony—however unintended—may be found in the teacher's complaints that rumors were circulating in the Ardèche that were hostile to Napoleon III. During the Second Republic, the government of Louis Napoleon Bonaparte had benefitted more than their Montagnard opponents from rumor. Building on elite fears of growing Montagnard influence, particularly but not exclusively in regions where secret societies had proliferated, the Bonapartists had manipulated and encouraged rumor to their advantage, preparing the way for the coup d'état.

SIX

Some Observations on the Transition to the Euro in France

The relatively weak popular support in France in the 1990s for "Europe" makes an attempt to assess the transition to the euro even more interesting. The Treaty of Maastricht was ratified by only 51.1 percent of voters. How would the Europeanization of money in France be accepted in a country with long traditions of state intervention or control, to say nothing of nationalism, and widespread attachment to necessary social programs (thus, resistance to budget cutting and to such endeavors as Prime Minister Lione I Jospin's program of finding temporary jobs for young people) and public services?[1] This chapter offers observations penned in the first months after the transition to the euro in France, with an emphasis on daily life. My reflections are not those of a political scientist or economist—I am neither—but of a historian who resides a good part of the time in a village of 350 people in the Bas-Vivarais in Ardèche.

Let me say at the outset that "Europe" and "Europeanization" have long seemed in many ways distant, even somewhat irrelevant for many if not most people in a relatively isolated village, even one in which tourism has become part of the local economy. "Europe" has brought a nice, sporty sign to welcome tourists to the village and indicate things that they might see, written in French, English, and German. "Europe" had paid one or two landowners to rip out vines and plant fruit trees, and then to knock down the fruit trees and to plant vines again (yet, because the money comes via the Ministry of Agriculture, it seems to be French in origin). Only fifteen families still work the land of the nearly two hundred families who tilled the "ungrateful soil" there in the middle of the nineteenth century. The first priority is to finish reforming the sanitation system, bringing Balazuc into anyone's norms by assuring the proper disposal of waste. This was recently completed. The hope is that then European money may help bring order to the rocky paths of the village. "European norms" have transformed the way goat cheese is produced. And now "Europe" has brought the euro into the daily life of sixty million people in France beginning on January 1, 2002, when 304 million people initiated the "euro conversion."

Political leaders wanted a smooth transition from the franc to the euro. The transition to the euro went remarkably well. It occurred without major problems and in good humor. The beloved owner of the only café open all year had said in the previous October that one of the reasons she was going to retire at the end of the year was the transition to the euro—she did not want to have to learn to take money and give change in a new currency. Yet, she is still there. The new currency caught on quickly. A German-American singer known as "Deutschmark Bob" simple changed his name to "Euro Bob." *Le Progrès de Lyon* put it this way on January 2: "The euro has become part of our daily life extremely quickly. No one could have imagined this at the beginning." To *Libération,* "Everything occurred as in a dream." Nicolas Herpin, a sociologist, put it this way in *Le Figaro:* "The most important fact is the ease with which the euro became the money of everyday life" (*Le Progrès de Lyon,* January 4, 2002; *Libération,* February 16–17, 2002; *Le Figaro,* February 16–17, 2002). According to statistics of the European Commission on January 4, France "stood at the head of the pack" with the Netherlands in how things seemed to be going, with a regular progression, day by day, in the percentage of transactions in the new currency. If daily life became temporarily more complicated, the dislocation was not as much as one might have anticipated, and not for very long. One editorialist celebrated the transition as "a veritable triumph of social technology" (Gérard Dupuy, *Libération*, February 16–17, 2002).

Preparations

In France, the euro's big coming-out party was well prepared with five years of work, in conjunction with the European Commission and its campaign, *"L'Euro facile"* (The Euro Made Easy). As everywhere in the euro zone, a massive campaign prepared consumers for the big change (occasionally called rather pompously "the pedagogy of the conversion," though descriptions like "making users aware" were more common).[2] Adapting with considerable success the European campaign (and, more than occasionally, giving the impression that they invented it), the Ministry of Economy, Finance, and Industry initiated meetings with the theme "The Euro for Everybody," and set up a website for questions. Checkbooks arrived in euros in September, and several big supermarkets had euro days. Banks began to give balances and expenses in both euros and francs. Some explanations of why France was going euro took the form of cartoons, in the tradition of the historic images of Épinal.

Pamphlets and brochures explaining the euro and its conversion bombarded the public. Municipalities put forward information on the transition, following the model of the campaign of *L'Euro facile*. "The Euro at School" brought anticipation of the euro to the young. All banks and insurance companies produced guides similar to that of the Société Générale, "The Euro and Your Company: Practical Guide to the Single European Currency," with color pictures of each coin, explaining the symbolism of their decorations. This glossy brochure reminded businesses to establish a "plan of action" for the conversion of, for example, the preparation of accounts and taxes, and to discuss the charge with employees, as well as showing how to convert from francs into euros. The Société Marseillaise de Crédit offered clients a tiny conversion table, *L'Euro facile!*, not much bigger than a folded euro banknote. The SNCF guide to the national railway, "To Facilitate the Euro for You: Practical Advice," featured a shooting star racing across a symbol of the euro. The Ministry of Economy, Finance, and Industry produced a flashy brochure, "Let's Discover Right Now Our New Currency" with a beautiful young woman, a contemporary, nightclub embodiment of Marianne, an up-to-date symbol of the republic. The SNCF made readily available the "SNCF Guide to Make the Euro Easy for You," with practical advice for the period January 1–February 17, the period when both currencies would be nervously coexisting. Such preparations were, to repeat, part of a coordinated campaign initiated by the European Union.

Day after day newspapers explained "the easy conversion"[3] from francs to euros, reminding readers of several reference points: 1.5 euros to 10 francs, 15 euros to about 100 francs, and 150 euros to 1,000 francs. They offered reassuring advice to the "euro-stressed-out" and the "euro-flipped-out," including simply buying lots of goods in advance and freezing them. In December, *Libération* ran a daily example of how much a familiar purchase would cost in euros: "And in euros, how much?" The monthly *métro* pass, two zones, was 291 francs or 44.36 euros; or one metro ticket, 8.50 francs or 1.30 euros; or, at a different level, and fairly removed from daily life, one gold ingot on December 4 was worth 65,595 francs, or 10,000 euros. The pamphlet "And in Euros? How Much Is It?" told readers that the *rmi* (minimum assistance to the unemployed) for one person after January 1 would be 397.66 euros per month (2,608.50 francs). Gambling casinos discretely began to add new gray and yellow tokens to replace change in francs, seven tons of tokens just for the machines in La Baule produced for the Barrière association. There, in the early morning hours of January 18, a hundred employees, in the company of police and technicians, changed the machines over to the new system (*Libération*, December 24, 2001).

As a result of a euro agreement organized by the European Commission with associations of retailers and consumers (the euro-logo agreement), in the weeks before the big day, training programs were initiated in supermarkets and in the *métros* of Paris, Lyon, and other cities. Several promoted euro days. Carrefour began training its checkout people in euros early in 2001 to sensitize the employees, so that each employee had at least eleven hours of training. Lessons included how to recognize a fake euro banknote. This task was made more difficult by the unwillingness of the Banque de France to release very many banknotes even for such lessons: 120 cashiers had to work with several small banknotes, none of which was more than 50 euros, and no coins, merely with a photocopy of some coins, so they could learn to recognize them. The instructions were clear: leave the coins and bills on the counter; do not confuse 200 francs with 200 euros (1,312 francs) and thus give the client seven times more change than was due; and reminding each, "You are responsible for your cash register; don't forget it!" (The clerks remain poorly paid, barely above the minimum wage, whether in euros or in francs.) And the clerks were not to round off anymore, as they had with centimes, as one euro cent would now be worth about ten centimes. With a tinge of Taylorism, instructions expressed concern that the average time it took to count money rendered and check for counterfeit bills and coins would pass from thirty-four to thirty-nine seconds; it was hoped there would be no more than five errors for every thousand clients paying in cash. The fear was, of course, that some clients would become so tired of waiting in line that they would simply abandon their food carts and leave in disgust (*Libération,* December 11, 2001).

In Paris and Lyon, the *métros* were at the forefront in preparing the conversion, for obvious reasons. The R.A.T.P. announced that all trips would be free from five o'clock in the evening until the closing of the *métro* not long after midnight, so that the transformation could be achieved in the ticket offices at each stations, while encouraging clients to buy their monthly *métro* pass early and to use their euro kits when possible. Two sets of machines would be required—one for euros, one for francs— although payment for tickets purchased ten at a time by credit card was strongly encouraged.

The euro kits were the trump card for the conversion. Fifty million of them, small plastic sacks of forty coins totaling 15.25 euros (100 francs), went on sale on December 14, 2001 (banknotes were not available until January 1). These kits were advertised as "handsome gifts for children," and they were. The starter kits were such a success that they began to run out in some places (the minister of the economy had asked people not to buy more than one), and some bank branches limited sale of them to their own clients only, a sign of things to come.[4]

In early November 2001, the government was expressing confidence that, although both the franc and euro were to coexist officially until February 17, the franc could be relegated to memory within several days after January 1, with the "*fast euro*" or "*un big bang*." Pierre Marleix, a member of the Comité notional de l'euro and representative of the FO-*consommateurs*, criticized "the euro enthusiast" who wanted to rush forward and not take full advantage of the planned period of transition. He noted discussion of the possibility of assessing a fine of 1,000 francs for merchants who continued to give change in francs and for consumers who refused to accept euros. Much would depend on the massive use of checks (use of which increased by 4 percent in January alone) and credit cards (the use of which increased by 14.4 percent in January) (*Libération*, November 5, 2001; *Le Monde*, February 17, 2002). In November and December, more than half of the merchants in France accepted payment by check in euros, which facilitated the transition. During the first week of December, one-third of all checks were already written in euros (as opposed to a tenth in September).[5] François Patriat, secretary of PME (Petite et moyenne enterprise, or small and medium businesses) and Consumers, reflected his *euro-enthusiame*, and, in the context of *euro-confiance* and *euro-vigilance*, introduced in early November the concept of *euro-impatience* (*Libération*, November 5, 2001). By the time February 17 rolled around, the transition had cost the 114 companies classified as very large firms 7 billion francs. The SNCF estimated its cost of conversion to the euro at about 320 million francs, after having bragged that it would be the first "to accommodate itself to the euro." This figure reflected total cost, not net cost, but most companies refused to try to estimate net cost of the transition in order to attempt to obtain subsidies from the state (*Le Monde,* February 17, 2002).

The euro became a part of daily conversation even before it was legal currency. On the popular nightly television program of political satire, *Les guignols de l'info*, President Jacques Chirac, whose rather brazen and unapologetic use of public funds to pay for his vacations and extravagant meals in his official residences has offended some, confidently demonstrated conversion from francs to euros, assuring citizens that vacations for his family and friends totaled no francs in expenses for him. Then he offered to show how to convert francs into euros, and, making a quick calculation, demonstrated that the conversion process is easy, that his vacation for family and friends had cost no euros.

And, as most everywhere, with so much work around *en noir* (off the books), lots of cash hidden or stored here and there came forward, a boom that please merchants. Laurent Fabius estimated that about 100 of 150 billion francs "hidden away in woolen socks have returned to the banks." A veritable flood of expensive purchases in Germany and Spain, in particular, suggested the obvious: a last-ditch effort to spend money earned in the underground economy, the so-called mattress money. German police arrested some German citizens carrying large sums of money across the border in Luxembourg and Switzerland, but such seizures were only a drop in the bucket, although this phenomenon seemed less obvious in France.

Many elderly people, who more than any other group expressed their determination to pay as much and as often by credit card when the transition went into effect, feared that they would be duped by merchants or landlords. With this is mind, the Ministry of Economy, Finance, and Industry, along with the National Institute for Retirement (Inrac), as part of its massive operation, "The Euro Together," organized half days of information sessions in retirement homes, where senior citizens organizations, and those responsible for state-owned, low rent housing (HLMs) with "euro training," carefully explained the value of the new currency, its banknotes, and coins. The European Commission directed a specific campaign, "*L'Euro pour tous*" (The Euro for Everyone), toward the population "at risk of exclusion" (along with campaigns directed toward businesses and consumers). The "population at risk" included people who were illiterate, very elderly, handicapped, or extremely poor. The program encouraged direct contact with as many as possible to help them learn "monetary language," the "indispensable instrument of social integration" (*Europe locale*, October 1999, special issue). Thus the French government provided people to accompany elderly people or those with handicaps (including the blind and deaf) to their banks and help them confront the new currency.

Care was taken to help another group that might have had reason for worry about the transition to the euro. A Senegalise singer called Nuru Kane, a veritable poet and musician, the winner of a competition held in 2000 by the Foundation of France and the Foundation of Saving Banks, was sent to various *foyers* housing African immigrant workers to acquaint them with the euro by singing the a song, "The euro, our money for everyone," from his CD *Dimano euro, aujourd'hui l'euro*, using a rhythm to explain the new currency, "as a field that we all cultivate together." Some immigrant workers had reason to be confused by the franc, and most still do not have access to banks.

Fears

The periods of preparation and of transition also inevitably became associated with public fears that had characterized the previous years: the perceived increase in criminality; anxiety about inflation and anticipated "pricing abuses" during the transition period, although prices were to be frozen until March 31, 2002; and national identity. Preparation for the March 2002 elections helped make "the lack of security" something of a public obsession. The conservative newspaper *Le Figaro* almost regularly shouted out headlines like "Delinquency is establishing itself everywhere" and "Violence explodes in the Paris *métro*" (*Le Figaro*, January 28 and February 13, 2002). Indeed, crimes and misdemeanors increased by 7.7 percent during 2001. In a poll taken between November 28 and December 6, 72 percent expressed their belief that the distribution of the euros to fifty thousand centers of distribution would accentuate the problem of public safety from crime. In the past several years, the number of attacks, occasionally murderous, on armored trucks transporting money had increased rather dramatically, along with the size and complexity of weapons carried by thieves and their willingness to kill without second thought. Thus the question of how virtually every corner of France was going to be provisioned with euros occupied considerable thought, with plans referred to as "*euro-vigilance*" (as in piracy vigilance, the anti-terrorism security measure). Some of the nervousness was generated by organizations of money transporters, whose leaders had had more than a few colleagues killed over the past few years. In late November 2001, the minister of the interior called for a "heightened level of vigilance," with eight thousand large deliveries of money in euros, starting with the 131 branches of the Banque de France, and then other banks, as well as the post offices and commercial retailers. The coins alone distributed in France weighed four times the weight of the Eiffel Tower. The plan of security had been prepared for two years, with national police trained specially and with military escorts in some cases, involving twenty-five hundred soldiers, in group of thirty each. Such a show of force seemed at least "dissuasive." Euros were stocked in eighty different places before distribution. Yet attacks were predicted, even by Marcel Vinzerich, who was responsible for the security of the euro (Channel 5, November 26, 2001) Pictures on television of heavily armed guards taking euro shipments around were themselves unsettling. Fontenay-sous-Bois in the Val-de-Marne took the honor for having the first holdup of a truck transporting euros. The director of BRED, a member of the group Banque Populaire, advised his employees to be particularly careful of potential holdups—"Even if you find yourself confronted with a person who appears rather suspicious to you, above all remain natural, do not play the hero"— advising them not to buzz anyone into the minizone of security at the bank's entrance if the person was wearing a motorcycle helmet (*Le Monde*, February 15, 2002).

Several cases of counterfeit euros appeared before the euro officially appeared. Particular attention was given by the Central European Bank to provide careful instructions about how to recognize counterfeit euros: touching the paper (made with cotton fibers) and certain places with relief printing on the back (designed in part with blind people in mind, who can recognize banknotes and coins by touch), looking at security thread within the transparency, and other keys, and so on. Moreover, the fear of counterfeiting led to the images of the real euros and their security features being released to the public only in September 2001 (*L'Express*, December 27, 2002).

The Big Day and Afterward

Curiosity, more than fear, and arguably sociability and a sense of working together as well, were the theme of the big day and those that followed.[6] About twenty-seven thousand *Tabacs* opened up on January 1, far more than usual (estimates ranged up to 80 percent). This led to a good line: "*Chez les buralistes, l'euro fait un tabac!*" (*Le Figaro*, January 1, 2002). Rural people making purchases on the first day were more apt to pay in euros than were their urban counterparts (70% to 40%). In some places, merchants even ran out of euros (*Libération*, January 2, 2002).[7] For his part, candidate Jospin two days earlier, before his ministers, had stated that the success of the euro "was not an accident, but rather the result of long and detailed preparation" of the government, largely stimulated by the European Commission. Early on the morning of January 1, he was out shopping in euros (for croissants, roses, chestnuts, and wine), first using his "euro kit" and then, when that was gone, waiting in line like everyone else for an ATM machine, seemingly happy to participate in "a true historical event." Candidate Jospin, who had earlier tried to stay as far away from the euro as possible, had to be convinced somewhat against his will to "go out with euros in hand" on January 1, and did so because of the political capital his old enemy Laurent Fabius was accumulating by associating himself with the euro as closely as he could. A few days later, Jospin congratulated citizens for having "come to grips with this with a smile, calmly, almost childlike in the face of such a potentially distressing event" (*Le Monde*, February 17, 2002; *Libération*, January 2 and 12, 2002).

On January 2, "euro guides" dressed in yellow, stood ready to aid confused Lyonnais travelers to make the conversions as best they could. Ticket prices were rounded where possible, 1.30 euro for a single ticket, and 9.30 for a carnet, but in the stations of the Lyon metro, many machines still only functioned with francs, despite reassuring posters most everywhere, "TCL *et l'euro, ça roule.*" A sweeper in a metro station patiently explained to a well-dressed, and grateful, man how to work the machine. Above ground, there were no signs of panic at condom machines. The SNCF recommended that clients pay by check or by credit card, use the ticketing machines whenever possible, or reserve by phone, minitel, or internet, and pay with exact change. Euro specialists in red vests were available in large stations, a veritable small army mobilized for the transition. Change would be returned in euros, and when the new currency was depleted, by bank transfer, necessitating the client have an RIB (Relève d'identité bancaire) slip, and, if not, a "ticket of overpayment," sort of an IOU. On trains, checks were accepted for as little as five euros for tickets (six for food). Merchants were obliged to accept both currencies for payment through February 17 (though, in principle, they were to give change in euros). Yet many complaints surfaced that a good many simply refused because of the long waits and chaos, and that clients were obliged to accept in change whatever came forward. *Le Monde* had offered to sell purchase coupons in Paris from mid-December to the end of February, for seventy-nine francs or twelve euros, for ten copies of their newspaper, to avoid lines during the transition: "Here, move to the euro without stress." Small converters (cheap at twenty francs, or three euros) were available but appear to have been rarely used—their service was psychological, providing a sense that they could be use if necessary. BNP-Paribas and *Le Point* magazine offered "memory aids." Amazingly enough, a free telephone number provided the caller with instantaneous, automatic conversion: one said, "100 francs" in the phone and the machine replied, "15.24 euros." One hundred thousand converters with the numbers presented in large-size format, along with vocal commands, were made available for people with difficulties seeing. In any case, double pricing was by far the most useful measure taken, again encouraged by the *Euro-facile* program.

Perforators systematically began defacing banknotes on January 2. By the following day, half of all transactions were in euros. So many francs came pouring in that to some branches, and stores as well, it seemed like the *Sorcerer's Apprentice*. As Laurent Yserd of BNP-Paribas put it, "The flood of francs is causing chaos in the cash registers of merchants." The owner of a *tabac* put it this way, "Following the first symbolic payments in euros people began to scrape the bottom of their chests of drawers and lifted up their mattresses. The result is an avalanche of francs" (*Libération*, January 5, 2002). Yet that day an estimated 60 to 80 billion francs remained hidden in socks (*Libération*, January 3, 2002). The European Commission and the government estimated that by mid-January in France about 90 percent of payments made in cash were made in euros (with payments by check and by credit card obliged to be in euros beginning January 1) (*Le Monde*, January 16, 2002). By January 14, 18 billion euros were in circulation, while the number of banknotes in francs circulating had fallen from 31.5 billion on December 31, 2001 to 22.5 billion, with between 0.8 and 1.1 billion euros worth of francs being turned in each day. Four of every five clients were paying in euros. According to the Banque de France, a third of banknotes in francs remained in circulation as of February 11, 2002 (the equivalent of 10.9 million euros), before eventually meeting their fate, being burned in a paper mill in Vic-le-Comte in the Puy-de-Dôme (*Le Monde,* February 17, 2002). By January 19, 19.8 billion euros were in circulation, and 11.3 billion francs had been turned in since January 1. Some charities directed appeals to citizens to contribute their last francs to their cause. (In our village of Balazuc, the mailman started a collection of twenty centime coins for charity.)

Jacques Chirac publicly thanked Laurent Fabius, minister of finance—but not Jospin, his rival in the upcoming elections—on February 15, while hurrying to take credit for his role: "At the origin of the euro was the political will to unify Europe, to give it a tangible reality and confer on the Union the force of a unified currency. This objective I have overseen since 1995." With the elections rapidly approaching (which in itself probably undercut public debate on the euro, and perhaps also reassured citizens by presenting a crucial event that was truly French, reaffirming national identity), Lionel Jospin belatedly rushed to take some credit. BNP-Paribas congratulated itself on the face that according to its (hardly neutral) survey, 94 percent of its clients indicated that the bank had responded well to questions and 87 percent approved of the overall response to the transition (*Libération,* February 3, 2002).

Snafus

But there were inevitably snafus in the transition. Large banknotes were taken to stores for small purchases. Such a strategy was based, to be sure, on convenience, but also on the chronic fear of consumers that their deposits at banks might seem suspicious and somehow be communicated to the tax offices. Although stores can refuse to accept large banknotes—it is up to the client to have change, or at least small banknotes—some agencies that did run out of small bills at the end of the first week of January simply suspended their operations for the day (*Libération,* January 5 and 23, 2002).

Early in December 2001, 74 percent of those surveyed feared

that errors, and particularly bank errors, would adversely affect them in the transition. Elderly people, again, were particularly concerned (*Le Monde*, December 16–17, 2001). Indeed, there were some cases of charges in francs being converted (inadvertently, one would assume) into euros, transforming small purchases into sizable ones, but hardly the hundreds of thousands of errors some had anticipated. Owners of credit cards who had charged 100 francs found themselves being charged 100 euros and had to check and complain, for example at a BP gas station, where 200 francs in petrol turned into a 200-euro credit card charge—most people buy gas with credit cards. Who knows how many such errors remained unseen or not rectified?

Strikes posed another challenge, though considerably less than had been anticipated (*"une grève en peut bien cacher une autre"*). But the strikes themselves can hardly be linked directly to the euro as such. In some places postal employees, nurses, and doctors prepared to go out, joining bank clerks, putting pressure on the government, which had given gendarmes a raise and allowed doctors to augment their modest consultation fee. Here, employers took advantage of what some viewed as an uncertain situation and the upcoming elections to put pressure on the government. Strikes affected some savings banks and post offices, but less than 20 percent of employees stayed out. In the Rhône-Alpes, 29 percent of employees stayed out, less than expected, and unions called for the strike's suspension.

For several days, lines stretched even longer than usual—about twice as long as normal—at autoroute tollbooths, although here too, payment with credit cards (which had been rapidly increasing) helped make things somewhat easier.[8] Yet, here too, the anticipated fear of total chaos proved unwarranted, and French drivers are used to lines at the tollbooths near Paris, Vienne, Montpellier, and Bordeaux, among other places.

All banks had longer lines than usual; indeed, one bank official estimated that the number of clients had multiplied by eight during the first days of the transition, before returning to normal. Some branches of Crédit Lyonnais would only change money for their customers, which was against the general agreement that had been made before the transition with the European Commission. Others said that they had no more euros. Some bank employees asked for identification from those standing in front of them with fistfuls of francs, fearful that they could be implicated for laundering money. Euro advisors stood ready to consult with clients. In some banks, one had to make an appointment to bring in sizable amounts of francs, particularly coins (commonly, 200 francs arrived in pieces of 5 centimes), drawing the criticism of Laurent Fabius. The announcement by branches that they would only serve their own clients drew the wrath of those who had waited patiently in line to change money. Thus post offices, which were closed on December 31 to facilitate the switch,[9] were mobbed with between 15 and 20 percent more clients than normal (four million more), because they had to accept everyone, and lines were truly long. Banks and the post offices ran out of certain coins. Some stores soon had no 50-centime and 2-euro coins, in particular (*Le Progrès de Lyon*, January 4, 2002). Some banks angered clients, including their own regular clients, by refusing to take change that was not rolled into a package, and some branches refused all change (*Le Progrès de Lyon*, January 4, 2002). Monoprix allowed clients to pay by credit card for a bill of only one euro.

Despite the claim that 90 percent of the distributors in France worked on January 1 (and 100 percent at the end of the week), trying to get cash from any bank machine on January 2 in Lyon made one think that one was in Buenos Aires (during the banking crisis of late 2001), unable to get any money out. Moreover, many machines were emptied within twenty-four hours, and then had to be refilled. Yet the glitches were limited to the first day or two, and by January 4, if the Département of the Rhône is typical, 95 percent of cash machines worked in euros (*Le Progrès*, January 4, 2002). By five in the afternoon on January 1, 2.2 million withdrawals from ATMs had taken place in France, 180 million euros pouring out, an average of 82 euros, more than the average withdrawal during the holidays.

The period between January 1 and February 17, the date on which francs would no longer have any legal value, necessitated considerable adaptability. Shop owners had no legal obligation to give only euros in change but had been advised to do so, in order that the supply of francs in circulation could be quickly reduced. Many cafés of any size had to have two cash registers, one for francs and the other for euros. Some of those cafés that were also PMUs (betting establishments/lotto ticket vendors) were required to have four, which necessitated hiring extra personnel. A good many of them simply gave back francs in change for all purchases. The owners of the Maison newspaper stand in Aubenas barked out, "I am not a bank," continuing to return francs in changed for francs rendered (a possibility that declined with the rapidly decreasing circulation of francs). Laurent Fabius, while not endorsing the strategy of returning francs for francs, nonetheless used almost the same expression on January 3: "Merchants are not bankers; banks should do their own work" (*Libération*, January 5, 2002). As usual, fears were voiced that small shops and cafés would somehow be forced to shut down.

Cafés had, in particular, reason for worry. The transition came at a time of economic worries, the warning that "Life with euros will not necessarily be a life of roses" (*Libération*, November 5, 2001).[10] As a time when the number of cafés had been declining rapidly in France, the euro inevitably fed into vague fears about closing down of small businesses. Two cafés that announced that they were for the euro (a small sample here, to be sure, taken in Rouen and St. Lys in the Haute-Garonne), nonetheless, complained about the inconveniences of the transition but expressed the view that the euro will ultimately facilitate tourism. The Chamber of Deputies in October 2001 voted to help small businesses by ending commissions on small payments made by credit card (less than 30 euros) in order to encourage payments by credit card and to contribute to a reduction in the use of checks.

Certainly the popularity of the euro increased with the return of summer vacationers who had left France and no longer had to worry about conversions into Belgian francs or, even worse, Italian lira. It was the same for truck drivers, who no longer had to pay fees for changing francs into pesetas, Belgian francs, or Deutsche marks. "It means time saved and less stress," said one. Yet French visitors abroad complained of bank charges for transactions in euros made in other countries. Another problem was that differences in price for the same item could be found across the border in Belgium, Spain, of that haven of cheaper pastis, Andorra. Moreover, to pay with credit card, or to take money from a money machine, costs something for French residents when they are outside of France (where it is free); in addition, foreign merchants, like French ones, are not obliged to accept checks in euros drawn on foreign banks.

Many people suddenly seemed like tourists in their own land (particularly those who did not have experience traveling outside of France and converting to other currencies). Everything seemed new, and perhaps even cheap. "Beware of euphoria," warned the president of Conso-France. "Imagine a skirt or a pair of pants that cost 500 francs before the sales, and which tomorrow will cost 50 euros. Some clients will get carried away. They will think that they cost 90 percent less!" In fact the reduction was really only about a third. A customer at Tati, an inexpensive department store, exclaimed, "It's great with the euro. One has the impression that everything is free, or almost" (*Libération*, January 8 and 12, 2002). An owner of a garage expressed his view that the hardest thing was the difficulty of establishing and understanding "the notion of value." A café owner said, "What strikes me is the absence of a sense of how much things cost in my clients. I have the impression of having cheated tourists who look at you in a quizzical way and ask if they paid enough" (*Libération*, January 12, 2002). Those plunking down a 200-franc banknote for a restaurant bill accepted change in euros, with little to no idea what it was worth, and probably somewhat embarrassed to count it up. A family dependent on the minimum wage would now receive 1,000 euros, not 6,700 francs a month; a person living alone would receive 405 euros. Once rent and heating costs are paid, not much remains. Associations work with some families with financial difficulties, as they need to know down to the centime the cost of everything. For them, the cost of managing only an approximate conversion, through miscalculation, could add to their woes. Moreover, poor people were likely to be afraid to reveal themselves as such, by looking as if they wanted to count the change. Thus, the transition to the euro, particularly the first period, arguably increased the risk for the "disadvantaged" of a strong feeling of further exclusion. In the words of Jacques Saliba, anticipating the change, "The fear of individuation or isolation is not a fantasy in the traditional community. It is etched in the real danger represented, for the survival of the individual, by the detachment or exclusion from a group" (Saliba 1999, 33). A woman at a market commented, "I am already sick of giving the impression of being an idiot at the market along with the other idiots, rocking back and forth, nervously fiddling with euros" (*Libération*, January 12, 2002).

As the new prices often included euros and cents, small amounts in cents and in change received annoyed some. "One has the impression of returning to the 1960s," related one restaurant owner on the rue de Belleville (*Le Monde*, January 12, 2002). I can remember a friend's indignation when the humble baguette went up from fifty-nine to sixty centimes, a jump of one centime (now, the staff of life went, in principle, from 4–4.6 francs to 0.61–0.70 euros). The use of centime coins had really ended in the late 1970s with inflation. As one bank managed put it, "Even as we have to convert directly into euros, we have never had to deal with so many centimes" (*Libération*, January 5, 2002).

Waiters here and there struggled to collect money and give back change to dining companions, each of whom insisted (*á l'américain*) on paying separately, one in francs, the other in euros. Many café owners chose to give back change in euros for euros rendered, and still give back francs for francs. In all, good humor seemed everywhere evident: "You are not going to quibble over two centimes," concluded a café owner in the Vaucluse. Here and there, change was given in candy. In early

January 2002, automatic booths for identity photos had not yet been converted, nor had many candy and drink machines and photocopy machines in schools and the universities (*Libération*, January 3, 2002). Coffee machines and parking meters (though in some cities problems developed) were converted entirely to euros by January 1. (Virtually all phone booths had already been converted to accept only phone cards purchased in advance.) Yet some machines gave change in francs, after accepting euros, but this was not too widespread. There were mistakes in programming machines; for example, some were programmed to accept fifty cents but not five euros. There were problems in parking lots, as many machines had not been converted to euros, and some clients had abandoned or forgotten their francs, and thus had to rely on credit cards (more than half pay by card, anyway, in public parking lots). A 10-baht (Thai) coin, which closely resembles in size and texture (but not value) a 2-euro piece, began turning up in coffee machines, witnessing the impact of wide-ranging French tourism. Between 13,000 and 14,000 machines had to be reprogrammed so they would no longer accept a 2-euro coin, until the problem could be resolved (*Libération*, December 27, 2001, and January 19–20, 2002). One- and two-euro coins were easily confused, and their resemblance with the old 10-franc coin caused confusion.

Determining the value of the new currency—and thus to speak the language of the new currency—is easiest for the largest expenses of any household: wages, rent, insurance, taxes (including the hated television tax), EDF (Electricité de France) bills, and so on, normally paid by check or by automatic deductions from bank accounts. Next, consumers are most likely to adjust to the prices of ten or twelve items of everyday use ("*le mémoire de prix*"), the baguette (for well into the nineteenth century, bread itself took up about half of the budget of poor consumers), metro tickets, and so on. The greatest difficulty for consumer is apt to be other purchases for which they pay across the counter or table. For example, determining tips became an immediate problem. A taxi driver protested that a client with a bill of 12.40 simply rounded up to 13 for the tip, much less than a normal tip, and that many clients did that. Yet the café owner of Place de la République, who priced coffee at 1.05 (confusing in itself), said people tipped more generously. Indeed waiters seem to have been among the big winners in the early month, as clients with the tradition strongly implanted of leaving additional small coins in francs now left twenty and fifty centimes pieces in euros, the fact not having really registered that fifty centimes in euros equaled more than three francs.

In all, many merchants had the sense that many clients "wanted to pass quickly to the euro and did not want to hear anything more about francs" (*Libération*, January 5, 2002). The "war of the franc," anticipated (and perhaps encouraged) by some, never occurred. After all, it had not been all that long ago that the Gaullist politician Phillipe Séguin called the euro a "historical stupidity" (1992). Jean-François Chevènement's turn against Socialist Party policies included the euro: "I think that we are on the Titanic. The orchestra is playing in this dream" (*Le Figaro*, February 16–17, 2002). The Committee in Defense of the Franc in January announced several events, but they never took place. Those who remained defiant "until the bitter end" out of unshakable opposition to the change, and who vowed to pay in francs as long as possible, were rare (*Libération*, January 2–3, 2002; *Le Figaro*, February 16–17, 2002). The possibility existed that people with money would find more security in foreign monies, like the dollar. But that has not happened. The euro had continued to rise vis-à-vis the U.S dollar (the euro value began to be quoted as of January 1, 1999), crossing the 0.90 threshold early in January 2002 and reaching near equality with the dollar and since rocketing by it. The successful transition in itself may have had a positive effect of a couple of days. In general, public confidence—particularly that of investors—in the euro probably has assisted this rise. On the micro level, it appears that the euro is associated with financial stability (particularly remembering the monetary instability of 1992 and 1993, when interest rates had to be raised to defend the franc).

Moreover, as a defining event that has affected virtually everyone, a sense of solidarity was apparent those first days. For one woman, "It is like the snow, it brings people together. Everyone talks about it" (*Libération*, January 12, 2002). That many (though still a small minority) of French vacationers leave the country during vacations has undoubtedly contributed to the transition.

Why was the transition so much easier than that which occurred at the beginning of the Fifth Republic with the passage from old to new francs (NF)? This time, old francs were not allowed to hang around with a different value, unlike the 1958–60 transition, when one old coin of 100 francs had become worth one "new" franc. Banknotes of 1,000 old francs, with "ten new francs" added in red, served in 1958–59 and lasted until 1963, when new bills in francs were issued, without the mention of NF. New coins in new centimes then followed.

Elderly people were the most apt to be confused by the transition to the euro. They remembered the transition from old to new francs. Young people not born during the de Gaulle era still used old francs to assess the value or sales of property, or of big hold-ups (*fric-fracs*), and millions of elderly people continued to use a thousand for ten francs. Certainly the press and particularly television helped carry on the tradition of speaking in old francs. I know people who still use old francs for any sum. At the Tuesday market of St. Lys, a butcher patiently explained to what was certainly one of his oldest clients what her small purchase represented in old francs, new francs, and euros. The advent of the euro only complicated things for many of them, and particularly in weekly markets, where credit cards are not use except for very large purchases (such as mattresses, sold at virtually every market). Yet, the transition has been easier even for them, in part because the franc was not transformed into a franc that had been revalued, leading to confusion. In any case, once the threshold of several euros has been passed, most people continue to convert into and speak of francs when discussing the cost of anything. One key factor in the relative ease of acceptance by elderly people (in comparison with last time around), however, was the fact that the percentage who had traveled abroad has increased exponentially since 1960.

The euro's symbol is not on the keyboard of computers, but the makers of Macs and P C s put out instructions. A European-wide survey at the end of December 2001 demonstrated (not surprisingly) that two-thirds of computer owners did not know how to make the symbol of a euro. An internet service after several pages on the subject offered, "The most simple solution: avoid using the character of the euro." This would become increasingly difficult (*Libération*, December 27, 2001).

Rounding Up?

European consumers had been promised that the transition between September 2001 and June 2002, or even its anticipation, would not accentuate inflation, as had the switch to the new franc in 1960. (Supermarkets could raise certain prices according to supply, but the overall rise for all products had to be held in line.) December brought extreme cold to many regions of France, and resulting rises in the price of some products could be blamed on the euro. [11] Store like Intermarché put forward signs reassuring clients that the sacred trust between client and storeowner would continue. Moreover, the posting of prices in both euros and francs continued. Those consumers, old and young, who believed that they had been cheated were encouraged to contact the "euro office" of their local Department of Consumption and the Repression of Fraud. Here again, this possibility followed European Union policy, specifically a recommendation in 1998 calling for the creation of such offices, as part of an agreement between consumer and retail associations.

There were several highly publicized cases of "rounding down." The SNCF proudly announced that the railroad would not raise prices, but rather, prices in euros would be "systematically rounded off to the advantage of the client." A parking fine of 75 francs became a fine of 11 euros, rounded down from 11.43, and a fine of 1,000 francs became 150 euros, and not 152.45. The minimum amount of capital necessary to start up a business (*capital social*) went from 50,000 francs to 7,500 euros, not 7,622.45 euros. The brochure "Justice and the Euro" stood ready to explain such conversions.

Yet, cafés, food store, and even prostitutes stood accused of having "rounded up" ("*à arrondir à la hausse*") despite the ban on any rise in prices during the period of transition. Even if statistics do not show much inflation, the impression was that merchants rounded up, as with coffee going from 6.5 francs not to 0.99 euros but to 1.20 euros in ordinary cafés, and reaching two euros and more in fancy ones. Warnings were frequently expressed on television about the "price abuses" during this "sensitive period." Hairdressers and the owners of restaurants and brasseries were routinely accused of sharply raising their prices. Polls of consumers found only half, and in most cases considerably less than half, expressed confidence in the supermarkets to carry out the transition fairly and without rounding up. Carrefour took out full-page ads promising consumers that the prices of such essential items as vegetables, eggs, coffee, and chocolate bars had been reduced in price. However, consumer insistence that prices were being rounded up also followed the transition to the decimal system in 1971 in Britain and Ireland, with fears, confusion and disruption in the habits of everyday life reflected in such a way. [12]

For the January sales, the government made an extraordinary effort to monitor prices (four had to be clearly marked, previous and sale prices in francs and in euros). Market police—notably two hundred gendarmes from the division against fraud—made sure that the equivalent value in francs was posted along with prices in euros. Whereas some bank branches were refusing to change 500-franc banknotes in January, department stores and commercial chains were happy to do so, although some complained, and none were obliged to do so. At Galeries Lafayette, foreign tourists waited patiently in line to spend wads of euros on Gucci, Longchamps, and Dior products. One survey of 210 products showed little inflation in December and January (*Libération*, February 16–17, 2002).

Regarding the "oldest profession," a client asked one prostitute on the rue St. Denis in Paris (this comes from a newspaper account, not from personal experience), "How much is that in euros?" "That will be 50 euros," came the response. The prostitutes of her working neighborhood had agreed on prices that reflected the step into a new world. Gone, ultimately, would be confusion and hesitation of German, Belgian, and Italian clients, though British and American men would still have reason to make rapid calculations in their head. "Fifty euros, that makes 328 francs. That's 28 francs more than the usual 300 francs. But in any case we are not going to convert the two numbers that come after the decimal point," complained her workmate on the sidewalk. "This isn't a tobacco shop. And we are not selling peanuts." Nearby, another prostitute reflected on the rounding up of prices: "Our prices haven't gone up in ten years. Thus we aren't going to be bothered by rounding up." Yet, as in countless other cash exchanges, there were limits to how far up one could round. Where a basic trick (*passé*) went for 200 francs, in euros this would come out to 30.49 euros, a clumsy sum. One lady said that she hoped to ask for 35 euros in the future, but that if a client balked, then she would agree to 30. In any case, the prostitutes in that particular neighborhood preferred to avoid change wherever possible, so the rounder, the better. Yet, as in other professions and in other places in France, the prostitutes of St. Denis feared to be cheated by clients giving them counterfeit banknotes that they could barely see in the dark (*Libération*, December 12, 2001).

At what might be considered the other end of some sort of spectrum, parish priests were also all for rounding up. A baptism went from 300 francs to 45.79 euros, more or less, a Mass for a marriage or a funeral, 900 francs to 137.37 euros. At the church of Notre Dame de Cligancourt, the price of a small candle went up from three francs to one euro, more than doubling. But when the collection at Mass came along, would parishioners round up or down? A national survey had demonstrated that 56 percent of the faithful put a 10-franc coin in the collection basket, and 15 percent a 5-franc coin. But if a euro replaced ten francs in the basket, churches could lose 34 percent of their income from that source. "We are putting out the message that one should give two euros, but the campaign is discrete . . . we cannot pressure the faithful." Some priests mentioned the change to the euro from the pulpit, other did not. In a few places, the Church handed out tables of conversion, with posters, "Christians, do the conversion: 10 francs + your generosity = 2 euros." Again, preparation and publicity seemed to be the key (*Libération*, December 28, 2001; *Le Canard enchaîné*, January 9, 2002).

Problems of Language and Identity

The franc's demise necessitated some adjustment in language: some popular expressions were quickly made obsolete, or required deft rethinking or rephrasing. What would happen, for example, to "the one symbolic franc," assessed for damages? There is already a "symbolic euro." The transition itself brought new terms (and even the use of rather obscure words like fungibility—the notion that the euro and the currencies of the twelve participating countries of the European Union were legally equivalent, upon the application of the accepted levels of conversion). Yves Cochet, minister of the environment, referred to *meuros*, for millions of euros, to replace MF, millions of francs (*Libération*, January 12, 2002). The Académie Française "advised against" the use of the term "Euroland" for the "new European monetary space," preferring the term "euro zone," which was already used by the Banque de France (session of January 7, 1999).

The advent of the euro generated discussion—indeed a ruling by the Académie Française in February 1999—on whether "euro" should have an "s" and be plural, though the euro remained singular because not all languages of countries that have adopted it use an "s" for plural, but the euro is plural on checks. This also raised the question of "cent," singular and plural (*un cent, des cents*), with some feeling that retaining "centimes" in place of "cents" (in order, in part, to eliminate the confusion between

"cents" and the French number "cent," although the pronun-
ciation is the same) would somehow make the euro French.
The presence of Marianne, "La Semeuse," and the liberty tree
on one side of coins produced in France is not quite the same
thing. The one- and two-euro coins include the liberty tree and
the inscription, "*Liberté, Éqalité, Fraternité,*" thus differentiat-
ing the coins produced in France from others. The decision to
have one side of the coin presenting a national theme was, to
be sure, a European decision, though France was among the
countries that desired a national side to the currency. (Belgium
and the Netherlands are monarchies—as well as Monaco and
the Vatican, for all intents and purposes—and if each banknote
and coin were designed without one side offering a specific reference to each participating country, they would have had to
change their constitutions.) Thus one side of the coins at least
gave the impression that something called France remains. One
man who had voted against the Treaty of Maastricht exclaimed,
"When, beginning on January 1, I saw in Boulogne euros minted
in France, I celebrated." A woman from Monaco was disappointed—on one day in December she went from place to place in vain
searching for "Monegasque euros," which had sold out. Quick
assessments of the look of the banknotes and coins abounded:
"It looks cheap." Some with vacation experience behind them
noted that the 2-euro coin resembles 1000-lira Italian coins (the
coin was designed by an Italian) and the small coins resemble
Dutch florins. Interestingly enough, the doors and windows on
banknotes (open doors are seen on the 10-, 100-, and 200-euro
banknotes; windows on the 20-, 50-, and 500-euro banknotes)
may be perceived as suggesting openness to immigration (as
well as modernity, peace, and so on), that is, "an open Europe,"
possibly giving the National Front another reason to oppose
the new currency (*Libération*, December 16, 2001, January 3
and February 16–17, 2002).

To be sure, the campaign of the European Union for a
smooth transition from national currencies to the union
was predicated on learning a new language.[13] Jacques Barus-

Michel, a psychologist, warned that the transition would take a long time, despite the seeming ease of the transition itself: "The franc is our mother tongue . . . The euro has easily entered our pocketbooks, but not yet into our heads." He suggested that after the excitement of having new coins and banknotes to examine, compare, and spend, a sort of fatigue had started to set in, "a feeling of vulnerability and even of suffering because of being always obliged to convert in one's head." Jean-Michel Servet, an economist specializing in monetary behavior, also warned that some people could eventually crack under the strain of the change, particularly those who receive payments in cash. (A neurologist from the big hospital at Orsay announced, oddly enough, that converting from francs to euros used a different part of the brain, presumably from that part which converted old francs to Belgian francs or German marks.) In a survey taken just after the franc ceased to be legal currency, 39 percent said that they missed the franc "a great deal" or "a little," the remaining 61 percent not at all. Women (49%), older people (44%), workers (52%), and people on the right (41%) seemed to be more nostalgic. Servet suggested that "we pay in euros, but we still count in francs . . . a society can live for a very long time paying in one currency and thinking in another," noting that in some places people still measure wine in barrels and the value of land in *jours* (*Libération*, January 29, February 16–17, and February 18, 2002; poll by *Dimanche Ouest-France).*

And what about the rich and fluid popular expressions for money? Time will tell whether the expression *cent balles* can be adapted to the euro. The value of a *balle* fluctuated, from one centime to one franc, with the shift to the new franc in 1960, coupled with inflation. As *Libération* put it, "Simple, perhaps we should provide ourselves with argot-converters, along with euro-converters." *Fric* (from, *fire, fricasser* via *fricot), l'oseille, l'avoine,* or *le blé,* and other ways of referring to money will still work, but *sous* and *balles* translate less well into euros. *Des ronds* poses no problem, because euro coins are still round, and probably also *pèze, grisbi* (cash in the world of organized crime), *pognon* (from *pogne, la main*) and the very recent *maille*. But what about *de la thune,* which was originally a five-franc coin? Of course, the euro will undoubtedly generate new terms from other languages adapted into French argot, arguably further threatening identity, at least in a minor way. Certain French slang terms changed with ease with the transition from the old franc to the new franc. A *brique* is now worth 1,524.39 euros. (The term came from the volume of banknotes of 1,000 old francs to make a million.) With 1960, the *brique* was rather easily converted into 10,000 francs. Will one *brique* be rounded up to 10,000 euros (seems unlikely), or will a *balle* be adopted to 0.1524 euro (rather clumsy and therefore impossible)? New slang terms stemming from the value of banknotes will certainly come along (as *un scalpa* for the 500-franc banknote with Pascal on the front, from *verlant,* or backslang), or be reinvented. Suggestions came pouring in even during early days: why not *eu* for a euro, but that would sound like *oeufs,* or *ro* from euro, rather like *ronds,* or *roro,* or *boules* (*Libération,* December 31, 2001).[14]

The transition to the euro also inevitably has raised questions about what difference over the long run this continued Europeanization will make to French identity. On the day of the big change, the conservative *Le Figaro* asked if it were "not a little bit of France which is disappearing?" According to the sociologist Smain Laacher, "Money is a vector of solidarity, of integration, of confidence in oneself, a marker of one's position in society. It is linked to the manner in which one sees the world and its hierarchy, and of representing it . . . It is a 'total social fact' closely related to society in its totality as well as to the identity of persons and groups." This is very different from the transition to the new franc from the old franc, much more than a simple problem of conversion or vocabulary, rather an entire economic and political project. One person surveyed before the changeover put it this way: "The euro doesn't make me smile, because it represents the standardization of everything, and in that one loses particularities." If problems of confidence in the euro emerge, then questions of identity are more apt to surface (*Libération,* December 31, 2001; *Le Figaro,* January 1, 2002; Saliba 1999, 23).

Is the disappearance of the franc another blow against the independence of the French language? De Gaulle once said, "A nation is a state, an army, a currency." Obviously this is an old debate, revived a few years ago by Jacques Toubon (dubbed Jack or John Too-Good by some wags). Spoken French is, to be sure, increasingly peppered by expressions in English (not just the old obvious ones like *le weekend* but *le look, stressé,* and *big love,* among other), so that it is possible to think that one is in Québec, where French is dotted with words absorbed from English, such as *les breaks de ma voiture.* If the franc has disappeared, and with the colossus of the English language becoming the way that business communicates in the global era, is the euro another strike against France remaining French? (The extreme right-wing National Front, interestingly enough, was the only political party to blast away at the euro.) Most of Europe now speaks a single language—that of a single currency.

As the franc passed into memory, at least four small town or villages were contending to be the site of a statue in honor of the franc—all with franc in this name: Frans (Ain), Francs (Gironde), Francierre (Somme), and Franqueville (Seine-Maritime). [15] Can the franc be so easily relegated to history ("Obituary notice . . . Never call me again the franc!" intoned *Le Figaro* on February 16–17) and to shops for coin collectors (banknotes and coins were printed in such great quantity that they seem unlikely to become terribly valuable)? The place of the franc in the history and collective memory of France is obviously considerable. It was created with a royal decree on December 6, 1360. (Ironically, the franc coin was apparently first struck in order to pay for the ransom of Jean II le Bon, who was held prisoner by the English after the defeat at Poitiers; the king was shown with his sword drawn, to show his captors that he would be strong again once freed. The coin was struck *"pour que le roi soit 'franc' des anglais,"* that is, free of the English, *rendre franc.* The franc was replaced by the écu d'or and then the livre royal, although the franc remained a synonym in principle for the livre well after it disappeared in 1641. The franc returned in 1795 as the assignat collapsed.) The franc was increasingly identified with France. Raymond Poincaré, after all, earned his reputation in history as "the savior of the franc" in 1926, and subsequent governments remained attached to the *"franc fort"* until 1983. The franc in Europe now is to be found only in Switzerland.

Will people in France remain convinced that the euro could be secure, that its value and stability are guaranteed, at a time when by some measures French prosperity stood ahead of only Spain, Portugal, and Greece within the European Union? Psychologists argue that the very notion of citizenship is tied to such confidence. Who or what would guarantee anything about the euro? Jean-Michel Servet, who warned that the transition may appear easier than it has been, concludes that "The abandonment of a currency is also a moment at which one thinks about the role of the state, or even more about the place of social protection." Here, the role of the state has been fundamental in reassuring people that they will not be cheated and that consumers will be protected, so that the new currency quickly becomes part of daily life, and trusted. The role for the government and of associations of consumers was to reduce suspicion of the new currency, and in that they succeeded. In doing do, they fully appropriated the carefully laid plans of the European Commission. Moreover, the apparent success of the euro put a face on the construction of a new Europe, which seemed to many to be identified no longer with faceless bureaucrats in Brussels, but with freshly printed banknotes and minted coins that they held in their hands (*Libération*, December 31, 2001; January 12 and February 16–17, 2002).

SEVEN

I Went Up to Amiens Today

A Tribute to Charles Tilly

I went up to Amiens today, out of nostalgia. Chuck and I had gone there long ago for some research in the Archives Départementales de la Somme. I write from Rouen, where I teach in May, and although I am often around here, I had not been up to Amiens for a long time. Thus, after hearing the sad news that Chuck had died, I wanted to go back. Of course, going on the road with Chuck was not the typical road trip of my college days. For one thing, he got up terribly early—it seemed like 3:00 a.m. but was probably closer to 4:30, and began to do sit-ups. Then he read and thought for what seemed like hours. I, too, had thoughts at that time in the morning, since I suddenly found myself awake, but my thoughts, such as they were, concerned what I would eat for lunch that day. Chuck and I were very different.

When Chuck first went off to Angers to begin his research on the counter-revolution in the West of France that has come to be called the Vendée, after one of the key *départements* in the conflict, he knew little French. Back in the late 50s, he was one of the very first generation of U.S. scholars to work in French departmental archives. Entering, he encountered the classically grumpy, blue-clad *gardien*. Slightly intimidated, Chuck froze when the man asked him what he wanted to see. He could not say anything. Finally, when the irritation of the *gardien* had become anger, Chuck was able to blurt out, *"Montrez-moi un document!"* (Show me a document!). The archival employee did just that, and then, when Chuck had conveyed the fact that he was interested in the counter-revolution during the French Revolution, hundreds and hundreds of documents followed.

In 1968, I started graduate school at Michigan in history, for not very compelling reasons. I had no idea what I would do, and was playing baseball in Ann Arbor in the summer and needed an excuse to stay around, so I took a history course. Still clueless about what I wanted to do, I enrolled in a seminar in the fall that seemed to focus principally on what French generals such as Marshall Soult thought about Louis-Philippe's July Monarchy. Someone—I cannot remember who—told me that I should read Charles Tilly, *The Vendée*. I did, one Saturday afternoon. Suddenly, it seemed that one could explain important events by looking at the bigger picture. Rebellions, indeed revolutions, had causes, and were part of change. Moreover, Chuck had just arrived at Michigan. I took his seminar the second semester of my second year. He was so nice and encouraging. I had become interested in the Revolution of 1848, and Chuck had on microfilm much of the relevant archival series, BB18 and BB30. He suggested that interesting things were going on in Limoges, and the region of the Limousin during the Second Republic. I wrote a seminar paper on the dynamics of police repression there. Several months later, following my oral exams (I had met Chuck so recently that he was not even on committee for my orals), I was off in France for research on my dissertation, with Chuck as the director.

In Ann Arbor, chez Tilly on Hill Street was the setting for now legendary Sunday evening seminars. Natalie Davis and Maurice Agulhon were among the speakers, but one could also hear graduate students discussing their dissertations. This was a perfect kind of apprenticeship, and the most important thing about it was that Chuck tolerated no kind of hierarchy, and everyone's ideas (even not so good ones) were equal. Wayne Te Brake, Bob Schwartz, Mike Hanagan, Miriam Cohen, Ron Aminzade, M.J. Maynes, and Bill Roy were among the participants in those days. And of course from the very beginning,

Chuck was always just plain Chuck, not Professor or Doctor or some other pompous title, and most of the rest of us have kept that tradition alive.

Chuck worked almost all the time. He was so busy—and yet so generous, always, with his time. (This made it very difficult to imagine ever turning in a paper late; if he could work like that, we should be able to do so, as well.) But he did not like to waste time. He always received so many letters, phone calls, and visits. (He once explained to me his "neutral corner" strategy for dealing with visitors, which would be to suggest not to meet in his office, but in some other place, so that he could decide when the talk was over after a reasonable amount of time and return to work.) Then with the computer age he always had hundreds of messages. He had almost no patience with small talk, and certainly not by e-mail. To get a response, one had to pose a specific question, "What is good on Albanian collective violence?" or "How are you?", and then he always wrote back, immediately.

He was so loyal to his students, colleagues, and friends. He claimed that the only time he ever wore a tie was when he and Louise flew out to Carol's and my wedding in New Haven in 1980. (That was about my case, too.) Their presence obviously meant a great deal. When we took up permanent residence in France, in Ardèche (a challenge as I teach at Yale and go back and forth), he came to see what our village was like. Though he seemed to enjoy himself, when he left I could tell he was thinking if I would really be able to get enough work done there. For about nine or ten years, Chuck had the lease for a tiny apartment in the second oldest building still standing in Paris on the rue François Miron in the Marais in Paris. I served as something of the agent for the apartment, and was there much more than Chuck. We had very different standards of maintaining the apartment. Once, when Chuck arrived after my departure, he described it as looking like the last days of Pompeii. He could be a bit compulsive: on one occasion, he spent the last twenty minutes of his visit tying pieces of string together so that they could be added to the apartment's ball of string. After France became much less of a focus for his research, he really did not return here very often.

Chuck remained committed to virtually same day service when it came to reading manuscripts—thousands and thousands of them over his career—especially those of his colleagues, former students, and students. Within the past six years, my editors at Oxford and Norton contacted him to see if he would have time to write a blurb. In both cases, they each called me in astonishment to say that he had read the book and provided a wonderful blurb the next day. He was like that.

Last year, Chuck agreed to give the keynote talk at a conference in Washington. He was not feeling well and was very tired, but all the same was there. I had been invited to introduce him, and he told me that he was tired, and would speak only 35 minutes, so I introduced him for 10 or 12. He was fantastic, brilliant, cogent, compelling. It was vintage Chuck. It was the last time I ever had the chance to hear him speak.

Chuck's fifty-one books, by latest count, and hundreds of articles have of course had enormous influence on history, as they did on sociology, political science, and one should probably add anthropology and economics as well. He once described himself as working in the no-man's land between sociology and history, but what he did basically was to create historical sociology. In my case, as a historian, he has influenced all my books on France in important ways (including the one I dedicated to him in 1992). Examples of what I learned from Chuck include: how to think about the revolutionary process; the need to keep the dynamics of economic, social, political, and cultural change up front—to "put this in neon," as he once said—within the context of the narrative history I sometimes do; the need to appreciate the complexity of cities and towns and relations between city and country; and much more. Chuck once wrote, "It is bitter hard to write the history of remainders," and that has always stuck with me. For *The Red City*, I first got the idea of pulling the comparison between the *corporation* of butchers based in the center of Limoges and the porcelain workers in the faubourgs from something once said. When I wrote *A History of Modern Europe from the Renaissance to the Present* and the subsequent editions, I have always kept in mind something that he told me long ago—that history should not be seen as a series of bins that one opens up and then closes, then moving on to another, but that such big themes as statemaking and capitalism provide a way of understanding and presenting the past.

Whenever as a student (and beyond) I came to a snafu in thinking about what I was working on or writing about, I would go to Chuck to seek his advice. He invariably said, "Look, there are three aspects to this," while holding his hands somewhat off to the side, oddly enough, in what seemed to be the shape of a box, one that suggested four aspects—but with Chuck, three or four was a simplification for the rest of us, because he could imagine about a hundred at any one time. (There is a photo of him on the inside jacket of one of his books, if I remember correctly, of him in that pose.)

Well, there are (at least) three ways of thinking about Chuck Tilly. He was the most brilliant person any of us will almost certainly ever know. His great influence on the social sciences will continue, through his own work and hopefully through his colleagues and former students. And he was a wonderful human being, someone of great good will and good humor, who cared about people and the human condition. He was the perfect mentor and colleague, a wonderful friend. How we will miss him.

SOURCE ACKNOWLEDGMENTS

"The *Demoiselles* of the Ariège, 1829–1831" originally appeared in *The Revolution of 1830 and the Origins of the Social Questions in France*, edited by John Merriman (New York: New Viewpoints, 1975), 87–118.

"The Norman Fires of 1830: Incendiaries and Fear in Rural France" originally appeared in *French Historical Studies* 9 (1975): 451–66. Copyright 1975 by the Society of French Historical Studies. All rights reserved. Republished by permission of the copyright holder and the present publisher, Duke University Press, www.dukeupress.edu.

"Incident at the Statue of the Virgin Mary: The Conflict of Old and New in Nineteenth-Century Limoges" originally appeared in *Consciousness and Class Experience in Nineteenth Century Europe*, edited by John Merriman (Homes and Meier, 1979), 129–48.

"Urban Space and the Power of Language: The Stigmatization of the *faubourg* in Nineteenth-Century France," originally appeared in *Social Science Information* 38, vol. 2 (1999), 329–51.

"On the Loose: The Impact of Rumors and *Mouchards* in the Ardèche during the Second Republic" originally appeared in *Europe in 1848: Revolution and Reform*, edited by Dieter Dowe, Heinz-Gerhard Haupt, Dieter Langewiesche, and Jonathan Sperber (New York: Berghahn Books, 2001), 869–88.

"Some Observations on the Transition to the Euro in France" originally appeared in *The Year of the Euro: The Cultural, Social, and Political Import of Europe's Common Currency*, edited by Robert M. Fishman and Anthony M. Messina (Notre Dame IN: University of Notre Dame Press, 2006), 37–61.

NOTES

Doing History on the Margins

1. Stephen A. Kippur, *Jules Michelet: A Study of Mind and Sensibility* (Albany NY: SUNY Press, 1981), 49–50.

2. Arlette Farge, *The Allure of the Archives*. Introduction by Natalie Zemon Davis (New Haven CT: Yale University Press, 2013) (first published in French in 1989), 6–7, 14, 46, 122. She adds, "It sneaks up imperceptibly, almost without warning. You can come to have such a fondness for the documents and for the archives themselves that you forget to be wary of the traps they can lay or the risk of not keeping enough distance from them" (69). One of my most memorable academic occasions was when I was invited to participate in a session on the documents of history in La Rochelle, along with Carlo Ginzburg and Alain Corbin, and a few others. Listening to the exchanges in our gathering, particularly those of Ginzburg and Corbin, was absolutely remarkable.

3. Christopher H. Johnson, *Utopian Socialism in France: Cabet and the Icarians, 1839–1851* (Ithaca NY: Cornell University Press, 1974).

4. Debra Silverman, *Art Nouveau in Fin-de-siècle France: Politics, Psychology, and Style* (Berkeley: University of California Press, 1989); Robert L. Herbert, *Impressionism: Art, Leisure, and Parisian Society* (New Haven CT: Yale University Press, 1988).

5. Barrie M. Ratcliffe has torn apart Chevalier's contentions: "Classes laborieuses, et classes dangereuses à Paris pendant la première moitié du dix-neuvième siècle? The Chevalier Thesis Reexamined," *French Historical Studies* 17, no. 6 (Autumn 1991): 542–74.

6. Archives Départementales de la Meuse, 71M 10, gendarmerie report June 23, 1825.

7. Along with the bombing of the Liceo theater in Barcelona that same year.

1. The *Demoiselles* of the Ariège

The research for this study was made possible by a faculty summer grant from the History Department of Yale University.

1. Paul Gonnet, "Esquisse de la crise économique en France de 1827 à 1832," *Revue d'histoire économique et sociale* 33, no. 3 (1955): 249–92.

2. On the significance of popular protest, see Charles Tilly, "The Changing Place of Collective Violence," in Melvin Richter, ed., *Essays in Theory and History* (Cambridge: Harvard University Press, 1970), 139–64; Charles Tilly, "How Protest Modernized in France, 1845–55," in W. O. Aydelotte, A. G. Bogue, and R. W. Fogel, eds., *The Dimensions of Quantitative Research in History* (Princeton: Princeton University Press, 1972), 210–24; and Louise Tilly, "La révolte frumentaire, forme du conflit politique en France," *Annales* 27 (May-June, 1972): 731–57.

3. Particularly relevant approaches include, Charles Tilly, "Food Supply and Public Order in Modern Europe," a working paper of the Center for Research on Social Organization, the University of Michigan, in Charles Tilly, ed., *The Formation of National States in Western Europe*; Albert Soboul, "The French Rural Community in the Eighteenth and Nineteenth Centuries," *Past and Present* 10 (November 1956): 78–95; and E. P. Thompson, "The Moral Economy of the Crowd in the Eighteenth Century," *Past and Present* 50 (February 1971): 76–136.

4. Gonnet, *op. cit.*; Roger Price, "Popular Disturbances in the French Provinces After the July Revolution of 1830," *European Studies Review* 1, no. 4 (1971): 323–55; James Rule and Charles Tilly, "Political Process in Revolutionary France, 1830–32," in Merriman, John M., ed., *1830 in France* (New York: New Viewpoints, 1975), 42–85.

5. François Baby, *La Guerre des Demoiselles en Ariège (1829–1872)* (Montbel, Ariège, 1972). Maurice Agulhon's discussion of the forest problem in the Var and its impact on the creation of rural radicalism during the Second Republic is invaluable, in *La République au Village* (Paris: Plon, 1972), 42–92. Baby figures the separate "appearances" of the *demoiselles* at 114 between 1829 and 1872, including 36 in 1829 and a peak 53 in 1820 (93). See also Louis Clarenc, "Le code de 1827 et les troubles forestiers dans les Pyrénées centrales au milieu de XIXe siècle," *Annales du Midi* 77, no. 73 (July 1965): 293–317. See, more recently, Peter Sahlins, *Forest Rites: The War of the Demoiselles in Nineteenth-Century France* (Cambridge: Harvard University Press, 1994).

6. Baby, *op. cit.*, and Clarenc, *op. cit.*, give a good picture of the importance of the forests and the general economic and social situation. See also Archives Départementales de l'Ariège (henceforth ADA), Pe 45, "Aperçu sur le service forestier de l'*arrondissement* de St. Girons" (September 29, 1830), and the reports of General Laffite to the Minister of War (henceforth MG), in the D^3 series of the Archives of the Ministry of War at Vincennes (henceforth AG). The prefect estimated that two-thirds of the population of the mountainous regions depended upon raising cattle or sheep for survival (Pe 45, Prefect of Ariège [henceforth PA] to Minister of the Interior [henceforth Int.], March 2, 1830). The state owned the vast majority of the forests in some cantons (Clarenc, 294).

7. Note Agulhon's chart of forest litigation in the Var, *op. cit.*, 50–73. The petitions of the communes of Unac, July 5, 1829, and "Observations presented by the mayor of Massat," n.d. (ADA, Pe 45) are particularly revealing. Baby, *op. cit.*, 31, noted the changing class composition of the forge-owners.

8. André Armengaud, *Les populations de l'Est-Acquitain au début de l'époque contemporaine* (Paris, 1961), 165. Baby, *op. cit.*, 30, says that three of the most insurrectionary cantons were becoming rapidly overpopulated between 1804 and 1841 (Massat, 21 percent growth in population; Cabannes, 34.5 percent; and Castillon, 41.4 percent).

9. "Observations presented by the mayor of Massat," n.d., ADA, Pe 45. The rising price of wood is noted by Agulhon, *op. cit.*, 46; Clarenc, *op. cit.*, 299; and Guy Thuillier, *Aspects de l'économie nivernaise au XIXe au XIXe siècle* (Paris: Colin, 1967), 106.

10. M. Baudrillart, *Recueil chronologique des règlements sur les forêts, chasses et pêches, III* (Paris, 1824); M. E. Meaume, *Des droits d'usage dans les forêts de l'administration des bois communaux et de l'affouage, I* (Paris, 1851); Suzanne Coquerelle, "Les droits collectifs et les troubles agraires dans les Pyrénées en 1848," *Actes du 78e Congrès National des Sociétés Savantes*, 1953, 345–363; Agulhon and Clarenc, *op. cit.* By notables, I am referring to important property-holders, both noble and bourgeois.

11. The number of prosecutions increased in the *arrondissement* of St. Girons from 192 in 1825 to 341 in 1828 (830 in 1833), Baby, *op. cit.,* 39. ADA, Pe 45, "Tableau par ordre chronologique des divers attentats commis . . . par les malfaiteurs connus sous le nom de Demoiselles," relates the story of the peasants searching for their deeds. "Rapaciousness" of notables indicated by the *sous-intendant militaire* in Foix to MG, AG D³ 127, August 17, 1829.

12. AG, E⁵ 2, General Laffite to MG, September 16, 1830. The general was given credit for putting down an uprising in the department in 1815, ADA, Pe 45, "Aperçu sur le service forestier de l'arrondissement de St. Girons"; AG, E⁶ 1, Laffite to FG, August 10.

13. ADA, Pe 45, PA to Int., February 3, 1829. Early resistance also was noted in the *arrondissement* of St. Gaudens in Haute Garonne, Commissioner of Forests in Toulouse to PA, July 6, 1829.

14. ADA, Pe 45, PA to Int., May 30, 1829.

15. ADA, Pe 45, PA to Int., August 6, 1829; Int. to PA, August 31; and PA to Int., September 7. Marrot apparently was able to buy the forest at a very low price because of the tradition of the rights of the commune of Moulis in the forest.

16. ADA, Pe 45, Sub-prefect of St. Girons (henceforth, SPSG) to PA, June 30 and July 20, 1829.

17. ADA, Pe 45, SPSG to PA, June 7, 1830.

18. AG, D³ 127, Commander of 10th Military Division (Toulouse, hereafter, 10th) to MG, August 20, 1829; ADA, Pe 45, PA to Int., August 20, 1829, and SPSG to PA, August 18, 1829. All of the administrative correspondence relative to the *demoiselles* is gathered in Pe 45, in four dossiers or *liasses*. Hereafter, ADA will refer to Pe 45, unless noted. In addition, the departmental archives include the *procès-verbaus* for ten trials of *demoiselles*, 1829 to 1831, in 2 U 193.

19. AG, D³ 129 10th to MG, February 14, 1830. Also letters of February 1 and 9.

20. AG, 10th to MG, February 21, 1830; ADA, SPSG to PA, February 18.

21. AG, 10th to MG, March 19, 1830, and ADA PA to Int., April 5, 1830.

22. ADA, Trinqué to PA, July 17, 1829. His first recorded complaint was a letter written to the prefect, June 17, 1829.

23. ADA, Int. to PA, June 9, 1830.

24. ADA, Int. to PA, June 9, 1830; PA to Int., May 24, 1830.

25. ADA, PA to Int., May 30, 1829.

26. The very first mention seems to be AG, Commander of Gendarmerie to MG, July 16, 1829, D³ 126, which dates their appearance earlier than François Baby indicates. Baby did not consult the useful AG. There is good evidence that the *demoi-*

selles were active initially in the *arrondissement* of St. Gaudens in Haute Garonne, Commander of Gendarmerie to 10th, July 3, 1829, AG.

27. ADA, Forest Inspector to Commissioner of Forests, July 6, 1829; ADA, PA to Int., June 12, 1829. One of the most accurate and complete descriptions is from the *arrondissement* of St. Gaudens in Haute Garonne, AG Commander of Gendarmerie of the *arrondissement* to MG, July 16, 1829. This disguise included a hood of cotton cloth.

28. ADA, Mayor of Saurat to PA, June 5, 1830, and June 8, 1830. Peasants from a nearby commune wore their native straw hoods.

29. Proclamation in ADA refers to the "criminal association of the *Demoiselles*"; ADA, PA to SPSG, February 23, 1830.

30. E. J. Hobsbawm and George Rudé, *Captain Swing: A Social History of the Great English Agricultural Uprisings of 1830* (New York: Pantheon Books, 1968), example from 206.

31. ADA, signed "Madamoiselle Lagrande."

32. The evidence confirms that the *demoiselles* were local peasants; ADA, letter of a justice of the peace to PA, July 16, 1829, and mayor of Saurat to PA, April 30, 1830. Indications of outsiders (Spaniards or deserters from other departments) among *demoiselles* are slight. The prefect, not normally a perceptive man, agreed that the peasants involved in the July 1829 disturbances were locals (ADA, PA to Int., July 20, 1829, and ADA, PA to Int., May 18, 1830).

33. Natalie Zemon Davis, "The Reasons of Misrule: Youth Groups and Charivaris in Sixteenth-Century France," *Past and Present* 50 (February 1971), 57.

34. Professor Davis asserts that "real life was always deeply embedded in these carnivals" and that the "mocking laugh of misrule intended to keep a traditional order" (45, 65). In her "Women on Top: Sexual Inversion and Disorder in Early Modern Europe," preliminary draft of a paper presented to the American Anthropological Association, 1972, Davis indicates that female attire and titles in collective protest was to be found in Lyon in the 1770s (10).

35. Baby, *op. cit.*, especially pages 126–139.

36. Davis, *op. cit.* It was significant that one important incident of pillage in the forests of the unpopular Astrié de Gudannes came on the day of the local *fête*, ADA, PA to Int., June 12, 1830, which Baby notes (105).

37. AG, D³ 129, 10th to MG, February 14, 1830; ADA, commander of the first subdivision of the 10th to PA, July 27, 1829. Brawls between the communes and the forest guards were common; e.g. ADA, SPSG to PA, July 16, 1829.

38. ADA, PA to Int., December 18, 1829; ADA, SPSG to PA, April 23, 1830 (example from royal forest of Bethmale); AG, D³ 128, 10th to MG, November 1, 1829. Other examples of attacks on forest guards and *charbonniers* include, ADA, under-inspector of forests in St. Girons to inspector in Foix, June 28, 1829, PA to Int., June 20, 1829, and July 3, 1829. Weapons usually included scythes, hatchets, sometimes rifles, and even bayonettes (ADA, mayor of Aulus to PA, June 14, 1830). The commander of the 10th complained that it was difficult to find *charbonniers* to go into the forests of the Ariège, AG D³ 126, July 25, 1829.

39. AG, D³ 126, Int. to MG, July 9, 1829. Secret police were used beginning in June 1829, ADA, PA to SPSG, June 30, 1829.

40. For example, ADA, *lawyer of propriétaire* to PA, June 14, 1830.

41. AG, D³ 127, 10th to MG, August 17, 1829, and Int. to MG, August 30. It seems that some members of the National Guard were present among some of the repressive forces in the summer of 1829, but these were certainly the elite in communes which were completely outside of the struggle.

42. ADA, PA to Int., March 8, 1830; ADA, PA to Bishop of Pamiers, June 30, 1829, and Bishop to PA, September 10, 1829. In addition, the SPSG convoked the mayors from the troubled areas, on orders from the prefect, ADA, PA to SP, September 5, 1829, and the prefect talked to a number of mayors on his tour of the arrondissement, ADA, May 18, 1830.

43. Baby, *op. cit.*, 60–61, indicates that priests sometimes helped the insurgents, and that the communes mentioned, Biert and Soulan, were communes in which the curés were, at least in 1809, members of the "Petite Eglise," which had refused to accept the Concordat and the authority of those priests ordained since 1803.

44. ADA, PA to Int., September 4, 1829. As the prefect wrote the Minister of Interior, ADA, May 24, 1830, "The commune of Massat wants all rights of pasturing without any exception." In December, the number of incidents sharply increased, including those in St. Lary, Augirein, and Villeneuve. This followed a period of relative calm. The Minister of War, whose job was to repress the disturbances, frequently suggested some conciliation, e.g., AG, D³ 129, MG to Minister of Finance, February 7, 1930. Few municipal councils formalized claims in the time following the decree in August, ADA, PA to Commissioner of Forests, November 28, 1829.

45. AG, D³ 127, 10th to MG, August 21, 1829; ADA, SPSG to PA, April 12, 1840. Troop movements can be followed in the General Correspondence in the AG, e.g., D³ 125, 10th to MG, May 31, 1829. Baby, *op. cit.*, 93, estimates the entire repressive force, including gendarmerie, at more than two thousand or one for every eighty-five people in the department. There were entire companies in communes like Massat, Boussenac, and Rivèrenert.

46. This was first suggested by the prefect, who generally preferred the hard line, ADA, PA to Int., September 4, 1829. On complaints, see ADA, Int. to PA, August 31, 1829, and PA to SPSG, September 5, 1829, particularly petition from Castelnau (ADA, SPSG to Pa, June 9, 1830), complaining that they were forced to lodge troops in their commune which were used to watch neighboring Esplas.

47. ADA, PA to Int., March 8, 1830. Arrests included those in Ustou, where the worksheds of the *charbonniers* were burned (AG, D³ 126, 10th to MG, July 23, 1829); trials involved arrested peasants from St. Lary, Seix, Sentenac-de-Sérou, Massat, Esplas, and Buzin, 2 U 193 ADA, ten *affaires*.

48. The most important was the trial and conviction of Bertrand Cointre, *dit* Falot du Company, which was announced and posted throughout the department, ADA, PA to Int., March 8, 1830. For example, one trial of ten *demoiselles* resulted in the conviction and sentencing of three (two got ten years and the other six months); witnesses could not, or would not, establish the identity of the others, ADA, PA to Int., June 7, 1830. On the two major trials, see Baby *op. cit.*, 82.

49. Proclamation of Prefect, ADA, March 15, 1830; ADA, *Procureur* of St. Girons to PA, April 7, 1830; Int. to PA, June 9, 1830; AG, D³ 130, Int. to MG, April 17, 1830. In

the Trinque case, 2500 francs went to the Crown as a fine, and 300 and 75 francs to the two guards. The use of this law, the law of 10 Vendémaire, An 4, was first suggested by the prefect, ADA, PA to Int., September 4, 1829.

50. ADA, mayor of Saurat to PA, June 8, 1830. The winter was apparently particularly harsh, including an avalanche in Bethmale, Archives Nationales (hereafter, AN), F⁷ 6767, PA to Int., February 5, 1830. Spring appearances were particularly marked in cantons of Massat, St. Girons, and Oust.

51. ADA, St. Martin (inspector?) to PA, September 4, 1829, notes the return of four hundred peasants from the Spanish harvests.

52. AN, F⁷ 6767, PA to Int., September 10, 1829. Only mention of dissent is the prefect's report that the young of the "*classes aisés* are generally imbued in the principles of independence which the liberal press sanctions and propagates," AN F⁷ 6767, PA to Int., March 11, 1830. Political interest undoubtedly centered in the *arrondissement* of Pamiers, which had 355 electors, as compared with 345 for the *arrondissements* of Foix and St. Girons combined.

53. ADA, 5 M 44, August 3 proclamation of the prefect; 5 M 62, proclamation of August 5. The wording of this petition may indicate that there was already an outbreak of disturbances in the forests.

54. ADA, 5 M 62, August 5; AG, D3 131, Laffite to MG indicates Laffite had arrived in Foix from Rouen.

55. ADA, 5 M 44, proclamation of provisional committee of administration, August 9, 1830. The departure of Charles X was not known until the eighth, as evidenced by the fact that the committee replaced one subprefect on the seventh because he would not swear loyalty to Charles X. Two more members were added to the provisional committee of administration on the 10th (proclamation, ADA, 5 M 62). Another proclamation on that day asked each commune to report on the local political situation, agricultural resources available to the commune, and whether the tricolor was flying.

56. Even David Pinkney's excellent political history of the revolution, *The French Revolution of 1830* (Princeton: Princeton University Press, 1972), underplays the impact of the revolution on the common man and largely limits discussion of the events in provincial France to political settling, such as dismissals and replacements and the threat of a pro-Bourbon uprising in the West and South. He views the general economic crisis and its popular protest as contributing to the acceptance of the overthrow of the Bourbons (225).

57. James Rule and Charles Tilly, "Political Process in Revolutionary France," in Merriman, John M., ed., *1830 in France* (New York: New Viewpoints, 1975), 42–85.

58. ADA, mayor and justice of the peace of commune and canton of Cabannes to *Procureur*, August 11, 1830; petition of communes of Cabannes canton, to departmental commission on the forest question, n.d.; AG, E⁵ 1, *Procureur* to MG, August 21, 1830.

59. AG, E⁵ 1, provisional committee of administration to MG, August 21, 1830; ADA, *procés-verbaux* of events, August 18, 1830. Damages were estimated at 40,000 francs.

60. ADA, complaint of owners, August 26, 1830. The commune of Fougax, where there was never an appearance of the *demoiselles*, seemed to have provided most of the participants, who were not disguised.

61. ADA, n.d., mayor of Rabat to the provisional committee.

62. ADA, mayor of Prayols to PA, September 12, 1830; mayor of Labastide-Sérou to PA, September 23; Marrot to PA, October 9. Other examples, pillage of property of the Mirepoix family, AG, E⁵ 2, 10th to MG, September 23; mayor of Saurat to provisional committee, September 5; and complaint of mayor of Ganac that commune of Brassac was furnishing *demoiselles* who were coming into the forests at night, ADA, to PA, September 22, 1830.

63. ADA, mayor of Saurat to provisional authority, August 20, cites the threatening letter. Details of forge-burning, ADA, mayor of Luzenac to provisional committee, August 20, and mayor of Ax to PA, August 20; AG, E⁵ 1, 10th to MG, August 22 and August 21; and AG, E⁵ 1, provisional authority to MG, August 21. At the same time, an intriguing incident seems to have occurred in Lavelanet, with Luddite overtones—an anonymous letter to the provisional authority on August 28 mentioned that a machine of some sort had been destroyed by individuals who claimed that the machine was taking work from them, ADA.

64. Pamiers incident, ADA, 5 M 44, subprefect of Pamiers to provisional authority, September 1: ADA, mayor of Vicdessos to provisional authority, August 23. The mayor of Vicdessos also claimed, in a letter of August 27, that the *demoiselles* were seen in the town the night before the people came to "do justice" to the tax collectors.

65. ADA, petition of mayor of Mongailhard to PA, September 2.

66. ADA, mayor of Mirepoix to provisional authority, and SPSG to PA, September 7, 1830; AG, E⁵ 2, de Portes, deputy, to Int. (Guizot, his friend), September 9, 1830.

67. ADA, mayor of Freychenet to provisional authority, August 28; AG, E⁵ 1, Laffite to MG, August 21. News of concessions spread quickly, AG, E⁵ 1, 10th to MG, August 26 and ADA, mayor of Cabannes to provisional authority, August 12. Concessions angered the new prefect, who wrote the mayors of two communes that "all acts of usage or of property which are bases on the disposition of this transaction [the concession] will constitute, until authorized by the King, an attack on the property of others and the communes will be held responsible," ADA, September 14, 1830.

68. ADA, mayor of Ax to provisional authority, August 23; mayor of Prayols to PA, September 12, 1830; AG, E⁵ 2, Commander of Gendarmerie of the *arrondissement* of St. Gaudens (Haute Garonne) to MG, September 1.

69. ADA, Mayor of Ax to provisional authority, August 23, 1830.

70. ADA, mayor of Engomer to SPSG, August 12, 1830.

71. This attitude seemed to be reflected in Paris in the face of increased militancy of the workers; David H. Pinkney, "*Laissez-faire* or Intervention? Labor Policy in the First Months of the July Monarchy," *French Historical Studies* 8 (1963), 123–28.

72. See note 45. There is no evidence that the number of troops and gendarmes in the department changed between April and the months of August and September.

73. AG, E⁵ 2, Laffite to MG, September 16, 1830.

74. AG, E⁵ 1, 10th to MG, August 26, 1830; MG to Int., August 31.

75. AG, E⁵ 2, Minister of Finance to MG, September 23, 1830 and decree of September 27; Laffite to MG, September 26, 1830.

76. ADA, petitions of Cabannes canton and commune of Montoulieu, n.d.

77. ADA, petition of commune of Montgailhard, September 2, 1830.

78. ADA, Inspector of Forests to PA, September 20, 1830, and report of the Commissioner of Forests at Toulouse, November 6, 1830. Amnesty noted by Baby *op. cit.*, 90–91.

79. ADA, report of the commission, December 18, 1830, in the form of twenty-two *arrêtes*, or decrees. Article 10 provided for a hearing of the mayors and municipal council before the forest administration indicated each ear the "defensible" or permitted areas of the forests. The communes were still held responsible for all violations of the forest code as modified. One previously burdensome stipulation was removed—the communes no longer had to attach a small bell to each animal pasturing (article 19). The tiny commune of Montoulieu finally received some right in the royal forests (see note 76).

80. ADA, report of the Commissioner of Forests at Toulouse, November 6, 1830. It also recommended the upgrading of the personnel of the forest guards in response to the public clamor about the guards' behavior.

81. AG, E⁵ 2, Laffite to MG, September 16, 1830. In one interesting case, again that of Massat, the commune actually purchased the disputed forest from the owners after the revolution (ADA, n.d. "Observations presented by the mayor of Massat"), later losing it back to the former *propriétaires* when the payments could, apparently, no longer be made (Baby, *op. cit.*, 89).

82. ADA, letter of a "captain" of the *demoiselles* to the provisional authority, August 30, 1830.

83. ADA, PA to mayor of Montgailhard, November 30, 1830; Inspector of Forests to PA, September 26, 1830 (reported that the new forest guard in Ax was being threatened); ADA 5 M 53, Int. to PA, December 14, 1830.

84. AG, E⁵ 9, 10th to MG, March 22, 1831, particularly in the Massat area. Rumors of their reappearance began in this area as early as August 1830 (ADA, mayor of Massat to SPSG, August 24).

85. Baby estimates the number of actual appearances, with disguise, of the *demoiselles* at seventeen between 1831 and 1848, most of these in 1831 and 1832 (*op. cit.*, 93, 214–15). The number of forges continued to grow, reaching 57 in 1844 (43 in 1818), Baby, *op. cit.*, 35. Armengaud, *op. cit.*, 195–210, describes the depopulation of the Ariège. Between 1841 and 1856 emigration exceeded immigration by 23,362, particularly during the period 1851–1856.

86. As suggested by Albert Soboul, "La question paysanne en 1848," *La Pensée* 18 (55–66), 19 (25–37), 20 (48–56), 1948; and more recently in, "The French rural community in the 18th and 19th centuries," *op. cit.* Baby considers the "War of the Demoiselles" to be unique, the "last French revolt to have made folklore its ornament, its motivations and its principal arm" (*op. cit.*, 149). He portrays this "war" as "not a revolutionary uprising ... it is folklore, essentially [p. 147] ... not a moment of the Revolution of 1830 but a simple *jacquerie* [p. 54]." While the disguise in the Ariège may have been unique, there were similar forest disturbances in many areas of France, recorded most accurately in the General Correspondence in the AG and in the BB¹⁸ series of the AN. Many of these involved the loss of the same rights as in the Ariège (see not 5, Agulhon, for example). The end of this folklore element to protest was itself another indication of the disappearance of the traditional peasant community.

87. Agulhon, *op. cit.* In the May 1849 elections, the *"démoc-soc"* list won between 40 and 50 percent of the popular vote in the Ariège (Maurice Agulhon, *1848 ou l'apprentissage de la république, 1848–52* [Paris: Seuil, 1973], 174).

88. Charles Tilly, "The Changing Place of Collective Violence" and "How Protest Modernized in France, 1845–55," *op. cit.*; and Tilly, "Collective Violence in the European Perspective," in *Violence in America*, in Hugh Davis Graham and Ted Robert Gurr, eds. (New York: Praeger, 1967).

2. The Norman Fires of 1830

1. Georges Lefebvre, *La Grand Peur de 1789* (Paris, 1932); Edith Thomas, *The Women Incendiaries* (New York, 1966); and Edgar Morin, *Rumour in Orléans* (New York, 1971).

2. For example, David Pinkney's *The French Revolution of 1830* (Princeton, 1972), 33–34, and Vincent W. Beach, *Charles X of France* (Boulder CO, 1971), 318–19.

3. AN, CC 549 and 550 contain many records of the fires; their number was set at 264 by the *procureur général* of Caen (henceforth PGC) in a report (CC 550) dated November 8, 1830. One hundred seventy-eight of these were between February 18 and July 7, noted by Baron Angot des Rotours, "Les Brûleurs de 1830 en Basse-Normandie," *Normania* III (Sept. 1930): 690; the latter discusses the case of the *fille* Bourdeaux who set the Bremoy fires, blamed her *curé* for telling her to do it, and later retracted the accusation. This information is found in AN, CC 550, report of PGC, Oct. 3, 1830. The Cauvicourt fire mentioned in AN, F⁷ 9317, Minister of Interior's note, May 22, 1830. The fires generally were believed to have struck the "less fortunate," at least according to the *procureur général* of Paris in a report of June 2, 1831.

4. AN, F⁷ 9317, report of the Prefect of the Manche (henceforth PM), April 13, 1830.

5. AN, F⁷ 9317, report of PM, May 11, 1830; another good description of the incendiary devices was given by the prefect of the Eure in a report dated June 21.

6. For example, AN, CC 549, PGC report of June 24 and July 2; AN, CC 550, *Affaire* Bailleul.

7. Various reports, including AN, F⁷ 9317, report of the Gendarmerie commander for the *arrondissement* of Chinon (Indre-et-Loire), July 28, and report of the Gendarmerie commander of the Côtes-du-Nord, July 6; CC 549, reports of the *procureur* of Mortain, April 13 and Oct. 25, 1830, and PGC, May 8 and June 6.

8. AN, CC 549, report of the first president of the *Cour royale* of Caen, April 29.

9. AN, F7 9317, prefect of the Calvados (henceforth PC) report of May 15 and May 18.

10. *Ibid.*, May 21.

11. *Ibid.*, May 18; and CC 549, police report of May 15.

12. AN, CC 550, PGC, Nov. 8; mentioned by Baron Angot des Retours, "Brûleurs de 1830," 706. The silent church bells are noted in PGC, letters of October 3 and 11.

13. F⁷ 9317, report of the prefect of the Deux-Sevrès, July 24.

14. The threat reported in AN, CC 549, report of PGC, May 28; reports on security measures include CC 549, letter of the Minister of Interior to PC, March 29 and May 8; CC 550, Minister of Interior to the President of the Council of Ministers, May 15; troop movements may be followed in the General Correspondence of the

War Ministry, D³ 130, Archives historiques du Ministère de la Guerre, Vincennes (henceforth AHMG).

15. AN, CC 549, PGC, report of April 24 and May 11.

16. AN, F⁷ 9317, PCG, report of May 28, and note of Minister of Interior, May 15; CC 549, report of PGC, June 7; CC 550, *Affaire Pauline*, judged July 7.

17. For example, AN, CC 549, report of the prefect of the Maine-et-Loire, July 19; and Louis Blanc, *History of Ten Years* I (Philadelphia, 1848), 100.

18. AN, CC 549, Minister of Interior's note, May 15; BB¹⁸ 1184, A⁷ 3594, report of PGC, May 22.

19. AN, CC 550, Minister of Justice to PGC, June 25, and reports of the *procureur* of Mantes [n.d.]; Baron Angot des Retours, "Brûleurs de 1830," 686–86; and H. Monin, "Une Epidemie anarchiste sous la Restauration," *Revue de sociologie international* II (Nov. 1894): 766; and Louis de Viel-Castel, *Histoire de la Restauration* XI (Paris, 1860–80), 75–78.

20. AN, CC 549, PM, report of June 6. There was another case where some *biens nationaux* property was burned, in Plélan-le-Petit, AN, F⁷ 9317, report of Gendarmerie commander in Dinan, July 16.

21. Comte de Guernon-Ranville, *Journal d'un Ministre* (Caen, 1873), 85; the fires were discussed at meetings on May 2, 5, and 23. See also *Le Moniteur universal* (Paris), suppl., Sept. 28, accusation of M. Mercier.

22. For example, AN, F⁷ 9317, report of the prefect of Maine-et-Loire, July 28; *La Gazette de France*, remark cited in H. Monin, "Epidemie anarchiste," 772.

23. AN, CC 549, PGC, reports of April 24, May 12, 24, and 28, and June 25.

24. AN, F⁷ 9317, Minister of Interior's note, June 9.

25. AN, CC 550, Minister of Justice to PGC, June 3.

26. AN, CC 550, PGC, report of Nov. 15, and *procureur général* of Angers to the President of the Chamber of Peers, Oct. 16.

27. AN, CC 550, "Dépositions . . . de Pierre Gamain, prévenu de crimes d'incendie," Oct. 29.

28. BB²⁰ 49, Cour royale d'Angers, *Affaire Pellé; procureur général* of Angers, report of Feb. 15, 1831.

29. *Moniteur*, suppl., Sept. 28, especially accusations of de Briqueville, Enouf, and Mercier; Baron Angot des Retours, "Brûleurs de 1830," 703–04; David Pinkney, *French Revolution of 1830*; CC 550, for example, report of the *procureur général* of Angers to the president of the Chamber of Peers, Oct. 16. The "revelations" of a man arrested in Toulouse, who claimed that Charles X and Polignac had paid him to set the fires, proved false, cited in Monin, "Epidemie anarchiste," 787–89.

30. AN, BB²⁰ 49, Cour royale d'Angers, especially *procureur général* of Angers to Minister of Justice, Feb. 15, 1831; the sixteen brought to trial included a *forcat libré* (alias Gaulthier), two mendicants (ages 13 and 14), an *eau de cologne* salesman, two *journaliers*, one merchant, one *artiste d'agilité et artificier*, one mill guard, one *pâtre*, one wife of a *carbaretier*, one *cultivateur*, one widow (of a *cultivateur*), one domestic, one man without a profession, and one *cultivateur-cabaretier*. Police made fifty arrests in this *ressort*.

31. Frederick B. Artz, "La Crise des assurances en 1830 et les companies d'assurances," *Revue d'histoire moderne* IV (March-April 1929): 96–105, esp. 103. Artz bases his interpretation primarily on three or four reports, which deal principally with the northern departments involved.

32. AN, CC 549, police report of July 15, duplicated in F⁷ 9317, and May 15; BB¹⁸ 1183, A 3537, report of the *procureur général* of Amiens, April 29.

33. AN, CC 549, prefect of police report, July 21, and PGC, report of June 7; F⁷ 9317, Gendarmerie commander of the Pas-de-Calais, report of May 26.

34. AN, CC 549, PGC, report of May 5; F⁷ 9317, prefect of the Aisne, report of May 28, and Minister of Justice to Minister of Interior, May 1.

35. For example, AN, CC 549, PC report of May 2 and PM, April 13, and F⁷ 9317, report of the prefect of the Pas-de-Calais, June 9, and of the subprefect of Avesnes (Nord), May 28. Of 207 fires listen in CC 550 for the *ressort* of Caen at least 93 were ascribed to insurance motives.

36. AN, CC 550, reports assembled for the commission of the Chamber of Peers, investigating the fires, Côtes-du-Nord, 3rd sess., 1830; Cantal, 4th sess., 1830; Toulouse, 3rd sess., 1830.

37. AN, CC 549, PC, report of May 2; and report of the *procureur* of Vire, April 21.

38. AN, F⁷ 9317, report of the prefect of the Loire-Inférieure, June 12.

39. AN, CC 550, Cour royale de Rennes, reports from the 4th sess., 1829; General Sabot, who had killed someone before moving to the commune, was condemned to death.

40. AN, F⁷ 9317, Gendarmerie commander of Maine-et-Loire, July 11.

41. AN, CC 550, Haute-Loire, 4th sess., 1829; Charente-Inférieure, 2nd sess., 1830.

42. AN, F⁷ 9317, Gendarmerie commander of Saint-Quentin (Aisne) reported the threat, May 16; CC 550, Minister of Interior to PM, May 27.

43. André Abbiateci, "Les Incendiaries devant de Parlement de Paris: Essai de typologie criminelle (XVIIIe s.)," in André Abbiateci, F. Billaçois *et al., Crimes et criminalité sous l'ancien régime* (Paris, 1971), 19.

44. AN, F⁷ 9317, report of the *procureur* of Argentan (Orne), May 23.

45. AN, F⁷ 9317, Minister of Interior's note, June 9; CC 549, PGC, report of June 9; F⁷ 9317, reports of Gendarmerie commander of Dieppe, June 20; PM, July 9; prefect of Côtes-du-Nord, July 8; and prefect of Ille-et-Vilaine, where most of the fires seem to have been set by vagrants and mendicants, May 10 and 24.

46. "Epidemie anarchiste"; like Baron Angot des Rotours, Monin summarizes some of the most interesting cases of domestics claiming that they were paid to set fires. Artz also cites Monin, 101–02. Baron Angot des Rotours seems most intent on clearing the Bourbons from accusations of involvement; to the extent that when he fixes blame he places it on the liberals for creating a political mood which made political incendiarism possible.

47. AN, CC 549, *procureur* of Vire, report of April 24.

48. A view held by the Gendarmerie commander in Dinan, AN, F⁷ 9317, report of July 16. BB¹⁸ 1182, A⁷ 3440, report of the *procureur général* of Limoges, April 17, gives a good example of an accidental fire attributed to "malevolence." Apparently

a few fires were started in order to get other villagers to share the burden of surveillance, CC 550, report of PGC, Nov. 8.

49. Paul Gonnet, "Esquisse de la crise économique en France de 1827 à 1832," *Revue histoire économique et sociale* XXXIII (1955): esp. 271–72.

50. The commission investigating the possible complicity of the Polignac ministry gathered reports from every *Cour royale* in France, listing the fires in each *ressort* from October 1829 until September 1830; fires were divided into categories such as "malevolence," "private vengeance," "insurance," "unknown cause," "accidental." Officials in virtually every judicial region (Rouen was an exception) were convinced by some of the following totals that there were more fires than "normal": Paris, 268; Bordeaux, 99; Nîmes, 71; Lyon, 63; Riom, 82; Bourges, 61; Montpellier, 51; Orléans, 79; Poitiers, 54; and Dijon, 20. I have not attempted to calculate any sort of "normal" occurrence of fires but have accepted the virtual unanimity of official opinion. Examples of the continuation of the fires may be found in the following: AG, E[5] 7, Commander of 18th Military Division report, Feb. 22, 1831; AN, BB[18] 1206, A[7] 7250, PGC report of May 25, 1832; BB[18] 1194, A[7] 5018, Minister of Interior to Minister of Justice, March 23, 1831, on the "multiplication" of fires in the Aisne, ascribed to "private vengeance," insurance motives, and "religious and political" fanaticism; BB[18] 1205, A[7] 7050, Interior to Minister of Justice, April 5, 1832; BB[18] 1194, A[7] 5170, report of the *procureur général* of Orléans, March 31, 1831. Some of the rumors and bands in the west were, of course, related to re-emergence of the *chouans* after the July Revolution.

51. The Swing "movement" in England at the same time offers a fascinating comparison; see Eric J. Hobsbawm and George Rudé, *Captain Swing: A Social History of the Great English Agricultural Uprising of 1830* (New York, 1968), who note that (200, quoting a press report) "the fire instrument, it appears, is of a slowly explosive character, and being deposited beneath the stack, after a certain period ignites and explodes."

52. Other examples of threatening placards can be found in AN, F[7] 9317, CC 549 and 550, as well as in Gonnet, "Esquisse de la crise économique." These examples are taken from AG E[5] 2, report of commander of First Gendarmerie Division, Sept. 2, 1830; AN, BB[20] 49, report of *procureur général* of Angers, Feb. 15, 1831; E[5] 3, report of Gendarmerie commandeer of Saint-Quentin, Oct. 21, 1830; and D[3] 127, report of Gendarmerie commander of Saint-Omer, Oct. 26, 1829. A thorough study of placards after the revolution would probably show more "political" content—that is, consciously against the "bourgeois rabble" and the like; placards complaining about the lack of work, of course, turn up in towns and cities after the revolution.

53. For an expansion of this view see John M. Merriman, ed., *1830 in France* (New York, 1975), esp. Merriman, "Introduction," and "The 'Demoiselles' of the Ariège, 1829–31" (reprinted in this volume), and James Rule and Charles Tilly, "Political Process in Revolutionary France, 1830–32." Ernest Labrousse, "1848—1830—1789: How Revolutions Are Born," in F. Crouzet, W. H. Chaloner, and W. M. Stern, *Essays in European Economic History* (London, 1969), is also relevant.

54. Suspicions of a political conspiracy lingered; for example, one of three suspects arrested after a fire in Coulonges-les-Sablons (Orne), Mouru *dit Laboureur*, had a letter dated September 17, 1830, telling him that "everything is going well" and including a

notation, "974261 of which 553271 furnished by the clergy, 421100 by the Royal Treasury" (AN, CC 550, *procureur* at Mortaigne, Oct. 18, 1830), leading one to suspect a *chouan* plot.

55. The fires, when they are broken down into probable origin, include the following (from CC 550): Aube, 8 insurance, 17 vengeance, 29 "unknown"; *ressort* of Riom, 19 vengeance, 1 insurance, 5 unknown (of 82); *arrondissement* of Douai, 3 unknown, 1 insurance, 1 set by a *fou* (of 13); *arrondissement* of Arras, 3 vengeance, 8 unknown, 4 insurance, 4 "malevolence"; *arrondissement* of Cambrai, 1 *fou*, 4 insurance, 1 vengeance, 4 malevolence; Yonne (from Nov. 1830 until Feb. 20, 1831), 3 malevolence, 2 unknown, 3 carelessness; and so on. These breakdowns are by no means complete, but are representative.

56. There is good evidence that patterns of collective violence of Frenchmen were changing and reflecting fundamental changes in economy and society, meaning that the French poor were not simply being "squeezed" by another economic crisis. The increasing domination of a national economy was gradually changing economic relations in rural areas as well as in towns and cities, and the growing ability of the centralized state to extract taxes and obedience undercut traditional forms of popular protest. See Charles Tilly, "The Changing Place of Collective Violence," in Melvin Richter, ed., *Essays in Theory and History* (Cambridge MA, 1970); and "Food Supply and Public Order in Modern Europe," in Charles Tilly, ed., *The Formation of National States in Western Europe* (Princeton, 1975); and Merriman, "*Demoiselles* of the Ariège."

3. Incident at the Statue of Mary

Research for this article was made possible by grants from the Whitney Griswold Fund and the Concilium on International and Area Studies, both at Yale University.

1. See John M. Merriman, *Agony of the Republic: The Repression of the Left in Revolutionary France, 1848–51* (New Haven CT: Yale University Press, 1978).

2. Edward Shorter and Charles Tilly, *Strikes in France, 1830–1968* (Cambridge: Cambridge University Press, 1974), 276.

3. Maurice Agulhon, *La République au village* (Paris: Plon, 1970).

4. Limoges was one of the fastest growing cities in France. Charles Pouthas, *La population française pendant la première moitié du XIXe siècle* (Paris: Presses Universitaires de France, 1956).

1806	21,757	1861	51,053	
1821	24,992	1872	55,134	
1826	25,612	1876	59,101	
1831	27,070	1881	63,765	
1836	29,706	1891	72,697	
1846	38,119	1901	76,832	(84,121)a
1851	41,360	1906	81,685	(88,597)
1856	46,564	1911	85,173	(92,181)

Source: *Almanach Limousin*, 1864, 1873, 1886, 1893; Census of 1906, etc. aUnofficial population figures.

5. See particularly, Alain Corbin, *Archaïsme et modernité en Limousin au XIXe siècle, 1845–1880* (Paris: Rivière, 1975), which is the definitive study of the Limousin during the middle years of the century; Camille Grellier, *L'Industrie de la porcelain*

en Limousin (Paris, 1908). Fascinating descriptions of the city are found in the War Archives in Vincennes, in MR 1298, 1300, etc. *The Almanach Limousin*, which was published annually from 1859 to 1914, is a remarkable source for the study of Limouges. See "Limoges depuis cent ans," in the *Almanach* for 1860 ff.

6. See Kathryn Amdur, "Unity and Schism in French Labor Politics; Limoges and Saint Etienne, 1914–1922" (Ph.D. diss. Stanford University, 1978), 57–60, 505–516.

7. Gaston Ducray, *Le Travail porcelainier en Limousin* (Angers, 1940), 197–98. Few studies of French cities effectively treat the relationship between the city and its suburbs; see Jean Bastié, *La Croissance de la banlieu parisienne* (Paris: Presses Universitaires de France, 1964); Robert J. Bezucha, *The Lyon Insurrection of 1834* (Cambridge: Harvard University Press, 1974); and Michael P. Hanagan, "The Logic of Solidarity: Social Structure in Le Chambon-Feugerolles, 1871–1914," *Journal of Urban History* 3 (1977): 409–26.

8. Rapport du Secrétaire de la Chambre de Commerce de Paris, June 15, 1855, exposition "Le Parisien chez klui au XIXe siècle," Archives Nationales, Nov. 26, 1976–Feb. 28, 1977.

9. This brief analysis is based upon a study of two faubourgs and a number of central city streets: the censuses of 1848 and 1906; and information provided by the *Almanach Limousin*, which I have read for the years 1859 through 1914. A large proportion of Limoges buildings housed boutiques, stores, or workshops, as noted by the Prefect of Haute Vienne in his report of May 6, 1819, in AN F 7 9711. The streets of prostitution were the center of much controversy; plans for their demolition were proposed throughout the century; see Louis Guibert, *Le Quartier Viraclud* (Limoges, 1897).

10. Between 1820 and 1835, for example, the average number of births was 1,136 as compared with 1,200 deaths; deaths outnumbered births 15,776 to 14,330 between 1849 and 1859 (*Almanach Limousin*, 1860), there being an excess of births only in 1850 and 1853. In 1881 (actually, December to December) there were 1,600 deaths and 1,676 births (of which 148 were illegitimate); the following year there were 1,729 births and 1,692 deaths, representing a relative decline in mortality. The fact that many people from the countryside died in the Limoges hospital, charity institutions, madhouses, or jails must be taken into consideration. Between 1884 and 1893 there was an excess of births in six out of ten years with the exception of 1882 and 1890–92. Corbin lists Limoges's net migration as follows

1846–50	4,076	1866–71	4,252
1851–55	5,526	1872–75	2,258
1856–60	4,986	1876–80	3,398
1861–65	1,029		

Source: Corbin, *Archaïsme et modernité*, 583.

11. The remarkable unofficial census of 1848 gives place of birth and *duration de domicile* of male heads of households; it is not complete, as a number of streets were missed, probably because of the *Affaire de Limoges* of April 27. I have plotted the birthplace of all porcelain workers and day laborers who appeared in the census. The census of 1906 was also at the mairie; it has now been put in a more organized archive

nearby. There were some important shifts within the porcelain industry, notably in the decline of "specialized" migrants from other porcelain cities such as Vierzon and Paris. My findings are tentative since this work is still in progress. In 1891, 56,406 of Limoges's population of 72,679 were born in Haute Vienne (2,814 in Corrèze; 2,074 in Charente; 1,947 in Dordogne; 663 in Seine; 451 in the Indre; 346 in Vienne, and so forth).

12. Eugen Weber, *Peasants into Frenchmen: The Modernization of Rural France 1870–1914* (Stanford: Stanford University Press, 1976). Theodore Zeldin, *France: Ambition, Love, and Politics* (Oxford: Oxford University Press, 1976).

13. Georges-Emmanuel Clancier, *La Vie quotidienne en Limousin au xixe siècle*. See also Clancier's novel, *Le Pain Noir*, which was serialized for French television.

14. Shorter and Tilly, *Strikes in France*, 276.

15. Census of 1906; Amdur "Unity and Schism," 516. According to the census of 1906, only slightly more than one-third of the shoemakers employed by Monteux, the largest shoemaking firm (50 Avenue Garibaldi, just up the street from Haviland porcelain), were born outside of Limoges. Amdur's sample, taken from the census of 1891, indicates that 42.4 percent of the shoemakers were born in Limoges; 41.2 percent in the department of Haute Vienne; 12.9 percent in neighboring departments; and 3.5 percent in the contiguous region. The fourteen years between the censuses is significant and indicates an increasing geographic stability in the industry, whose peak period of growth began in the 1880s.

16. John M. Merriman, "Social Conflict in France and the Limoges Revolution of April 27, 1848," *Societas* 4, no. 1 (Winter 1974): 21–38.

17. According to G. Désiré-Vuillemin, "Les liens entre population ouvrière citadine et population rurale demeurent nombreux, les échanges incessants." "Une Grève révolutionnaire: les porcelainiers de Limoges en avril 1905," *Annales du Midi* 83 (Jan/March 1971): 21.

18. See Amdur's summary of labor politics in Limoges in the decades before the war, "Unity and Schism," especially 73–143; Désiré-Vuillemin, "Une Grève," passim; Pierre Cousteix, *Une Esquisse du movement ouvrier à Limoges depuis le xixe siècle* (Angoulême, 1929). See also the following refutations of the "uprooting hypothesis": Oscar Lewis, *Anthropological Essays* (New York: Random House, 1970); Janet Abu-Lughd, *Caire: 1001 Years of the City Victorious* (Princeton: Princeton University Press, 1971); Joan W. Scott, *The Glassworkers of Carmaux* (Cambridge: Harvard University Press, 1974); Charles Tilly, "The Chaos of the Living City" in *An Urban World* ed. Charles Tilly (Boston: Little, Brown, 1974), 86–108; Charles Tilly and Lynn Lees, "The People of June 1848," in *Revolution and Reaction: 1848 and the Second French Republic*, ed. R. D. Price (London: Croom Helm, 1975), 170–209; Charles Tilly, Louise Tilly, Richard Tilly, *The Rebellious Century* (Cambridge: Harvard University Press, 1975).

Tensions between the center city and the faubourgs seem to have been acute in nineteenth-century French cities. Michelle Perrot, *Les Ouvriers en grève*, vol. 1 (Paris: Mouton, 1974), 220, has described Paris and its suburbs thusly: "La banlieue, sa réalité, ses représentations: beaux thèmes qui s'enflent en ce versant du siècle. Aux yeux des contemporains, trois traits la caractérisent: elle est misérable . . . violente et redoutable, mélange explosif de paysans déracinés, d'immigrants inadaptés, repaire des nouvelles 'classes dangereuses'; faits divers, rapports de police abondent en récits de rixes et d'agressions." Yet in some cities and in certain faubourgs, there may have been mitigating factors, such as the range of migration, availability of work, and commonality of cultural heritage.

19. *Almanach Limousin*, 1862, 12–13; Louis Guibert, a Legitimist, noted that "Il faut habiter longtemps notre ville pour savoir jusqu'à quel point le culte des bons saints y est pousée" (*Almnach Limousin*, 1862, 2–3). See also reports in AG MR 1300.

20. AG (Ministry of War Archives), MR 1300.

21. See Adrien Delor, *La Corporation des bouchers à Limoges* (Limoges, 1877); "La Boucherie de Limoges," *Almanach Limousin*, 1862; Joseph Petit, *Une Ancienne Corporation et ses survivances* (Paris, 1906); Septime Gorceix, "La Corpration des bouchers et la confrèrie de Saint Aurelien," in *Limoges à travers les siècles* (Limoges, 1946), 35–39; and M. le Marquis de Moussac, *Une Corporation d'autrefois encore vivante aujourd'hui* (Paris, 1892). The butchers' nicknames were duly noted in *Almanach Limousin* each year, together with their addresses.

22. "Limoges depuis cent ans," *Almanach Limousin*, 1862, 2–3.

23. ADHV Annex, 2V 3, reports on the ostensions; and Louis Guibert, "Les Ostensions," in the *Almanach Limousin*, 1862, 63–71.

24. *Journal des Débats*, February 16, 1943.

25. The public works in Limoges and their politics during the Second Empire may be followed in a series of articles which appeared in the yearly *Almanach Limousin*. Limoges's leading citizens were extremely sensitive about the city's bad reputation, which went back hundreds of years. A traveler wrote in 1753, "Le séjour de Limoges n'est pas agréable; les rues en sont étroites, mal percées et obscures. Les maisons, baties en bois, présentent le plus triste coup d'oeil; il n'y a pas une place décente, pas un édifice public remarquable." (Cited in *Almanach Limousin*, 1860).

26. "Limoges depuis cent ans," *Almanach Limousin*, 1862, 29–30.

27. AG MR 1300.

28. Marguerite Le Saux, "Approche d'une étude de la déchristianisation: l'évolution religiuse du monde rural dans trois cantons de la Haute Vienne (Ambazac, Le Dorat, Limoges) a milieu du XIXe siècle à la première guerre mondiale" (Mémoire de Maîtrise, Université de Poiters, 1971), which deals with only the rural communes of the canton of Limoges; anticlericalism manifested itself after the Revolution of 1830 and during the period of the 1871 Commune. See also M. Robert, *La Société limousine, 1870–1914* (Limoges, 1971), 125. The influence of the Revolution of 1848 and the spread of socialism in 1848–51 was undoubtedly a factor in the weakening of religion in rural Haute Vienne, leaving little more than the superstition and the cult of the "magic fountains."

29. See Mona Ozouf, *Fête révolutionnaire* (Paris, 1977).

30. On L'Union coópérative, to which five thousand families belonged, see the report of the Procureur Général of Limoges, January 10, 1895, in AN BB 18 1992.

31. M. le Marquis de Moussac, *Une Corporation d'autrefois encore vivante aujourd'hui* (Paris, 1892), 81.

32. Adrien Delor, *op. cit.*, 40–46.

33. Paul Ducourtieux, "Les Statues de la Vièrge au carrefours du vieux Limoges," *Limoges Illustré*, May 15, 1906. The butchers had a bad reputation in the countryside

market towns. For example, they successfully boycotted the market in Laurière after preventing anyone else from buying cattle while offering only a low price and threatening local officials; 1M 142; report of the Police Commissioner, August 7, 1855. The statue mutilation was noted in the *Almanach Limousin* of 1865.

34. This, of course, is an enormous and fascinating topic, as municipal politics in Limoges were bitter and important; the *Almanach Limousin* published yearly summaries of the meetings of the municipal councils. Much of the prewar period was dominated by the struggles of mayor and deputy Émile Labussière and his rival, the Radical Doctor Chénieux, as well as the clerical party.

4. The Language of Social Stigmatization

1. See John M. Merriman, *Aux marges de la vie: faubourgs et banlieues en France 1815–1871* (Paris, 1994) and *Limoges, la ville rouge* (Paris, 1990). In this paper, I am taking further some arguments and material that I developed in *Aux marges de la ville.*

2. Antoine Bailly, "Géographie sociale et marginalité: sa pertinence géographique," in André Vant, *Marginalité sociale, marginalité spatiale* (Paris, 1986), 50.

3. Bernard Vincent, "Les Marginaux et les exclus dans l'histoire" (Paris, 1979), 8, 13.

4. Bronislaw Geremek, "Criminalité, vagabondage, paupérisme: le marginalité à l'aube des temps modernes," *Revue d'histoire modern et contemporaine* 21 (July-September 1974), 348; see his *Les Marginaux parisient aux xive et xve siècles* (Paris, 1976).

5. Bronislaw Geremeck, op. cit., 85, 89, adding (95) that it is risky to speak of "veritable 'kingdoms' of misery."

6. Steven Kaplan, "Les Corporations, les 'faux ouvriers' et le faubourg Saint-Antoine au xviiie siècle," *Annales E.S.C.* xliii, no. 2, (Mars-Avril 1988): 353–78.

7. Ibid., 354, 356–57, 361–65, 369. In contrast, Kaplan notes that "The Faubourg Saint-Antoine was thus according to its partisans a type of utopian, an enclave of freedom (but not of license) in a universe of obstacles, inquisition and artificial doctrines" (360). Thus Kaplan argues that on the eve of the Revolution, "The faubourg . . . becomes despite itself a subversive space" (370).

8. See Leonard N. Rosenband, "Jean-Baptise Réveillon: A Man on the Make in Old Regime France," *French Historical Studies* 20, 3 (Summer, 1997): 481–510.

9. Ibid., 374, taken from Levacher-Duplessis, *Réponse des délégués des marchands en détail et des maîtres artisans de la ville de Paris aux rapports et délibérations des conseils généraux de commerce et des manufactures* (Paris, 1817), 23.

10. Quoted by Pierre Aycoberry, "Au-delà des remparts: 'vrais colonais' et banlieusards au milieu du xixe siècle," *Le Mouvement social* 118 (Janvier–Mars 1982): 38.

11. Quoted by Arlette Farge, "Un espace urbaine obsédant: le commissaire et la rue à Paris au xviiie siècle," *Les Révoltes logiques* 6 (1977): 11–12.

12. T. J. Clark, *The Painting of Modern Life: Paris in the Art of Manet and His Followers* (New York, 1985), 238.

13. However, another contemporary investigator, Antoine Frégier, treated the faubourg with a special kind of concern, because of the drunkenness he associated with the periphery.

14. Eugène Buret, *De la misère des classes laborieuses en Angleterre et en France* (Paris, 1840), I, 316, 341–42, 345–46; II, 22, 225–26.

15. MR 1209 (1841).

16. Including, most recently, by Barrie Ratcliffe, "Classes laborieuses et classes dangereuses à Paris pendant la première moitié du XIXe siècle? The Chevalier Thesis Re-examined," *French Historical Studies* 17, no. 2 (Autumn 1991): 542-74.

17. George Rudé, *The Crowd in the French Revolution* (New York, 1959); David H. Pinkey, "The Crowd in the French Revolution of 1830," *American Historical Review* 70, no. 1 (October, 1964): 1–17, and many others.

18. Charles Tilly, "The Chaos of the Living City," in Tilly, ed., *An Urban World* (Boston, 1974), and the work of George Rudé and David Pinkney, cited above.

19. Richard Cobb, *The Police and the People* (London, 1970).

20. Louis Chevalier, *Dangerous and Laboring Classes*, op. cit., 65.

21. Ibid., 86, 102, the latter quoting Hugo's preoccupation with the "murder of the barrière de Fontainbleau," and the description in *Les Misérables* of the tenement of Gorbeau (102–03) that had stood on the Boulevard Saint-Jacques.

22. Ibid., 83–90.

23. Ibid.

24. T. J. Clark, op. cit., 67, quoting Denis Poulot's classic *Le Sublime*.

25. A point made by T.J. Clark, op. cit., 58–59, 69, quoting *L'Assommoir*: "Underneath the rising tide of luxury from Paris, there was the misery of the faubourg, spoiling and befouling this new city in the making, put up in such haste." See Maarten van Buuren and Arja Firel, "Splendeur et misère: Le Paris du Second Empire d'Émile Zola," in Marie-Christine Kok Escalle, *Paris: De l'image à la mémoire* (Paris, 1997).

26. Copies of the minister of the interior's letter, December 14, 1844, can be found in many departmental archives, including A.D. Aube, M 1180.

27. Susanna Barrows quotes Émile Zola, who, in response to the storm that followed the publication of *L'Assommoir* as a serial in 1876, wrote in *Le Bien public* that "If I were forced to draw a conclusion, I would say close the cabarets, open the schools . . . And I would add: clean up the faubourgs . . ." ("After the Commune: Alcoholism, Temperance, and Literature in the Early Third Republic," in John M. Merriman, ed., *Consciousness and Class Experience in Nineteenth-Century Europe* [New York, 1979], 215.)

28. April 18, 1832.

29. André Latreille, et. al., *Histoire de Lyon et du lyonnais* (Toulouse, 1975), 325. Girardin added, of course, "Every manufacturer lives in his factory like the colonial planter in the midst of his slaves," reflecting the fear from within industrial cities, as well.

30. A. D. Bas-Rhin 3M 48, cp June 11, 1832.

31. A. D. Loir-et-Cher 1M 91, prefet December 12, 1838.

32. F7 6779, gendarmerie report, Charente-Inférieure, February 1, 1832.

33. A. D. Maine-et-Loire, 1M 6/25, sp May 3, 1829.

34. A. D. Saône-et-Loire, M 111, prefect September 7, 1840; A.D. Gard, 4M 48, cp April 20 and following.

35. Quoted by William Langer, *Political and Social Upheaval, 1832–1852* (New York, 1968), 337, 345–46.

36. Ibid., 837; 445 Bellevillois were tried by court martial in the wake of the June Days.

37. Yvette Baradel, Georges Bischoff, André Larger, Yves Pagnot, et al., *Histoire de Belfort* (Le Coteau, 1985), 103.

38. Jean Rougerie quoted in Fernand Braudel and Ernest Labrousse, eds., *Histoire économique et sociale de la France* 3, no. 2 (Paris, 1976): 799.

39. Jeanne Gaillard, *Paris, la ville, 1852–1870* (Paris, 1977), 203.

40. Cited by Gérard Jacquemet, op. cit., 819; Jacquemet, "Belleville aux xixe et xxe siècles: une méthode d'analyse de la croissance urbaine à Paris," *Annales E.S.C.* xxx, 1975, quoting Léon Beauvallet, *Les quatres âges de Paris* (Paris, n.d.) and T. Labourrieu, *Les bandits de Montfaucon* (Paris, 1869), 441–42.

41. See *Aux marges de la ville*, chapter 8.

42. For a synthesis of this argument, see *Aux marges de la ville*, chapter 9.

43. Alain Faure, "Classe malpropre, classe dangereuse? Quelques remarques à propos des chiffonniers parisiens au xixe siècle et de leurs cités," in Lion Murard and Patrick Zylberman, *L'Haleine des faubourgs* (Fontenay-sous-Bois, 1978), 91–92.

44. Michelle Perrot, "Dans la France de la Belle Epoque, les 'Apaches', premières bandes de jeunes," in Bernard Vincent, et. al., op. cit., 387–88, 392–94.

45. Jean-Paul Brunet, *La ville rouge*; Tyler Stovall, *Bobigny*; Annie Foucault, *Bobigny*.

46. *Larousse de la langue française* (Paris, 1979).

47. Emile Littré, *Dictionnaire de la langue française* (1863).

48. Ibid.; "faubourg" is noted as being influenced by faux by the *Grand Larousse de la langue française* (1973) and the *Grand Dicionnaire encyclopédique Larousse* (Paris, 1983).

49. *Nouveau Larousse illustré*.

50. *Grand Robert de la langue française* (1985).

51. Ibid.

52. 1973. The *Grand Robert* notes that faubourg also means, in argot, "postérieur d'une femme" and, again, the same dictionary, choosing an example of a *banlieusard*, or resident of the suburbs: "He is ashamed of himself, ashamed of never rising, in his liaisons, above the employee, the secretary, the little suburban woman" (1985, quoting J. Doutourd, *Les Horreurs de l'Amour*, 406).

53. See Jean-Claude Dalotel, Jean-Claude Freiremuth, and Alain Faure, *Aux origines de la Commune: le movement des réunions publiques à Paris, 1868–1870* (Paris, 1980).

54. See David Harvey, *Consciousness and the Urban Experience* (Baltimore, 1985); Merriman, *Aux marges de la ville*, chapter 8.

55. See *Aux marges de la ville*, chapter 7 and Merriman, *The Agony of the Republic* (New Haven, 1978).

56. *Aux marges de la ville*, chapter 6.

57. Ibid., chapter 5.

58. The following is drawn from my *Limoges, la ville rouge* (Paris, 1990), which first appeared in English as *The Red City: Limoges and the French Nineteenth Century* (New York, 1985).

5. On the Loose

The author would like to thank Carol Merriman, Elinor Accampo, Susan P. Connor, Paul Hanson, Carole Lacherey, and Heinz-Gerhard Haupt for comments on earlier versions of the paper, one of which was presented at the Kolloquium, Europa in den Rrevolutionen von 1848, Academie Frankenwarte, Würzburg, Germany, October 1996, and a shorter version at the Consortium on Revolutionary Europe, Baton Rouge, Louisiana, February 1997.

1. See, for example, his "La Monteé à Paris." *In Paris and its Provinces 1792–1802* (London, 1975), 26–27.

2. Georges Lefebrvre, *The Great Fear of 1789: Rural Panic in Revolutionary France* trans. Joan White (New York, 1973); Bronislaw Baczko, *Ending the Terror: the French Revolution after Robespierre*, trans. Michel Petheram (Cambridge, 1994); Richard Cobb, *The Police and the People: French Popular Protest, 1789–1820* (Oxford, 1970). See also Arlette Farge and Jacques Revel, *The Vanishing Children: Rumor and Politics before the French Revolution* (Cambridge MA, 1991), 95, who underline the fact that "rumour was an intrinsic part of the city's life"; Arlette Farge, *Subversive Words: Public Opinion in Eighteenth-Century France*, trans. Rosemary Morris (University Park PA, 1995); Daniel Roche, *The People of Paris: an Essay in Popular Culture in the Eighteenth Century*, trans. Marie Evans (Berkeley, 1987); and Paul Hanson "Rumor and its Resonance in the French Revolution," paper presented at the Consortium on Revolutionary Europe, Baton Rouge, Louisiana, February 1997.

3. John M. Merriman, "The Norman Fires of 1830: Incendiaries and Fear in Rural France," *French Historical Studies* 9 (1976): 451–66.

4. Alain Corbin, *Le village des cannibals* (Paris, 1990). In fact, such incidents seem to have been extremely rare. For another, see Peter McPhee, "Un meurtre dans le Sud de la France en 1830: violence, mémoire et tradition démocratique," *Bulletin du Centre d'histoire contemporaine du Languedoc Méditerranéen* 56 (June 1995): 3–30.

5. On atrocities believed to have been perpetrated by German troops and the reaction of the French population, see Ruth Harris, "The 'Child of the Barbarians': Rape, Race and Nationalism in France during the First World War," *Past and Present* 141 (November, 1993): 170–206.

6. Edgar Morin, *The Rumor of Orléans*, trans. Peter Green (New York, 1971); Edith Thomas, *The Women Incendiaries*, trans. James and Starr Atkinson (New York, 1966)

7. See Robert Darnton, *The Literary Underground of the Old Regime* (New York, 1985).

8. *Webster's Third New International Dictionary* (1986). Baczko writes that a "false rumour is a real social fact," and "the more a public rumour is false, implausible and fantastic, the more its history promises to be rich in lessons," and that one can use the study of rumor to learn of the "conditions that make its emergence and circulation possible, about the state of mind, the mentalités and the imagination of those who accepted it as true." Baczko, *Ending the Terror*, 3. Thanks to Susan Connor for alerting me to these particular quotes.

9. Richard Cobb, *The Police and the People*, 322, writes of World War II: "Then also rumour found ready credence even in the highest places: the B.B.C. informed its listeners in 1944, a few months before the invasion that French children in the Nord had been so reduced by famine that, if they had the slightest fall, they broke a limb."

10. Ted W. Margadant, *French Peasants in Revolt: The Insurrection of 1851* (Princeton, 1979); Peter McPhee, *Les Semailles de la République dans les Pyrénées-Orientales 1846–1852* (Perpignan, 1995). See McPhee's criticism of the "tickle-down" studies of

Agulhon, Margadant, and this author in McPhee, *The Politics of Rural Life: Political Mobilization in the French Countryside 1846–1852* (Oxford, 1992). See also Alain Corbin, *Archaïsme et modernité en Limousin au xixe siècle, 1845–1880*, 2 vols. (Paris, 1975).

11. J. Dagnan, *Le Gers sous la Second République*, 2 vols. (Auch, 1928–39), 509. Yet, use of the telegraph could also propagate rumors, which reached Paris from provincial officials with great speed.

12. See Maurice Agulhon, *La République au village* (Paris, 1970) [English-language edition, *The Republic in the Village*, trans. Janet Lloyd (Cambridge, 1982)]. For dissenting views, see Eugen Weber's entertaining but impressionistic *Peasants into Frenchmen: The Modernization of Rural France, 1870–1914*, (Stanford, 1977) and Peter Jones, *Politics and Rural Society: The Southern Massif Central c. 1750–1880* (Cambridge, 1985). For a nuanced look at Montagnard ideology, see Edward Berenson, *Popular Religion and Left-Wing Politics in France, 1830–1852* (Princeton, 1984).

13. McPhee, *The Politics of Rural Life*, 223.

14. André-Jean Tudesq, *Les grands notables en France*, 2 vols. (Paris, 1964), still a classic study. A rumor circulating in June had British guns being unloaded on the coast of the Vendeé (A.N. bb30 364).

15. McPhee, *Politics*, 128, citing Roger Price, *The French Second Republic: A Social History* (London, 1972), 126.

16. ada 5M 10, Subprefect of Tournon, 29 January 1850; Elie Reynier, *La Seconde République dans l'Ardèche (1848–1852)* (Privas, 1948), 89.

17. ada 5M 10, Subprefect of Tournon, 19 September 1850.

18. Margadant, *French Peasants in Revolt*, especially chapter 6; Merriman, *Agony of the Republic*, chapters 2–7.

19. ada 5M 10, circular of the Minister of the Interior (J. Baroche) to prefects, 6 April 1850. Two months later, he wrote prefects that "I am assured that the greater part of the former clubbists and the leaders of the revolutionary party are seeking to spark a movement on the occasion of the completion of the new electoral register." Soldiers for this insurrection would be drawn from men who had lost the right to vote by the law of 31 May 1850. This in itself was a frightening though, because the law had eliminated voters who had not resided in one place for a specific period of time, thus raising the spectre of a revolt by those perceived as *marginaux*. The minister called yet again on his prefects to observe the comings and goings of suspected Montagnards and to report the various rumors circulating in the provinces (Ministry of the Interior circular, 29 Jun 1850).

20. Reynier, *La Seconde République*, 103–4.

21. ada 5M 10, letter and police report of 17 September 1850. Furthermore, a search of a workshop whose workman had also been denounced by a secret police agent for allegedly having made knives for a noted Montagnard turned up but two knives ordered from a cutler.

22. Writing of Bourg St. Andéol and its region, Arnaud wrote, "The men of this region are all big and hardy, with mustaches and beards that strike terror." (5M 10 Arnaud, 18 September 1851).

23. ada 5M 10, n.d.

24. ada 5M 10.

25. ADA 5M 10, police spy, 18 and 19 August 1850.

26. Reynier, *La Second République*, 88–89.

27. ADA 5M 10, Lt. Gend. Largentière, 23 February 1850.

28. ADA 5M 10, undated report of police spy from September 1850.

29. ADA 5M 10, Captain Gend., 29 November 1850.

30. ADA 5M 10, Gendarmerie report, 19 June 1850 and *procès-verbal*.

31. ADA 5M 10, police report of September 1850.

32. Philippe Vigier, *La Second République dans la région alpine* 2 vols. (Paris, 1963), 280–86. "The insurrectional parties here are more ready to act than at any time since the revolution of February."

33. Vigier, 287; McPhee, *The Politics of Rural Life*, 207.

34. Dagnan, *Le Gers*, 430.

35. ADA 5M 10, subprefect of Largentière, 28 November 1850.

36. ADA 5M 10, subprefect of Largentière, 27 November 1850.

37. ADA 5M 10, n.d.

38. Margadant, *French Peasants in Revolt*, 208, citing reports in ADA 10M 13.

39. ADA 5M 10, 16 September 1850.

40. Margadant, *French Peasants in Revolt*, 208, citing reports in ADA 5M 13.

41. Ibid., 210.

42. A.N. BB30 394, 10 September 1851.

43. ADA 5M 10, Arnaud, letter of 11 September 1851. Arnaud apparently knew the prefect, asking that letters to him be sent by the brother of the *fonctionnaire*, whom he apparently also knew.

44. See n. 2.

45. ADA 5M 10, Subprefect of Largentière, 29 September 1851.

46. ADA, 5M 10, Subprefect of Largentière, 3 October 1851. Some of the news reported the prefect of the Ardèche might not have wanted to hear, as when the *mouchard* working the arrondissement of Tournon compared the prefect's reputation in Annonay with that of Privas: in the latter, Montagnards joked about the prefect's name, while in Annonay, "they regard you as a very adroit scoundrel, very fine, a swine who respects nothing and to whom all means are good" (report of 2–7 October 1851).

47. ADA 5M 10, gendarmerie report, 13–14 October and Subprefect, 14 October, 1851.

48. ADA 5M 10, Subprefect, 18 October 1851.

49. ADA 5M 10, summary report for October.

50. ADA 5M 10, Arnaud, 16 September 1851.

51. ADA 5M 10, Vigier, 28 October and Subprefect, 28 November 1851.

52. The *mouchard* working the arrondissement of Tournon reflected such prejudices, as well Annonay "was a city of workers, and, thus of rioters." In contrast, Arnaud revealed more grudging respect of those upon whom he was spying, at least those of Bourg St. Andéol: "Real men live in Bourg St. Andéol! They are calm, reflective, democratic, but with a fire that smolders under the ashes. Here, I see nothing but ignorant prattlers, pretentious orators of the countryside and the taverns: in Bourg, there are workers, who are kept busy and do not waste their energy in a weekly drinking bout, they even go to bed at an early hour," reading newspapers

and anticipating 1852—"They stroll, they play *boules.*" 5M 10, Arnaud, 20 September 1851; Tournon police spy, 2–7 October 1851.

53. ADA 5M 10, gendarmerie lieutenant of Aubenas, 31 October and Subprefect of Largentière, 14 November 1851. The *mouchard* in the arrondissement of Tournon had consulted with the mayor of Annonay.

54. ADA, 5M 10, report, n.d., [October] 1851.

55. Thanks to Elinor Accampo for pointing out this connection to me. See Lynn Hunt, ed., *The French Revolution and Human Rights: A Documentary History* (New York, 1995), 90.

56. ADA 5M 10, Arnaud, letters of 9, 15, 16, and 17 September 1851.

57. A.D.A. 5M 10, Arnaud, 16, 19, 23, and 24 September 1851. Yet, 21 September he claimed that a *rouge* had told him that the *commissiare de police* [presumably of Privas] had identified him as an agent of the Montagnards. In any case, the *commissaire de police* gave him twenty-four hours to leave the Ardèche, but was apparently convinced that he could not be sent away if he had a fever.

58. ADA 5M 10, Subprefect of Tournon, 13 October 1851.

59. The *mouchard* working the arrondissement of Tournon had been a café owner in Avignon, though where he came from originally, we cannot say. His accent would have been somewhat similar to that of Ardèchois, but not quite the same and he did not speak the same patois, though might have understood some of it, if he was indeed originally from the Vaucluse, where a Provençal-based patois was spoken among ordinary people.

60. Dagnan, *Le Gers,* 608–9.

61. McPhee, *Politics,* 223.

62. Ibid., 224.

63. Eugène Ténot, *Paris in December, 1851, or, The Coup d'État of Napoleon III* (Paris, 1870), translation of *Paris en décembre 1851: Étude historique sur le coup d'état* (Paris, 1868), 42–47. See also his *La province en décembre* (Paris, 1869).

64. Margadant, *French Peasants,* 139–142. See Eric Darrieux, "Résister décembre 1851 en Ardèche: essai d'histoire sociale d'une insurection," PhD diss., Université Lumiere Lyon-2, 2008.

65. Ibid., 295.

66. Ibid., 256. In Paris, too, false rumors momentarily increased popular defiance. As resistance spread on the central right bank, "rumors of bad news from Louis Napoleon—mostly false—were received with avidity" (Ténot, *Paris,* 169–170, 180–181, 185, giving many examples). The army diffused false rumors to justify the massacre of civilians following incidents in which shots were allegedly fired from houses, for example on the boulevards Montmartre and Bonne-Nouvelle. To Ténot, "The impression produced in Paris by this fatal event was immense, beyond all that may be imagined. The news spread rapidly, augmented by popular rumor. The unspeakable fright of those who escaped was transmitted to the masses, and it congealed them . . . The revolutionary movement, which was initiated in the first half of the 4th day of December with so much power that it seemed as if it was to carry the entire city with it, was therefore broken" (Ténot, *Paris,* 225, 236–37).

67. For Margadant, "These inaccurate and exaggerated accounts of insurgency were a natural concomitant of the oral communications networks through which villagers exchanged information with townspeople. By democratizing their leadership to include semiliterate and illiterate peasants, and by renouncing written means of communication within the underground, Montagnard organizers had encouraged the circulation of unconfirmed rumors in the countryside . . . Many branch leaders were themselves unaccustomed to verifying political information in the newspapers. Instead of dominating the flow of news by virtue of their superior literacy, militants often shared with everyone else a penchant for numerical exaggeration, emotionalism, and wishful thinking. Bourgeois Republicans in the towns might await precise, written news from Paris before deciding whether to support a *prise des armes*, but artisans and peasants in the bourgs and villages often responded with enthusiasm to oral messages heralding a general uprising" (*French Peasants*, 256–57). One might well quarrel, as would Peter McPhee, with this characterization of rural people as depending on instruction from slick urban bourgeois republicans, but the role of rumor in swelling the ranks of insurgents remains worthy of note.

68. Corbin, *Archaïsme*, vol. 2, 835. Thus, Morny addressed his prefects on 10 December, the anniversary of Louis Napoleon's election as president; "You have just experience in 1851 the social war which was to have broken out in 1852. You will have recognized it by its typical features of murder, brigandage, and incendiarism" (Margadant, *French Peasants*, 312, citing Adrien Dansette, *Louis Napoléon à la conquête du pouvoir* [Paris, 1961], 366).

69. Ténot, *Paris*, 247–248.

70. A.N., F1c III Ardèche 7, Perfect of the Ardèche, 14 July 1852.

71. A.N. F1c III Ardèche 7, Prefect, 4 August 1852.

72. A.N. F1c III Ardèche 7, Boiron, *instituteur* of St. Just, 1 February 1853, writing to the prefect. Four years later, on 7 July 1857, the prefect reported of rumors based in Aubenas, the center of "perverse men, incorrigible spirits," waiting for the right time to stir up trouble again. Fearing of the effects of these rumors on the countryside, he ordered the arrest of two "propagators of false news."

6. The Transition to the Euro

1. Attempts by the Jupé government to cut the budget for education and social programs in 1995 brought demonstrations and strikes, as had that by the Balladur government a year earlier to reduce minimum wage. See Howarth (2002), who notes that the independence of the Banque de France in 1994 could not have come without pressure from European Monetary Union: "The efforts of French governments to establish and then reinforce a European social policy from the mid-1980s can be seen as a French strategy to limit the competitive disadvantage, in the context of the single European market, created by expensive social programmes and generous workers' rights, and by correspondingly high taxes and social charges on companies" (169). To be sure, European Monetary Union was principally managed by the socialists in power in France. In 1976–1980 Raymond Barre had already overseen budget cuts for the sake of Europe, as did François Mitterrand and Jacques Delors in 1983. The rise of the European interest rates and the ability of the franc to resist deval-

uation helped maintain key support for the euro. See also Howarth (2001), which more fully explores forms of "power motives" (particularly with the aim of minimizing the domination of Germany, but also of the U.S. dollar) in shaping French policy on monetary coorperation and European integration and the pursuit of antiinflationary policies and an attempt to protect the franc. Here, Howarth sees French support for monetary union and European integration as, following Stanley Hoffmann, "a reaction to the near collapse of traditional sources of French international and European political power" (182), with the end of the cold war eroding France's position as something of an independent voice.

2. See Vissol (1999).

3. "*La conversion facile.*" From francs to euros: add to the amount its half, then divide by ten; e.g., 100 francs plus 50 francs divided by 10 equal 15 euros. From euros to francs: subtract a third from the amount, then multiply by ten; e.g., 6 euros minus 2 euros times 10 equals 40 francs.

4. *Libération*, December 13, 2001, available at tabacs, banks, post offices, and Bank of France. Only 18 percent of those surveyed indicated that they would keep the kits as souvenirs.

5. According to the Fédération bancaire française, *Le Monde*, December 16–17, 2001.

6. In a poll taken early in December 2001, only 11 percent of those surveyed described themselves as "indifferent" to the arrival of the euro.

7. The official exchange rate was 1 euro = 6.55957 francs.

8. However, Thierry Vissol, representing the project "*euro-facile*" for the European Commission noted, "One had imagined that people would rush to get their credit cards, and that is the opposite of what happened" (January 29, 2002).

9. Stamps with a franc amount inscribed would be valid until no more were left (a 3-france stamp became a 0.46 euro stamp). Stamp collectors rushed to buy stamps with their value in francs posted on them, or with nothing given, to collect before overwhelmed with stamps with euros. The old stamp of three francs comes out to be 0.4573 euro, rounded up to 0.46. With the passage to the euro, nineteen stamps of varying values were available in contrast to thirty in francs.

10. Some studies suggest that about half the population polled believe that things had become more expensive with the euro, while about half held the opposite.

11. The inflation rate for the six-month period beginning with September 2001 stood at about an annual rate of 2.5 percent.

12. I owe this point to Thierry Vissol. For the *hypermarchés*, the confidence of consumers stood at 50 percent for Champion; 47 percent for Leader Price; 45 percent for Auchan; 40 percent for Carrefour; 33 percent for Intermarché; and 29 percent for Leclerc (*Le Figaro*, February 16–17, 2002).

13. See, for example, *Euro locale*, October 1999 (*numéro special*), emphasizing "*la découverte d'un nouveau monde.*"

14. In Corsican, the euro became the *scudu*, sounding like *écu*, the predecessor of the euro.

15. The Association du franc français estimated the cost of the proposed statue to be 10–12 million francs, or 1.52–1.83 million euros.